OCTAGON CONFERENCE

September 1944

PAPERS

AND

MINUTES OF MEETINGS
OCTAGON CONFERENCE

AND

MINUTES OF COMBINED CHIEFS OF STAFF

MEETINGS IN LONDON, JUNE 1944

EDITED AND PUBLISHED BY THE

OFFICE, U.S. SECRETARY
OF THE COMBINED CHIEFS OF STAFF

1944

Published by Books Express Publishing
Copyright © Books Express, 2011
ISBN 978-1-780394-01-5

Books Express publications are available from all good retail and online booksellers. For publishing proposals and direct ordering please contact us at: info@books-express.com

TOP SECRET

TABLE OF CONTENTS

MESSAGES

PAGE

SCAF 78	Progress of Operations Report, Supreme Commander, Allied Expeditionary Force	3
FACS 78	Combined Chiefs of Staff reply to SCAF 78	9
MEDCOS 181	Progress of Operations Report, Supreme Allied Commander, Mediterranean	11
NAF 774	Progress of Operations Report, Supreme Allied Commander, Mediterranean	17
OCTAGON-IN-9	Progress of Operations Report, Supreme Allied Commander, Southeast Asia	21
SCAF 79	Publicity on MULBERRY	27
FACS 79	Publicity on MULBERRY	29

TOP SECRET

TABLE OF CONTENTS

PAPERS

C.C.S.		PAGE
320/27	Allocation of Zones of Occupation in Germany *(Memorandum by the Combined Chiefs of Staff)*	31
417/8	Operations for the Defeat of Japan 1944-45 *(Memorandum by the United States Chiefs of Staff)*	33
417/9	Over-all Objective in the War Against Japan *(Note by the Secretaries)*	37
452/26	British Participation in the War Against Japan *(Memorandum by the British Chiefs of Staff)*	39
452/27	British Participation in the War Against Japan *(Memorandum by the United States Chiefs of Staff)*	41
452/29	Allocation of the Two Remaining Combat Cargo Groups and the Two Remaining Air Commando Groups *(Memorandum by the United States Chiefs of Staff)*	43
452/31	Directive to Supreme Allied Commander, Southeast Asia Command *(Note by the Secretaries)*	45
520/6	Control of Strategic Bomber Forces in Europe Following the Establishment of Allied Forces on the Continent *(Note by the Secretaries)*	49
618/3	Machinery for Coordination of United States-Soviet-British Military Effort *(Memorandum by the British Chiefs of Staff)*	53

TOP SECRET

TABLE OF CONTENTS

PAPERS

C.C.S.		PAGE
618/4	Machinery for Coordination of United States-Soviet-British Military Effort . . . . *(Note by the Secretaries)*	56
643/1	Estimate of the Enemy Situation, Pacific-Far East (as of 8 September 1944) . . . . *(Report by the Combined Intelligence Committee)*	59
654/7	Program for the OCTAGON Conference . . . . *(Note by the Secretaries)*	77
654/8	Basic Policies for the OCTAGON Conference . . . . . . *(Note by the Secretaries)*	79
660/1	Prospects of a German Collapse or Surrender (as of 8 September 1944) . . . . *(Report by the Combined Intelligence Committee)*	81
674	Assumption of Command of DRAGOON Forces by Supreme Commander, Allied Expeditionary Force . . . . *(Note by the Secretaries)*	91
674/1	Assumption of Command of DRAGOON Forces by Supreme Commander, Allied Expeditionary Force . . . . *(Memorandum by the United States Chiefs of Staff)*	95
675	Priorities for Personnel Shipping Subsequent to Termination of Hostilities in Europe . . . . *(Memorandum by the British Chiefs of Staff)*	97
675/1	A Combined Memorandum on Troop Movements, Covering the Period October 1944 to March 1945 . . . . *(Report by U.S. and British Military Services)*	99

TOP SECRET

TABLE OF CONTENTS

PAPERS

C.C.S.		PAGE
675/2	Combined Personnel Movement Problem Arising During the First Year After the Defeat of Germany *(Memorandum by U.S. Transportation, British Movement and Combined Shipping Authorities)*	103
676	General Progress Report on Recent Operations in the Pacific *(Memorandum by the United States Chiefs of Staff)*	109
677	Future Operations in the Mediterranean *(Memorandum by the United States Chiefs of Staff)*	117
677/1	Future Operations in the Mediterranean *(Memorandum by the United States Chiefs of Staff)*	119
678	Planning Date for the End of the War Against Japan *(Memorandum by the British Chiefs of Staff)*	123
678/1	Planning Date for the End of the War Against Japan *(Note by the Secretaries)*	125
679	Redeployment of Forces after the End of the War in Europe *(Memorandum by the United States Chiefs of Staff)*	127
680/2	Report to the President and Prime Minister *(Note by the Secretaries)*	129
681/2	Communication of the Results of OCTAGON Conference to Marshal Stalin and Generalissimo Chiang Kai-shek *(Note by the Secretaries)*	141
682	Operation HIGHBALL *(Memorandum by the British Chiefs of Staff)*	147

TOP SECRET

TABLE OF CONTENTS

PAPERS

C.C.S.		PAGE
684	RANKIN Planning in the Mediterranean Theater *(Memorandum by the British Chiefs of Staff)*	149
687	Release of Amphibious Craft from OVERLORD to Other Theaters *(Memorandum by the United States Chiefs of Staff)*	153

TOP SECRET

TABLE OF CONTENTS

MINUTES OF MEETINGS

LONDON CONFERENCE, June 1944

	PAGE

C.C.S. 162d Meeting (London) 155
    Progress of Operation NEPTUNE
    Campaign in Italy

C.C.S. 163d Meeting (Middlesex) 159
    Operations in Europe
    Operations in the Pacific and the Far East
    Record of Discussion

C.C.S. 164th Meeting (London) 165
    Operations to Assist OVERLORD
    Operations

C.C.S. 165th Meeting (London) 177
    Operations
    War in the Pacific

C.C.S. 166th Meeting (London) 181
    Progress of OVERLORD
    French Resistance Groups
    War in the Pacific
    Operations in Southeast Asia Command
    Control of the United States Twentieth Air Force

TOP SECRET

TABLE OF CONTENTS

MINUTES OF MEETINGS

OCTAGON CONFERENCE

	PAGE
C.C.S. 172d Meeting	189

    Chairmanship of the Combined Chiefs of Staff
    Personnel Shipping
    Agenda and Hour of Meeting
    Situation Report from SCAEF
    Situation Report from the Mediterranean
    Combined Intelligence Report on the Situation in Europe
    Command of DRAGOON Forces
    Machinery for Coordination of United States-Soviet-British Military Effort
    Zones of Occupation in Germany
    Control of Strategic Bomber Forces in Europe

C.C.S. 173d Meeting 201

    Approval of the Minutes of the 172d Meeting of the Combined Chiefs of Staff
    Control of the Strategic Bomber Forces in Europe
    Machinery for Coordination of United States-Soviet-British Military Effort
    Report on the Enemy Situation in the Pacific
    General Progress Report on Recent Operations in the Pacific
    Strategy for the Defeat of Japan
    Basic Policies for the OCTAGON Conference
    Future Operations in the Mediterranean
    Next Meeting, Combined Chiefs of Staff

TOP SECRET

TABLE OF CONTENTS

MINUTES OF MEETINGS

OCTAGON CONFERENCE

	PAGE
C.C.S. 174th Meeting	207

    Approval of the Minutes of the 173d Meeting of the Combined Chiefs of Staff

    Control of the Strategic Bomber Forces in Europe

    British Participation in the Pacific

    Future Operations in Southeast Asia

    Planning Date for the End of the War Against Japan

    Operations of the Twentieth Air Force

    Communications to Marshal Stalin and Generalissimo Chiang Kai-shek

    Next Meeting, Combined Chiefs of Staff

C.C.S. 175th Meeting 223

    Approval of the Minutes of the 174th Meeting of the Combined Chiefs of Staff

    Final Report to the President and Prime Minister

    Communication of the Results of OCTAGON

    Redeployment of Forces after the End of the War in Europe

    Combined Personnel Movement Problem Arising the First Year after the Defeat of Germany

    Operation HIGHBALL

    Release to the Press of Information on MULBERRY

    Possible Statement to be made to the Press by the President and Prime Minister

    Progress of the Campaign in the Pacific

    Hour of Next Meeting

TOP SECRET

TABLE OF CONTENTS

MINUTES OF MEETINGS

OCTAGON CONFERENCE

	PAGE
C.C.S. 176th Meeting	231

    Approval of the Minutes of the 175th Meeting of the Combined Chiefs of Staff

    RANKIN Planning in the Mediterranean Theater

    Release of Amphibious Craft from OVERLORD to other Theaters

    Allocation of Zones of Occupation in Germany

    Situation in China

    Communiqué for Release to the Press

    Concluding Remarks

TOP SECRET

TABLE OF CONTENTS

MINUTES OF OCTAGON PLENARY MEETINGS

	PAGE
First Plenary Meeting	235

    Review of the Strategic Situation of the United Nations
        a. DRAGOON
        b. Campaign in Italy
        c. Campaign in Burma
    British Participation in the War Against Japan
    Treatment of Germany

Second Plenary Meeting	243

    Report to the President and Prime Minister
        a. Operations in Italy
        b. Over-all Objective for the War Against Japan
        c. Redeployment of Forces after the End of the War in Europe
        d. Allocation of Zones of Occupation in Germany
        e. Directive to Supreme Allied Commander, Southeast Asia
    Location of the Central Tripartite Control Commission in Germany
    Communication of the Results of OCTAGON Conference to Marshal Stalin and Generalissimo Chiang Kai-shek
    Release of Information on MULBERRY
    OCTAGON Communiqué

INDEX	253

TOP SECRET

PROGRESS REPORTS ON OPERATION "OVERLORD,"
OPERATIONS IN THE MEDITERRANEAN AND SOUTHEAST ASIA

SCAF 78
MEDCOS 181
NAF 774
OCTAGON-IN-9

At the request of the Combined Chiefs of Staff (C.C.S. 654/4) the Supreme Commander, Allied Expeditionary Force, the Supreme Allied Commander, Mediterranean and the Supreme Allied Commander, Southeast Asia submitted brief reports for consideration at *OCTAGON* giving the progress of operations in their theaters and their intentions for the near future.

TOP SECRET

PROGRESS OF OPERATIONS REPORT, SUPREME COMMANDER, ALLIED EXPEDITIONARY FORCE

References:

CCS 172d Meeting, Item 4
CCS 680/2, Paragraph 8

The report from the Supreme Commander, Allied Expeditionary Force, was considered by the Combined Chiefs of Staff in their 172d Meeting and the proposals therein were approved. The reply from the Combined Chiefs of Staff was dispatched as FACS 78.

PRIORITY

From: Supreme Headquarters, Allied Expeditionary Forces, Forward on Continent

To: War Department
Quebec, Canada (Relayed from WAR as number 28393)
CG, European Theater of Opeations, Rear Echelon, London, England
Allied Force Headquarters, Caserta, Italy
Supreme Headquarters Allied Expeditionary Forces, Main

Nr: FWD 14376   SCAF 78   9 September 1944

Progress of the battles on the Continent has been thoroughly covered in my daily and periodic reports. Consequently I am transmitting a brief outline only of the present situation together with a more complete statement of my intentions in response to the request of the Combined Chiefs of Staff contained in reference cable (WX 26682 7 September 1944).

PART I

SITUATION AS OF 9TH SEPTEMBER 1944.

Today, on D plus 95, almost the whole of northern France has been liberated as have substantial parts of Belgium. Our forces have entered Holland and are close to the German Frontier at more than one point. In Brittany only the Channel Islands, Brest, Lorient and St. Nazaire hold out, and on the channel coast only Le Havre, Boulogne and Calais. The hostile occupation in force of the Dutch Islands at the mouth of the Schelde is certain to delay the utilization of Antwerp as a port and thus will vitally influence the full development of our strategy.

In the south of France the Seventh Army in its rapid advance to the north has already reached Besancon and will shortly join forces with the central group of armies.

Enemy resistance, which has shown signs of collapse during the past few weeks, is stiffening somewhat as we approach the German Frontier. Nevertheless my belief is that the only way he can effectively oppose our advance into Germany will be by reinforcing his retreating forces by divisions from Germany and other fronts and manning the more important sectors of the Siegfried Line with those forces. It is doubtful whether he can do this in time and in sufficient strength but, were he to succeed, he will be likely to concentrate on blocking the two main approaches to Germany, i.e., by way of the Ruhr and the Saar. Of these he will probably regard the approach to the Ruhr as the more important, but in any event he will employ his forces to oppose a deep penetration.

Naval operations have in general proceeded according to plan, and attempts by the enemy to interfere with our sea lines of communications have been countered effectively. Consequently our losses due to enemy action have been light. However, the unexpected small losses in the assault were largely counterbalanced by the effects of a northeasterly gale in June and by the longer shipping turn-round time than had been anticipated. The scale of enemy minelaying and his use of new types of mines have strained our minesweeping resources to the utmost. These factors and systematic demolitions have retarded the development of ports.

Air operations have also proceeded as planned. The POINTBLANK program has been and is being pressed very successfully. Current priorities being as follows: Oil, production of aircraft parts, armored fighting vehicle parts industries, automobile plants.

The advance of the ground forces have largely removed the flying bomb and rocket threats and necessity for substantial air effort against CROSSBOW.

PART II

INTENTIONS IN THE NEAR FUTURE.

General.

My intention is to press on with all speed to destroy the German armed forces and occupy the heart of Germany. I consider our best opportunity of defeating the enemy in the west lies in striking at the Ruhr and Saar confident that he will concentrate the remainder of his available forces in the defense of these essential areas. The first operation is one to break the Siegfried Line and seize crossings over the Rhine. In doing this the main effort will be on the left. Then we will prepare logistically and otherwise for a deep thrust into Germany. The immediate missions assigned the army groups are set forth below.

Northern Group of Armies.

Antwerp having been seized, the northern group of armies and that part of the central group of armies operating northwest of the Ardennes will breach the sector of the Siegfried Line covering the Ruhr and seize the Ruhr.

TOP SECRET

The First Allied Airborne Army supports the northern group of armies in the attainment of first objectives. An operation to seize the crossings over the Rhine and in the area Arnhem-Nijmegen has been twice postponed on account of weather and only awaits favorable weather conditions. Plans for other airborne operations in support of both groups of armies have been prepared.

Central Group of Armies.

The central group of armies less that portion operating northwest of the Ardennes will:

a. Capture Brest.

b. Protect the southern flank of the Allied Expeditionary Force.

c. Occupy the sector of the Siegfried Line covering the Saar and then seize Frankfurt. This operation is to start as soon as possible in order to forestall the enemy in this sector but troops of the central group of armies operating against the Ruhr northwest of the Ardennes must first be adequately supported.

d. Take advantage of any opportunity to destroy enemy forces withdrawing from southwest and southern France.

The ports of Lorient, St. Nazaire, Nantes and the area of Quiberon Bay are no longer essential for maintenance of United States forces. Central group of armies have therefore been instructed that it is unnecessary to reduce St. Nazaire and Lorient by force of arms and that the German garrisons isolated in these areas may for the present merely be contained.

Link up with DRAGOON Forces.

Recommendations have been transmitted to the Combined Chiefs of Staff that operational control of *DRAGOON* Forces will pass to this headquarters on the 15th September 1944. At present the *DRAGOON* Forces have been directed on the area Dijon-Besancon-Vesoul in preparation for further advance on Mulhouse and Strassburg.

Future intentions.

Once we have the Ruhr and the Saar, we have a strangle hold on two of Germany's main industrial areas, and will have largely destroyed her capacity to wage war whatever course events may take. During the advance to the Ruhr and the Saar we will be opening the deep water ports of Le Havre and

TOP SECRET

Antwerp or Rotterdam which are essential to sustain a power thrust deep into Germany. I wish to retain freedom of action to strike in any direction so far as the logistical situation permits. At the moment and until we have developed the channel ports and the rail lines therefrom, our supply situation is stretched to the breaking point, and from this standpoint the advance across the Siegfried Line involves a gamble which I am prepared to take in order to take full advantage of the present disorganized state of the German armies in the west. The possibilities for further advance, depending on the situation at the time, are:

a. The Ruhr via Hanover on Hamburg or Berlin.

b. Frankfurt via Leipzig or Magdeburg on Berlin.

c. A combination of both.

Secondary operations such as the occupation of the Nuremburg-Munich area will depend on the logistical situation at the time.

The stage at which *TALISMAN* conditions will obtain cannot be forecast. Operation *TALISMAN* will be conducted as an extension of the military operations in progress when and if *TALISMAN* conditions arise. The necessary instructions to all concerned for the disarmament of the enemy forces, the occupation of specific targets in the Allied spheres and for the care and repatriation of prisoners of war are ready for issue and some are being issued.

Logistical developments.

Lines of communications are strained to keep up with present advances, and every effort is being made to develop railroads and ports to support rapid exploitation. Our main requirement is deep water ports east of the Seine. Brest and Le Havre will probably be opened initially for the central group of armies and Low Countries port initially for the northern group of armies. When the full capacity of rail lines operation from the original lodgement area to Paris, the Valenciennes coal field and north Belgium has been developed, considerably augmented forces can be supported in the advance into Germany. Air supply and special supply arrangements are being utilized to the maximum to support our rapid advance.

Operation other than OVERLORD Operation against the Channel Islands.

A force formed from sources outside the *OVERLORD* troop basis and consisting of 1 infantry brigade, reinforced, is being held in readiness in the United Kingdom to occupy the Channel Islands in the event of surrender by

TOP SECRET

the garrison. Steps are being taken to induce surrender by means of psychological warfare, and I do not intend to take the Islands by force of arms.

Operation into Norway.

In the event the enemy withdraws from Norway or surrenders I propose to send to Norway an Allied force of the order of 1 British division and 1 United States regimental combat team, together with certain Norwegian troops.

Operation POINTBLANK.

Strategic air forces will continue POINTBLANK operations to a successful conclusion. Priorities may change from time to time in accordance with the situation.

End

OCTAGON-IN-11   (10 Sept 44)

TOP SECRET

PRIORITY

Combined Chiefs of Staff
12 September 1944

Supreme Headquarters
Allied Expeditionary Force
Forward Echelon, France

War Department
Washington, D. C.

Number *OCTAGON* 16

TOPSEC to SHAEF France for Eisenhower, FACS 78 from the Combined Chiefs of Staff.

1. The Combined Chiefs of Staff approve the proposals set out in SCAF 78.

2. In transmitting this approval, the Combined Chiefs of Staff draw your attention: —

a. To the advantages of the northern line of approach into Germany, as opposed to the southern. They note with satisfaction that you appear to be of the same mind.

b. To the necessity for opening up the northwest ports, and particularly Antwerp and Rotterdam, before the bad weather sets in.

End

OCTAGON-OUT-16   (*12 Sept 44*)   *1842Z*

TOP SECRET

MEDCOS 181
NAF 774

PROGRESS OF OPERATIONS REPORT, SUPREME ALLIED COMMANDER, MEDITERRANEAN

References:

CCS 172d Meeting, Item 5
CCS 173d Meeting, Item 8
CCS 680/2, Paragraphs 11-13

Reports from the Supreme Allied Commander, Mediterranean were considered by the Combined Chiefs of Staff in their 172d and 173d Meetings. The agreed reply from the Combined Chiefs of Staff is shown in Enclosure "B" to C.C.S. 677/1.

TOP SECRET

OPERATIONAL PRIORITY

From: AFHQ

To: British Chiefs of Staff
        Joint Staff Mission for United States Joint Chiefs of Staff
        SHAEF

Nr: FX 91375,   MEDCOS 181,   2 September 1944

Following is a review of the situation in the Mediterranean Theatre.

I. *OPERATION "DRAGOON."*

1. Thanks to the skill with which it was mounted and carried through by all three services Operation *DRAGOON* has been an outstanding success. Once ashore the skill of the commanders combined with the determination and speed of manoeuvre of all forces coupled with effective assistance from the French Forces of the Interior have produced a situation in which the whole of southeastern France east of the Rhone and south of Lyons as far east as Nice is under the control of the Allied armies. Some 50,000 prisoners have been captured and very heavy losses have been inflicted on the enemy though some 1½ divisions have escaped to the north after having suffered heavy losses in men and material. The capture ahead of schedule of the ports of Toulon and Marseilles coupled with our unexpected success in securing control of the Port de Bouc practically undamaged have resulted in a situation in which by the middle of September the ports of Southern France will be able to handle any foreseeable demands which may be placed upon them. Subsequently the logistical bottleneck will be the capacity of the railway leading north through the Rhone Valley, but thanks to the speed of our advance and the consequent reduction in the expected scale of demolitions, Seventh Army expect to be able to maintain a force of one armoured division and four infantry divisions north of Lyons by 15th September at earliest. By 1st October it is estimated that a double line of railway will be working as far as Lyons which will by that date place the supply facilities for Allied armies operating in southeastern France on a satisfactory basis. A preliminary estimate, taking into account facilities offered by the use of the Rhone Canal, some 10,000 tons per day might be delivered in the Lyons area from that date. The general tactical plan of Commander Seventh Army which I have approved is that after the capture of Lyons the general grouping of his forces will be that the French Armee "B" will undertake the protection of the right flank facing the Franco-Italian frontier and will operate east of the Rhone with an axis of advance Bourg-Besancon. In the

TOP SECRET

execution of its security mission along the Franco-Italian frontier it will be assisted by the United States Divisional Airborne Division, and First Special Service Force. At the same time the VI American Corps will be regrouped so as to operate west of the Rhone on the line Autun-Dijon-Langres with the object of making contact with the American Third Army. I would propose that at this stage of the operations the command of the forces in France should be transferred to General Eisenhower. While the forces at present employed under the command of the Seventh Army might not appear to be of sufficient magnitude to warrant the formation of 6th Army Group, I consider that in view of the length of communications the very heavy responsibilities for port maintenance and civil affairs and matters connected with the French resistance movement together with the possibility that forces from the right wing of American armies already in France might either be placed under its command or maintained from Mediterranean ports, it is desirable that the 6th Army Group should take over command of southern France. Anticipating that this will be approved by the Combined Chiefs of Staff I am sending General Devers to consider plans with General Eisenhower. As regards administration, I have sent a planning representative to SHAEF to discuss the time when SHAEF should assume administrative responsibility. I would suggest that this matter be left for final settlement between SHAEF and my Headquarters. As regards the large areas in France west of the Rhone, I consider that no military action is required to deal with such small German forces as are still in this area and which are being rapidly rounded up by the French Forces of the Interior, and I feel that any divergence of regular troops would be a waste of effort.

2. *Air.*

I have recently discussed with General Eaker and General Spaatz proposals for the disposition of United States tactical air forces between Italy and southern France which have my full approval and which are now being discussed with General Eisenhower. Their general effect would be that continued offensive operations in the autumn and winter by the Allied armies in Italy would continue to receive very powerful air support from United States Army Air Force fighter-bombers as well as by medium bombers. The detailed deployment and distribution of the tactical air forces cannot and need not be decided until we see the outcome of the present offensive in the Po Valley. Meanwhile I am satisfied that that offensive as well as the operations in the *DRAGOON* area are receiving most adequate and effective support. At the same time certain administrative measures such as holding up the shipping to France of aviation engineers and steel planking have been taken to facilitate any redeployment of the tactical air forces that may be decided upon.

TOP SECRET

II. *ITALY*.

In the Italian Theatre the enemy now has a total of some 26 divisions which are estimated to be the equivalent of some 16 to 17. As a result of the deterioration in the situation in northern France the Germans have withdrawn two Panzer Grenadier Divisions from this theatre which have now been identified in central France. On the other hand the success of our cover plans which have been designed to make the enemy think that one of our objects was to secure Genoa and the Ligurian Coast together with the enemy's fear that the landings in southern France might be the prelude to an invasion of Italy from the west, have resulted in the enemy disposing some five divisions, including three Italian divisions to meet this threat. As a result his forces holding the Gothic Line have been considerably weakened, and until the last few days the enemy did not apparently appreciate the threat to his left flank. He has, however, now realised to some extent the seriousness of this threat and has moved two divisions into the line northwest of Pesaro and further movements to this flank may well be expected. With the reduction in the number of divisions available to him consequent upon the decision to launch Operation *DRAGOON*, General Alexander changed the plan for the major offensive in Italy, which was to be launched at the end of August. Whereas in the original plan the main blow was to be launched on the general axis Florence-Bologna with the object of breaking the enemy's centre and pinning the eastern portion of his forces back against the sea, the new plan is to launch the main blow along the Adriatic Coast north of Ancona where the Apennines present the least obstacle to movement. This main offensive was started on 26th August and is being conducted by the Eighth Army with a force of nine divisions. Good progress is being made and considerable penetration of the Gothic Line have been made on a front extending some 20 miles westwards from Pesaro. As soon as the enemy starts to move reserves to this area, General Alexander plans to start a second offensive to be launched by the Fifth U.S. Army which now commands the XIII British Corps northeast of Florence in the direction of Bologna. I have every hope that as a result of these two offensives the Allied armies will secure control of the line Padua-Verona-Brescia within a few weeks and thus secure the destruction of Kesselring's Army by preventing its withdrawal through the Alpine passes. To complete this task it will be necessary to have available the full resources now at General Alexander's disposal. Further the limited communication facilities which are available to the enemy in northern Italy point to the fact that the use of the air will be a major factor in completing his destruction and facilitating our advance. There will therefore be ample scope for the employment of medium bomber forces throughout the whole operation and it is also to be noted that if medium bombers are established in the Florence-Ancona area, heavy and sustained attacks can be

TOP SECRET

delivered by such air forces well into Austria. In view of the developments which are daily occurring in the general war situation it does not appear to me possible to undertake any further definite commitments. Should, however, the war be further prolonged and the enemy endeavour to withdraw from Greece and the Balkans with the object of holding a line from Trieste through Zagreb and Belgrade to Turnu Severin and the Transylvanian Mountains, the best course would be to regroup our forces and to move northeastwards with the object of securing control of the Ljubljana Gap. Such an operation would require the maximum co-operation with Tito's forces and the occupation of the port of Trieste. Amphibious resources in this theatre are not available to mount a seaborne attack on Trieste this year and consequently unless German resistance collapses it is unlikely that another major offensive could be mounted until the spring of 1945. Concurrently with an advance northeastwards it will be well to clear the enemy completely from northwestern Italy and this should be completed as rapidly as possible with the minimum forces required to establish control and law and order. Provided that demolitions through the Maritime Alps are not too severe it might well be possible to establish land communication with the forces in France.

III. *BALKANS.*

1. All information goes to show that the enemy is faced with an increasingly difficult situation throughout the Balkans and the Islands of the Aegean. This situation is likely to be further accentuated by the situation in Roumania and the probable defection of Bulgaria. Though it is estimated that a proportion of the troops are suitable from the training and equipment point of view for use elsewhere, there is little evidence at the moment that any substantial withdrawal is taking place. However, I anticipate that the Germans now faced with the necessity of finding some reserves in the Balkan area will be forced to regroup and make available four or five divisions if they are to hold either the Bulgarian frontier or the Zagreb-Belgrade line later.

2. *Balkan Air Force.*

Since its formation, the Balkan Air Force has been successful in maintaining pressure against the enemy forces in Yugoslavia and Albania and inflicting continuing losses upon him. On 1st September as a result of consultations with Marshal Tito a concentrated attack on enemy communications in the Balkans began with the object of further embarrassing him and preventing the regrouping of forces. This operation has the code name *RAT-WEEK* and appears suitably timed. Stimulation of Partisan activity in Greece and Albania is also in hand.

TOP SECRET

3. *Greece.*

Arrangements are in hand in the event of German withdrawal or surrender for the rapid occupation of Athens with its ports and airfields with a view of ensuring order and stability and the commencement of relief measures.

4. *RANKIN "C."*

I wish to draw the attention of the Combined Chiefs of Staff to the unsatisfactory situation in which I am placed with regard to the policy to be pursued in the event of a German collapse. If prompt and effective action is to be taken it is essential that I should receive immediate direction as to the extent of my commitments in regard to occupational forces and as to the formation which I am permitted to employ to carry out the tasks assigned to me.

T.O.O. 022130Z

End

CM-IN-4369   (6 Sept 44)   0041Z

TOP SECRET

URGENT

From: Allied Force Headquarters, Caserta, Italy

To: War Department
Headquarters Communications Zone, European Theater of Operations, US Army, France
Supreme Headquarters, Allied Expeditionary Forces,
London, England

Nr: FX 93838   NAF 774   8 September 1944

The general situation in this theatre has already been reported to the Combined Chiefs of Staff in MEDCOS 181. The following is an amplification of this telegram, taking into account the developments which have occurred since it was written.

I. *OPERATION "DRAGOON."*

This is developing most satisfactorily. All arrangements for transfer of control to SHAEF are in hand and I have nothing further to add.

II. *ITALY.*

I am confident from the progress of General Alexander's offensive from 26th August until the present date that the enemy will be driven completely from the Gothic Line. On the other hand, he is fighting very hard behind its eastern sector and I am not yet in a position to guarantee that this offensive will achieve decisive results. Considering, however, that the enemy has been forced to engage the bulk of his reserves to meet the thrust of the Eighth Army, I feel confident that as a result of the second offensive to be launched very soon by the Fifth Army the destruction of Kesselring's Army may yet be achieved.

Should Kesselring's Army be so hammered that it is unable to carry out an orderly withdrawal, I consider that with our great superiority in armour there is every chance of achieving really decisive results similar to those which have been secured in France. On the other hand, if he has time and opportunity to carry out a coordinated demolition programme, and particularly if bad weather should restrict the movement of armoured vehicles off the roads and limit operations of the air force as it may well do, then he may well be able to withdraw a considerable proportion of his forces intact and we may find them facing us behind the Po. Bearing in mind however that he is unlikely to have sufficient troops to hold the Po indefinitely, the course of operations would probably be a gradual withdrawal behind the line of the Alps and the Piave.

To sum up, it appears therefore that operations will develop in one of two ways:

a. Either Kesselring's forces will be routed, in which case it should be possible to undertake a rapid regrouping and a pursuit towards the Ljubljana Gap and across the Alps through the Brenner Pass, leaving a small force to clear up northwest Italy, or,

b. Kesselring's Army will succeed in effecting an orderly withdrawal, in which event it does not seem possible that we can do more than clear the Lombardy Plains this year. Difficult terrain and severe weather in the Alps during winter would prevent another major offensive until spring of 1945.

III. *THE BALKANS.*

Up to date information goes to show that the enemy is engaged in a large scale withdrawal from the Aegean Islands and from southern Greece with the object of finding mobile forces to hold the Bulgarian frontier and Yugoslavia.

At the same time, I anticipate that the enemy will retain static garrisons at important points and airfields with the object of preventing unopposed entry into the Balkans.

It would appear however that owing to the rapid advance of the Russian Army to Turnu Severin, and according to latest reports, the success of air and Partisan attacks on his Balkan communications (mentioned as *RATWEEK* in part III of MEDCOS 181) it seems to be probable that the enemy will be unable to achieve his purpose, nor will he be able to withdraw any substantial forces to assist him in his battles in Italy or in Central Europe.

I therefore consider that we can anticipate a situation in which the bulk of the German forces south of a line Trieste-Ljubljana-Zagreb and the Danube is immobilized and will so remain until their supplies are exhausted in which case they would be ready to surrender to us or will be liquidated by Partisan or Russian forces.

As long as the battle in Italy continues, I have no forces to employ in the Balkans except:

a. The small force consisting of two paratroop brigades and an improvised brigade group from Alexandria which is being held ready to

TOP SECRET

occupy the Athens area and so pave the way for the commencement of relief and the establishment of law and order and the Greek Government in the first of the countries which is likely to be liberated, and,

b. The small land forces Adriatic which are being actively used primarily for commando type operations.

Further, to intensify the enemy's difficulties in the Aegean, a force of four carriers with cruisers and destroyers is now on its way under the command of Admiral Troubridge to the Aegean to carry out attacks on all enemy seaborne movement.

End

MEDCOS 181 is CM-IN-4369 (6 Sept 44)

CM-IN-7313   (9 Sept 44)   0017Z

TOP SECRET

OCTAGON-IN-9

PROGRESS OF OPERATIONS REPORT, SUPREME ALLIED
COMMANDER, SOUTHEAST ASIA

Reference:

CCS 174th Meeting, Item 4

The report from the Supreme Allied Commander, Southeast Asia was noted by the Combined Chiefs of Staff in their 174th Meeting.

TOP SECRET

From: Southeast Asia Command, Kandy, Ceylon

To: War Department
Quebec, Canada (Relayed from WAR as No. 28363)
Supreme Headquarters, Allied Expeditionary Forces,
London, England

Nr: 266   8 September 1944

Reference WARX 26742. TOP SECRET for Combined Chiefs of Staff information British Chiefs of Staff cite 273.

PART I

PROGRESS OF OPERATIONS.

1. *11th Army Group.*

a. XV Ind. Corps. Operations in Arakan largely confined to active and offensive patrolling much hampered by monsoon conditions and thick jungle. No major changes in dispositions, though units of 81st (WA) Division have been moved to counter possible Japanese threat to our Chittagong-Dehazari line of communications from the Moythe-Labawa area.

b. XXXIII Ind. Corps.

(1) *Enemy.* No reports yet of any strong Japanese defensive position capable of holding up our advance for any appreciable period either in the Dabaw Valley or on the Tiddim Road. In the former there are reports of small numbers of Japanese at Yazagyo and Yedok, and on the Tiddim Road there may be an attempt to hold us up in the area just north of Tonnang. The Japanese on the Chindwin and Tiddim front show every sign of complete disorganization and lack of coordinated control. There are signs, however, of an attempt to gather together the remnants of 15th and 31st Divisions east of the Chindwin.

(2) *Own troops.* Operations to clear the enemy from west of the Chindwin have proceeded satisfactorily and there are now no enemy on this side of the river north of Sittaung. The latter was occupied by our troops on 4th September and active patrolling is taking place northwards and southwards on the west bank of the Chindwin down the Tiddim Road, has progressed speedily and has now reached MS 114, 48 miles north of Tiddim.

Japanese opposition has not been strong and the rate of progress has been largely dictated by the state of the road.

In the Rabaw Valley, our rate of advance has been satisfactory though hampered by swollen streams. Leading troops have now reached a point approximately half way between Memu and Kalemyo, without encountering any serious opposition.

2. *Northern Combat Area Command and Yunnan force.*

a. 36th Division has reached Pinbaw in the Mogaung-Katha railway corridor. Patrols have entered Hopin without encountering enemy resistance. 29th Brigade has reached Pinbaw. 72nd Brigade is based in the area of Namana.

b. On the Myitkyina-Bhamo Road Chinese forces have reached Kazu. Patrols are operating five miles south of Kazu without making enemy contact. It is reported that there are no Japanese troops north of Nalong.

c. The Japanese are withdrawing from the Hopin area, and a Prisoner of War report gave Mawhun as the next area of strong resistance in the Hopin-Indaw corridor. There are indications of a build-up along the Katha-Shwebo-Bhamo line.

d. Present directive to Northern Combat Area Command remains to secure the Myitkyina-Mogaung area. In pursuance of this directive the line Pinbaw-Kazu has been occupied.

e. Offensive operations by Yunnan force are in progress in the areas of Tengchung, Lungling and Sungshan.

3. *Air.*

Allied air forces have now gained almost complete air superiority in this theater. The following air activities are now in progress:

a. A strategic air offensive against enemy lines of communication and supply bases by bombers and long range fighters. These operations include the bombing of the Burman-Siam railway, and mine-laying in the main rivers and harbours of Burma.

b. Direct support by Third Tactical Air Force of our land forces pursuing the enemy towards the river Chindwin and Tiddim, and XV Corps in the Arakan.

c. Direct support by Tenth U.S. Army Air Force of the Northern Combat Area Command Forces advancing from Mogaung and Myitkyina, and of the Chinese forces west of the Salween.

d. Transport of troops and supplies to forward areas.

PART II

IMMEDIATE INTENTIONS.

4. *Enemy Situation in Burma.*

a. Ground. Japanese have at present nine divisions in Burma and 10th division expected shortly. Three divisions on the Chindwin and two in north Burma are estimated as 30 percent to 40 percent effective, two in northeast Burma probably 60 percent effective, remaining two in Arakan 100 percent effective. Continued arrival of replacements at recent rates would enable Japanese forces to be brought up to 80 percent effectiveness by end of year.

Present indications Japanese may try and carry out offensives in Arakan and Salween early in dry season, probably with primary object of causing diversion and thus gaining time to reform their forces.

b. Air. Current first line strength in SEAC is estimated at 450 aircraft with 165 in Burma-Siam/South Fic of which 70 (all fighters) are in Burma. By the end of the monsoon there may be a total of 410 first line aircraft in SEAC of which Burma-Siam/South Fic would have an estimated 200 (of which half are fighters).

5. *Intentions.*

a. The intention is to take advantage of the enemy disorganization by pressing as far as possible down the Tiddim Road and the Kabaw Valley and if opportunity offers to secure Kalewa and Kalemyo.

The Japanese are unlikely to resist us in strength north of the areas Yazagyo (in the Kabaw Valley) and Tonzang (at Milestone 133 on the Tiddim Road), but may do so there or further south. It is too early to say whether they will. If they do not the present operations should result in the capture of Kalemyo by about mid-November.

If, on the other hand, they do, then an airborne operation will be necessary. Conditions in the Kabaw Valley prohibit movement of

TOP SECRET

medium artillery and tanks until the roads are sufficiently dry, and Mawlaik must be secured in due course to remove any threat from that area. Having secured Kalemyo the intervening ground is of such a difficult nature that there may be some delay before we can capture Kalewa. Preparations must therefore be continued for an airborne operation.

b. In the Arakan, 3rd SS Brigade will be used to carry out minor amphibious operations to threaten the enemy line of communications and possibly divert his strength from the Kaladan Valley. 3rd SS Brigade would be released from these operations as necessary for *DRACULA*.

c. In northeast Burma I intend to continue operations to secure the Mogaung-Myitkyina area.

d. Air operations on existing scale will continue with intention to harass enemy land and water lines of communication and continue tactical support of land forces.

End

OCTAGON-IN-9   (10 Sept 44)   1920Z

TOP SECRET

SCAF 79
FACS 79

PUBLICITY ON "MULBERRY"

References:

CCS 175th Meeting, Item 7
2d Plenary Meeting, Item 4

On 15 September 1944, the Combined Chiefs of Staff in their 175th Meeting considered a request from the Supreme Commander, Allied Expeditionary Force for instructions as to the release to the press of stories regarding *MULBERRY*. The agreed reply was dispatched as FACS 79.

TOP SECRET

From: Supreme Headquarters, Allied Expeditionary Forces, Forward on Continent

To: War Department
Quebec, Canada (Relayed from WAR as No. 29208)
Supreme Headquarters, Allied Expeditionary Forces,
London, England

Nr: FWD 14565   SCAF 79   11 September 1944

Consider time is approaching when there would be no objection on the part of this headquarters to the release of *MULBERRY* stories to the press, but we are aware there may be security implications affecting other theaters, and we shall not release unless so instructed by you.

No evidence that details construction, operation or capacity have been compromised and all steps have been taken to continue to safeguard security.

End

OCTAGON-IN-62   (12 Sept 44)   2257Z

TOP SECRET

PRIORITY

From: OCTAGON

To: War Department
Supreme Headquarters, Allied Expeditionary Force,
London, England

Nr: OCTAGON 41   FACS 79   16 September 1944

    With reference to SCAF 79 the Combined Chiefs of Staff have agreed that security implications affecting other theaters preclude the release of information on *MULBERRY*.

                                                        End

NOTE: SCAF 79 is CM-IN-11043 (12 Sept 44) CC/S

CM-IN-15405   (17 Sept 44)   0035Z

TOP SECRET

C.C.S. 320/27

ALLOCATION OF ZONES OF OCCUPATION IN GERMANY

References:

CCS 172d Meeting, Item 9
CCS 176th Meeting, Item 4
2d Plenary Meeting, Item 1 k.
CCS 680/2, Paragraph 33

The Combined Chiefs of Staff in their 176th Meeting considered C.C.S. 320/26, a memorandum by the United States Chiefs of Staff, and approved the proposals therein subject to minor amendments agreed upon during discussion. The amended paper as approved by the Combined Chiefs of Staff was circulated as C.C.S. 320/27.

TOP SECRET

C.C.S. 320/27   16 September 1944

COMBINED CHIEFS OF STAFF

ALLOCATION OF ZONES OF OCCUPATION IN GERMANY

Memorandum by the Combined Chiefs of Staff

Upon the collapse of organized resistance by the German Army the following subdivision of that part of Germany not allocated to the Soviet Government for disarmament, policing, and the preservation of order is acceptable from a military point of view by the Combined Chiefs of Staff.

For disarmament, policing and preservation of order:

The British forces under a British Commander will occupy Germany west of the Rhine and east of the Rhine north of the line from Koblenz following the northern border of Hessen and Nassau to the border of the area allocated to the Soviet Government.

The forces of the United States under a United States Commander will occupy Germany east of the Rhine, south of the line Koblenz-northern border of Hessen-Nassau and west of the area allocated to the Soviet Government.

Control of the ports of Bremen and Bremerhaven, and the necessary staging areas in that immediate vicinity will be vested in the Commander of the American Zone.

American area to have in addition access through the western and northwestern seaports and passage through the British controlled area.

Accurate delineation of the above outlined British and American areas of control can be made at a later date.

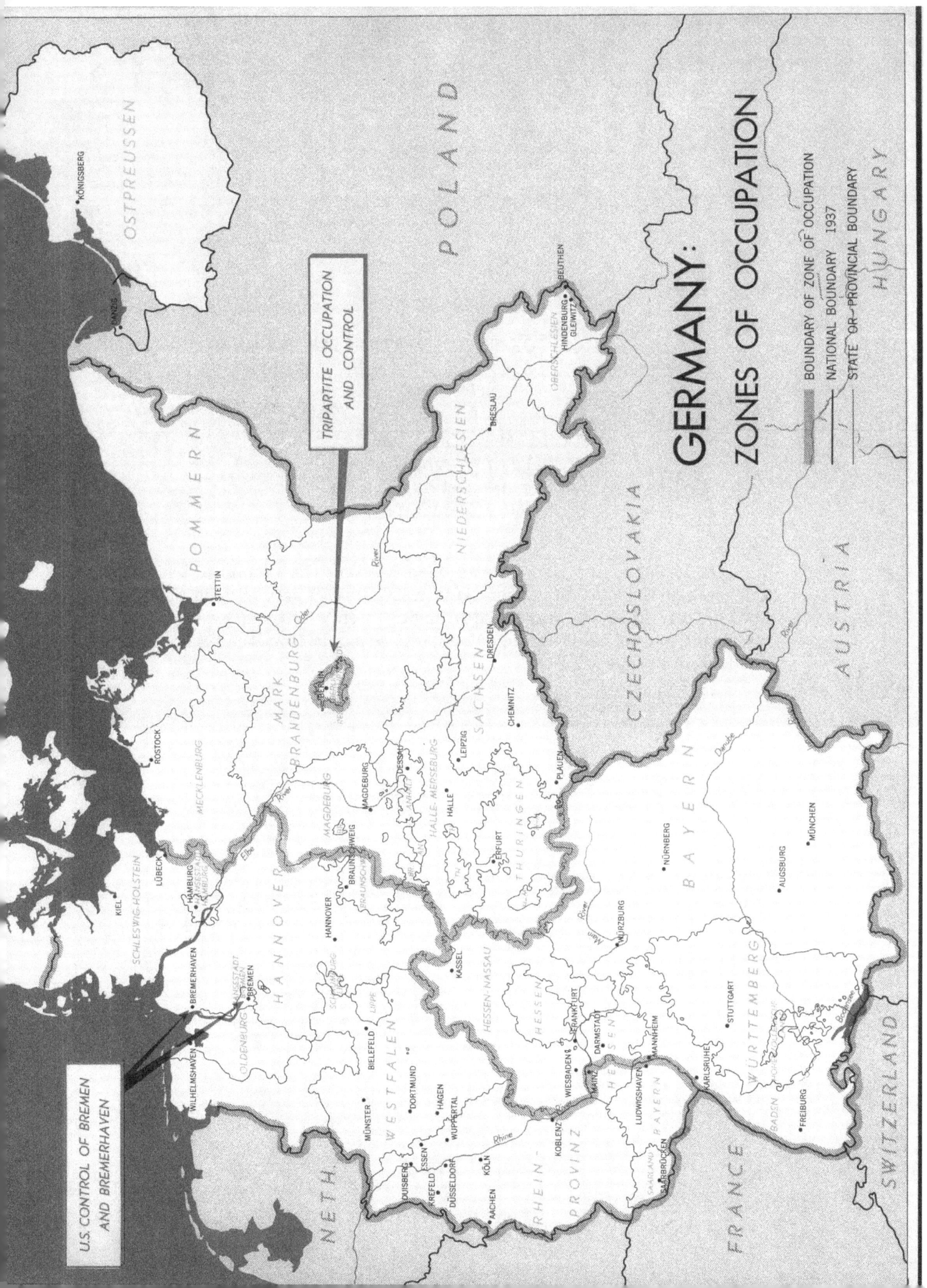

TOP SECRET

OPERATIONS FOR THE DEFEAT OF JAPAN 1944-45

References:

CCS 173d Meeting, Item 6
CCS 175th Meeting, Item 9
2d Plenary Meeting, Item 1 *e.*
CCS 680/2, Paragraph 22

    On 13 September 1944 in their 173d Meeting the Combined Chiefs of Staff accepted the schedule of operations in C.C.S. 417/8 as a basis for planning. However, certain of the target dates having been overtaken by events, the Combined Chiefs of Staff agreed to omit the schedule from the report to the President and Prime Minister.

TOP SECRET

C.C.S. 417/8 9 September 1944

COMBINED CHIEFS OF STAFF

OPERATIONS FOR THE DEFEAT OF JAPAN 1944-45

References:

    a. CCS 417 Series
    b. CCS 426 Series

Memorandum by the United States Chiefs of Staff

1. The agreed over-all objective in the war against Japan has been expressed as follows:

To force the unconditional surrender of Japan by:

    (1) Lowering Japanese ability and will to resist by establishing sea and air blockade, conducting intensive air bombardment and destroying Japanese air and naval strength.

    (2) Invading and seizing objectives in the industrial heart of Japan.

2. Pursuant to the above, the United States Chiefs of Staff have evolved a course of action for planning purposes. The schedule of major operations comprising this course of action follows:

Target Date	Objective
15 October 1944	Talaud
15 November 1944	Sarangani Bay
20 December 1944	Leyte-Surigao Area
1 March 1945	Formosa-Amoy Area
or	
20 February 1945	Luzon

TOP SECRET

If the Formosa operation is undertaken, the following operations have been approved for planning purposes:

April 1945	Bonins
May 1945	Ryukyus
March to June 1945	China coast (Foochow-Wenchow Area)
October 1945	Southern Kyushu
December 1945	Tokyo Plain

A course of action to follow the Luzon operation, if undertaken, is under study.

3. It is believed that operations should be devised to accomplish the defeat of Japan at the earliest possible date and to that end plans will retain flexibility and provision will be made to take full advantage of favorable developments in the strategic situation which may permit taking all manner of short cuts. It is proposed to exploit to the fullest the Allied superiority of naval and air power and to avoid, wherever possible, commitment to costly land campaigns. Unremitting submarine warfare against enemy shipping will be continued. Very long range bomber operations against Japan proper will be continued from China bases and will be instituted from bases being established in the Marianas and from bases to be seized in the future. The air forces in China will continue to support operations of the Chinese ground forces and will also provide the maximum practicable support for the campaign in the Pacific.

4. It is agreed that every effort should be made to bring the U.S.S.R. into the war against Japan at the earliest practicable date and planning for such contingency is continuing.

5. The views of the United States Chiefs of Staff on British participation in the war against Japan and operations in the Southeast Asia Command are contained in C.C.S. 452/21 and C.C.S. 452/25.

6. It is recommended that the Combined Chiefs of Staff note the foregoing.

TOP SECRET

C.C.S. 417/9

OVER-ALL OBJECTIVE IN THE WAR AGAINST JAPAN

References:

2d Plenary Meeting, Item 1 *d*.
CCS 680/2, Paragraph 21

C.C.S. 417/9 circulated the restatement of the "over-all objective in the war against Japan" as accepted by the Combined Chiefs of Staff, 11 September 1944, by informal action. This acceptance was subject to the agreements recorded in C.C.S. 417/5, reaffirming the existing agreements (C.C.S. 426/1, paragraphs 4 and 10) relative to the priority of Operations OVERLORD and DRAGOON and the existing agreements relative to the effect on the over-all objective of extension of operations in the Pacific.

TOP SECRET

C.C.S. 417/9　　　　　　　　　　　　　　　　　　　　　11 September 1944

COMBINED CHIEFS OF STAFF

OVER-ALL OBJECTIVE IN THE WAR AGAINST JAPAN

Note by the Secretaries

The Combined Chiefs of Staff, by informal action, have accepted the following restatement of the over-all objective in the war against Japan (in substitution for that contained in paragraph 3 of C.C.S. 417/2), subject to the agreements recorded in C.C.S. 417/5 as to the assurances requested by the British Chiefs of Staff in C.C.S. 417/4:

"To force the unconditional surrender of Japan by:

(1) Lowering Japanese ability and will to resist by establishing sea and air blockades, conducting intensive air bombardment, and destroying Japanese air and naval strength.

(2) Invading and seizing objectives in the industrial heart of Japan."

A. J. McFARLAND,

A. T. CORNWALL-JONES,

Combined Secretariat.

TOP SECRET

C.C.S. 452/26

C.C.S. 452/27

BRITISH PARTICIPATION IN THE WAR AGAINST JAPAN

References:

CCS 174th Meeting, Item 3
1st Plenary Meeting
CCS 680/2, Paragraph 25

In C.C.S. 452/18, dated 15 August 1944, the British Chiefs of Staff put forward their views with regard to the employment of the British Fleet in the war against Japan. The United States Chiefs of Staff replied on 8 September (C.C.S. 452/25), accepting the British proposal for the formation of a British Empire task force under a British commander to operate in the Southwest Pacific Theater under General MacArthur's supreme command.

In C.C.S. 452/26, presented at *OCTAGON* on 11 September, the British Chiefs of Staff requested the views of the United States Chiefs of Staff regarding the employment of the British Fleet in the main operations against Japan. The views of the United States Chiefs of Staff were expressed in C.C.S. 452/27.

The Combined Chiefs of Staff, in their 174th Meeting, considered the subject of British participation in the war against Japan and their agreements are recorded in the report to the President and Prime Minister (C.C.S. 680/2, paragraph 25).

TOP SECRET

C.C.S. 452/26   11 September 1944

COMBINED CHIEFS OF STAFF

BRITISH PARTICIPATION IN THE WAR AGAINST JAPAN

Memorandum by the British Chiefs of Staff

1. We have seen the views of the United States Chiefs of Staff in C.C.S. 452/25 concerning British participation in the Pacific in the war against Japan, and we note that no mention is made of the employment of the British Fleet in the main operations against Japan, for which we expressed a preference in C.C.S. 452/18.

2. In view of the important political considerations involved, we request a formal expression of the views of the United States Chiefs of Staff on our first preference—namely, the employment of the Fleet in the main operations against Japan.

TOP SECRET

C.C.S. 452/27　　　　　　　　　　　　　　　　　　　　13 September 1944

COMBINED CHIEFS OF STAFF

BRITISH PARTICIPATION IN THE WAR AGAINST JAPAN

Memorandum by the United States Chiefs of Staff

1. The United States Chiefs of Staff would welcome a British naval task force in the Pacific to participate in the main operations against Japan. They consider that the initial use of such a force should be on the western flank of the advance in the Southwest Pacific. They assume that such a force would be balanced and self-supporting.

2. The United States Chiefs of Staff repeat their acceptance of the British proposal to form a British Empire task force in the Southwest Pacific. It is realized that the time of formation of such a force depends to a considerable extent on the end of the war in Europe as well as on *DRACULA* and on the requirements of projected operations in the Southwest Pacific.

TOP SECRET

C.C.S. 452/29

ALLOCATION OF THE TWO REMAINING COMBAT CARGO
GROUPS AND THE TWO REMAINING AIR COMMANDO GROUPS

Reference:

CCS 174th Meeting, Item 4

On 14 September 1944 (C.C.S. 452/29) the United States Chiefs of Staff informed the Combined Chiefs of Staff with regard to the allocation of the two remaining combat cargo groups and the two remaining air commando groups.

The Combined Chiefs of Staff in their 174th Meeting took cognizance of the statement contained in C.C.S. 452/29 during their discussion of Item 4.

TOP SECRET

C.C.S. 452/29　　　　　　　　　　　　　　　　　　　14 September 1944

COMBINED CHIEFS OF STAFF

ALLOCATION OF THE TWO REMAINING COMBAT CARGO GROUPS AND THE TWO REMAINING AIR COMMANDO GROUPS

Memorandum by the United States Chiefs of Staff

The United States Chiefs of Staff have agreed to allocate one combat cargo group and one air commando group to the China-Burma-India Theater in order to assure adequate resources for Admiral Mountbatten to clear and secure the land line to China. The remaining combat cargo group and air commando group have been allocated to the Southwest Pacific in an effort to fill at least part of the deficiency in resources for operations in that area.

TOP SECRET

C.C.S. 452/31

DIRECTIVE TO SUPREME ALLIED COMMANDER,
SOUTHEAST ASIA COMMAND

References:

CCS 174th Meeting, Item 4
2d Plenary Meeting, Item 1 *g*.
CCS 680/2, Paragraph 28

On 13 September 1944 a memorandum by the British Chiefs of Staff (C.C.S. 452/28) proposed a directive to the Supreme Allied Commander, Southeast Asia Command for future operations in Southeast Asia.

The Combined Chiefs of Staff in their 174th Meeting, Item 4, amended and approved the directive which was then circulated as C.C.S. 452/30.

During discussion in the Second Plenary Meeting, C.C.S. 452/30 was further amended. The directive to the Supreme Allied Commander, Southeast Asia Command, as amended and approved by the President and Prime Minister, was circulated as C.C.S. 452/31

TOP SECRET

C.C.S. 452/31   22 September 1944

COMBINED CHIEFS OF STAFF

DIRECTIVE TO SUPREME ALLIED COMMANDER,
SOUTHEAST ASIA COMMAND

Note by the Secretaries

The directive to the Supreme Allied Commander, Southeast Asia Command, as approved by the President and Prime Minister, is attached hereto for information.

A. J. McFARLAND,

A. T. CORNWALL-JONES,

Combined Secretariat.

TOP SECRET

ENCLOSURE

DIRECTIVE TO SUPREME ALLIED COMMANDER,
SOUTHEAST ASIA COMMAND

1. Your object is the destruction or expulsion of all Japanese forces in Burma at the earliest date. Operations to achieve this object must not, however, prejudice the security of the existing air supply route to China, including the air staging post at Myitkyina, and the opening of overland communications.

2. The following are approved operations:—

   a. The stages of Operation *CAPITAL* necessary to the security of the air route, and the attainment of overland communications with China.

   b. Operation *DRACULA*.

The Combined Chiefs of Staff attach the greatest importance to the effective discharge of the task under paragraph 2 *a* and to the execution of Operation *DRACULA* before the monsoon in 1945, with a target date of 15th March.

3. If *DRACULA* has to be postponed until after the monsoon of 1945, you will continue to exploit Operation *CAPITAL* as far as may be possible without prejudice to preparations for the execution of Operation *DRACULA* in November 1945.

TOP SECRET

C.C.S. 520/6   14 September 1944

COMBINED CHIEFS OF STAFF

CONTROL OF STRATEGIC BOMBER FORCES IN EUROPE FOLLOWING THE ESTABLISHMENT OF ALLIED FORCES ON THE CONTINENT

References:

CCS 172d Meeting, Item 10
CCS 173d Meeting, Item 2
CCS 174th Meeting, Item 2
CCS 680/2, Paragraph 7

Note by the Secretaries

    The Combined Chiefs of Staff in their 174th Meeting approved the directive in C.C.S. 520/4 as amended by C.C.S. 520/5, and the directive as approved (Enclosure) was dispatched to the Deputy Chief of the Air Staff, RAF, and the Commanding General, United States Strategic Air Forces in Europe, by the Chief of the Air Staff, RAF, and the Commanding General, United States Army Air Forces, for action and furnished to the Supreme Commander, Allied Expeditionary Force, and the Supreme Allied Commander, Mediterranean, for information.

                                                     A. J. McFARLAND,
                                                     A. T. CORNWALL-JONES,
                                                     Combined Secretariat.

TOP SECRET

ENCLOSURE

CONTROL OF STRATEGIC BOMBER FORCES IN EUROPE

DIRECTIVE

Subject: Control of the Strategic Bomber Forces in Europe

To: Deputy Chief of the Air Staff
Commanding General, United States Strategic Air Forces in Europe

From: Chief of the Air Staff
Commanding General, United States Army Air Forces

1. The Combined Chiefs of Staff have decided that executive responsibility for the control of the strategic bomber forces in Europe shall be vested in the Chief of the Air Staff, RAF and the Commanding General, United States Army Air Forces, jointly.

2. The Deputy Chief of the Air Staff, RAF and the Commanding General, United States Strategic Air Forces in Europe, are designated as representatives of the Chief of the Air Staff, RAF and the Commanding General, United States Army Air Forces, respectively, for the purpose of providing control and local coordination through consultation.

3. The over-all mission of the strategic air forces is the progressive destruction and dislocation of the German military, industrial and economic systems and the direct support of land and naval forces.

4. Under this general mission you are to direct your attacks, subject to the exigencies of weather and tactical feasibility, against the systems of objectives and in the order of priority now established by the Supreme Commander, Allied Expeditionary Force. When you decide that changes in objectives or priorities are necessary, you will issue the necessary directives and inform the Chief of the Air Staff, RAF and the Commanding General, United States Army Air Forces.

5. Objectives other than those covered in paragraph 4 above will be attacked in accordance with the following:

a. Counter air force action. As the result of air action against the production, maintenance and operation facilities of the German Air Forces (G.A.F.), its fighting effectiveness has now been substantially reduced. At the same time our combined air strength has been vastly increased. In these circumstances we are no longer justified in regarding the G.A.F. and its supporting industry as a primary objective for attack. Our major effort must now be focused directly upon the vital sources of Germany's war economy. To this end policing attacks against the G.A.F. are to be adjusted so as to maintain tactical conditions which will permit of the maximum impact upon the primary objectives. No fixed priority is, therefore, assigned to policing attacks against the G.A.F. The intensity of such attacks will be regulated by the tactical situation existing.

b. Direct support. The direct support of land and naval operations remains a continuing commitment upon your forces. Upon call from the supreme commanders concerned either for assistance in the battle or to take advantage of related opportunities, you will meet their requirements promptly.

c. Important industrial areas. When weather or tactical conditions are unsuitable for operations against specific primary objectives attacks should be delivered upon important industrial areas by both Bomber Command RAF and USStAFE (using blind bombing technique as necessary).

d. S.O.E. operations. All SOE/OSS operations undertaken by units of RAF Bomber Command and United States Strategic Air Forces in Europe will be in accordance with the requirements of the Supreme Allied Commanders, who will issue the requisite orders from time to time, under existing procedure.

e. Attacks in support of the Russian armies. Attacks in support of operations by the Russian armies should be delivered as prescribed from time to time by the Combined Chiefs of Staff.

f. Fleeting targets. There may be certain other targets of great but fleeting importance for the attack of which all necessary plans and preparations should be made. Of these an example would be the important units of the German Fleet in harbor or at sea.

6. You are responsible that the operations of the strategic air forces are coordinated with the operations of the tactical air forces in the theaters.

TOP SECRET

C.C.S. 618/3
C.C.S. 618/4

MACHINERY FOR COORDINATION OF UNITED STATES-SOVIET-BRITISH MILITARY EFFORT

References:

CCS 172d Meeting, Item 8
CCS 173d Meeting, Item 3
CCS 680/2, Paragraphs 17-20

On 12 September 1944 (C.C.S. 618/3) the British Chiefs of Staff presented for consideration at *OCTAGON* certain proposals to effect close liaison between the Combined Chiefs of Staff and the Soviet General Staff on strategic and operational matters in Europe.

The Combined Chiefs of Staff in their 172d Meeting approved the recommendations of the British Chiefs of Staff in C.C.S. 618/3 and instructed the Secretaries to draft for approval a message to the Heads of the United States and British Military Missions in Moscow.

The proposed messages were circulated as C.C.S. 618/4 and approved by the Combined Chiefs of Staff in their 173d Meeting.

TOP SECRET

C.C.S. 618/3   12 September 1944

COMBINED CHIEFS OF STAFF

MACHINERY FOR COORDINATION OF UNITED STATES-SOVIET-BRITISH MILITARY EFFORT

References:

    a. CCS 129th Meeting, Item 3
    b. CCS 618 Series

Memorandum by the British Chiefs of Staff

THE PROBLEM

1. The United States and British Chiefs of Staff agree that it is necessary to create additional machinery through which the military efforts of the United Nations forces on the European fronts may be coordinated. The form of this machinery is considered below.

FACTS BEARING ON THE PROBLEM

2. Close liaison is needed between the Combined Chiefs of Staff and the Soviet General Staff on matters of strategy and military policy in Europe. It will, moreover, be highly desirable to open discussions with the U.S.S.R. on the war against Japan as early as politically practicable.

3. In June 1944 Marshal Stalin raised the question of improving the machinery for coordinating the military efforts of the Allies, and in July, Marshal Vassilievsky informed General Deane that the Soviet General Staff were interested in the matter and would like to know the proposals of the Chiefs of Staff in this respect.

4. As agreed at *SEXTANT*, the creation of any form of United Chiefs of Staff Committee would be unacceptable.

TOP SECRET

DISCUSSION

5. We consider the necessary liaison between the Combined Chiefs of Staff and the Soviet General Staff would be achieved by the creation of a Combined British, United States and Soviet Committee in Moscow, provided that it is clearly understood that this Committee:—

(a) Is purely consultative and advisory and has no power to make decisions without reference to the Combined Chiefs of Staff or the Russian General Staff respectively.

(b) Deals solely with strategic and operational matters and does not impinge upon the work that is at present being done by the European Advisory Commission, such as civil affairs, etc.

6. On the Russian side there has been reluctance in the past to discuss matters of any importance with the British and United States Missions, owing to the fact that the latter have usually to deal with officials of no authoritative standing. This difficulty should be overcome in the future provided that the Russian representative on the Committee is a senior member of the Russian General Staff. The Heads of the United States and British Missions already represent their own Chiefs of Staff and so might well serve as members of the Committee. Their rank should be similar to that of the Russian Member.

CONCLUSION

7. We conclude:

(a) That it would be to the advantage of the United Nations war effort to set up a Combined Military Committee in Moscow as a consultative and advisory body dealing only with strategic and operational matters.

(b) That the Committee should consist of senior representatives of the Russian General Staff and the British and United States Chiefs of Staff.

RECOMMENDATION

8. We recommend that the Heads of the British and American Missions in Moscow be instructed to approach the Soviet General Staff with the proposal to establish a Combined Committee in Moscow.

TOP SECRET

C.C.S. 618/4   12 September 1944

COMBINED CHIEFS OF STAFF

MACHINERY FOR COORDINATION OF UNITED STATES-SOVIET-BRITISH MILITARY EFFORT

Note by the Secretaries

In accordance with the instructions of the Combined Chiefs of Staff in the C.C.S. 172d Meeting, the Secretaries propose that the British Chiefs of Staff and the United States Chiefs of Staff send the messages attached hereto as Enclosures "A" and "B" to Generals Burrows and Deane respectively.

A. J. McFARLAND,

A. T. CORNWALL-JONES,

Combined Secretariat.

TOP SECRET

ENCLOSURE "A"

MESSAGE FROM THE BRITISH CHIEFS OF STAFF
TO GENERAL BURROWS

1. It is desired that you propose to the Soviet General Staff that a tripartite Military Committee be set up in Moscow consisting of senior representatives of the Russian General Staff, of the United States Chiefs of Staff, and of the British Chiefs of Staff. The idea of the British Chiefs of Staff is that this Committee would deal with strategical and operational matters, but you should make it clear:—

   a. That it will be purely consultative and advisory and will have no power to make decisions without reference to the respective Chiefs of Staff and the Russian General Staff.

   b. It must not impinge upon the work that is at present being done by the European Advisory Commission, such as civil affairs, etc.

2. The British Chiefs of Staff consider that formation of this Committee should assist in eliminating the delays now existent in dealings between the Russians and the U.S. and British Military Missions. A cardinal point in the proposal, however, is that the Russian representative on the Committee should be a senior member of the Russian General Staff. On the U.S. and British sides the Heads of the present Missions would represent the United States and British Chiefs of Staff respectively, each being responsible to his own Chiefs of Staff.

3. In view of the approach of the Russian, U.S. and British forces toward each other, you should initiate action at once with the Soviet General Staff in order that the Committee may begin to function in the near future.

Enclosure "A"

TOP SECRET

ENCLOSURE "B"

MESSAGE FROM THE UNITED STATES CHIEFS OF STAFF TO GENERAL DEANE

1. It is desired that you propose to the Soviet General Staff that a tripartite Military Committee be set up in Moscow consisting of senior representatives of the Russian General Staff, of the United States Chiefs of Staff, and of the British Chiefs of Staff. The idea of the United States Chiefs of Staff is that this Committee would deal with strategical and operational matters, but you should make it clear:—

   a. That it will be purely consultative and advisory and will have no power to make decisions without reference to the respective Chiefs of Staff and the Russian General Staff.

   b. It must not impinge upon the work that is at present being done by the European Advisory Commission, such as civil affairs, etc.

2. The United States Chiefs of Staff consider that formation of this Committee should assist in eliminating the delays now existent in dealings between the Russians and the U.S. and British Military Missions. A cardinal point in the proposal, however, is that the Russian representative on the Committee should be a senior member of the Russian General Staff. On the U.S. and British sides the Heads of the present Missions would represent the United States and British Chiefs of Staff respectively, each being responsible to his own Chiefs of Staff.

3. In view of the approach of the Russian, U.S. and British forces toward each other, you should initiate action at once with the Soviet General Staff in order that the Committee may begin to function in the near future.

Enclosure "B"

SECRET

C.C.S. 643/1

ESTIMATE OF THE ENEMY SITUATION, PACIFIC-FAR EAST
(as of 8 September 1944)

Reference:

CCS 173d Meeting, Item 4

The Combined Chiefs of Staff in their 173d Meeting took note of the report by the Combined Intelligence Committee (C.C.S. 643/1).

SECRET

C.C.S. 643/1 9 September 1944

COMBINED CHIEFS OF STAFF

ESTIMATE OF THE ENEMY SITUATION, PACIFIC-FAR EAST
(as of 8 September 1944)

References:

a. CCS 506/2
b. CCS 643

Note by the Secretaries

1. The Combined Chiefs of Staff in paragraph 4 *f* of the Enclosure to C.C.S. 506/2, as amended by "Decision Amending C.C.S. 506/2," dated 9 June 1944, directed the Combined Intelligence Committee to prepare estimates of the enemy situation in the Pacific and Far East and European Theater, and keep such estimates up to date. It was further directed that these estimates, with subsequent amendments when necessary, should be circulated to the Combined Chiefs of Staff for information.

2. The estimate of the enemy situation in the European Theater is contained in C.C.S. 660/1.

3. The enclosed report of the Combined Intelligence Committee, an estimate of the enemy situation in the Pacific and Far East, is submitted for consideration by the Combined Chiefs of Staff.

A. J. McFARLAND,
A. T. CORNWALL-JONES,
Combined Secretariat.

SECRET

ENCLOSURE

ESTIMATE OF THE ENEMY SITUATION, PACIFIC-FAR EAST

Report by the Combined Intelligence Committee

THE PROBLEM

1. To estimate the enemy situation and intentions in the Pacific and Far East.

SUMMARY

2. *Political and psychological.* (See Appendix "A.") Japan has sought to enlist the support of her most populous conquered areas by powerful propaganda and by grants of specious independence. For the present, Japan desires to avoid war with the U.S.S.R. in order to be free to direct all her energy against her enemies.

As a result of their fundamental beliefs, the morale of the Japanese populace, and especially of the armed forces, has remained relatively high, but a continuing series of sharp defeats will tend further to confuse and bewilder the Japanese. Such defeats, combined with a collapse of Germany, might conceivably cause a reshuffling of the ruling clique followed by an attempt to secure a negotiated peace. Japanese propaganda has already shifted from self-assured offensive to defensive.

3. *Economic factors.* (See Appendix "B.") Production of high-priority armament items such as aircraft may continue to expand for some time, even though the rapid growth of Japan's basic industry has been levelling off since the beginning of 1944. Further substantial growth of the Japanese steel and other basic industries is believed impossible in the light of the present Japanese shipping position. Shipping is now barely adequate to sustain current production rates in the basic industries, and sinkings exceed launchings. The largest and most essential economic commitment for shipping is within the Inner Zone.* Japan is continuing to develop raw material sources in the Inner Zone

---

* Japan Proper, Korea, Manchuria, North China, Formosa, and Karafuto (Japanese Sakhalin).

in an attempt to achieve self-sufficiency there, but is unlikely to achieve this goal. She is particularly dependent on the Outer Zone for oil. Inner Zone production and stockpiles of fuel oil are at best estimated as sufficient for about nine months but may be much less. In other essential raw materials not available in sufficient quantity in the Inner Zone, Japan is believed to have stockpiles to carry her for longer periods.

Japan's civilian supply position is stringent but not yet critical with respect to food and is generally bad and deteriorating with respect to other commodities, e.g., clothing.

4. *Military factors*. (See Appendix "C.") Realizing that the war potential of her enemies is increasing much more rapidly than her own, Japan has been compelled to adopt the strategic defensive. She hopes that tenacious resistance along successive lines of defense may eventually result in war weariness and possible division among the United Nations, which would enable her to conclude a satisfactory peace. In the past year her air force has deteriorated in quality of personnel and has operated less aggressively; her navy has suffered serious losses; only her ground forces have maintained their strength and fighting qualities.

Although Japan will continue to use caution in the employment of her air power and especially her battle fleet, we believe, nevertheless, that Japan now intends to make vigorous efforts to resist any Allied penetration of her inner defense line Japan-Formosa-Luzon-Mindanao. Her ground forces will offer maximum resistance at all points with little regard for losses; her air power will be committed to a scale of defense proportionate to the strategic importance of each area, and her battle fleet will attack should local circumstances develop which seem to offer opportunity for an effective blow.

In the Bonins, at Palau, and at Halmahera local Japanese ground forces will resist to the maximum extent of their capabilities, but without strong naval and air support.

5. *Intentions in specific areas*. (See Appendix "D.")

a. Japan Proper. As the war draws nearer to Japan we may expect to find an increasingly large percentage of her naval and air forces based nearby and all home defenses considerably strengthened.

SECRET

 b. Northern Pacific. Japan will continue her present policy of gradually strengthening her garrisons and other defenses in the Kuriles and Japanese Sakhalin.

 c. Manchuria. In view of the Soviet threat, Japan is unlikely to release any appreciable ground forces from Manchuria unless they can be quickly restored. She will continue to maintain a strong defensive position there, but is unlikely to undertake any offensive action unless she becomes convinced that the U.S.S.R. is about to enter the war against her.

 d. China. We believe that the Japanese are now conducting operations with the intentions of neutralizing Allied air forces in China and also of establishing overland communication from Manchuria to south China. Japan hopes, by such moves, to improve her strategic position in central and south China.

 e. Burma. The Japanese will continue to attempt to deny the Allies a land route to China and to maintain their position in Burma as an anchor for their western perimeter defenses. They will only undertake limited offensive action for the purpose of breaking up Allied operations.

 f. Malaya-Sumatra. Although this area is of great importance to the Japanese, both for its own resources and as a barrier on the approaches to the South China Sea from the west and south, we anticipate no substantial reinforcement of it until a major threat is more clearly apparent.

 g. East Indies. We believe that Japan will maintain her hold on the East Indies as long as possible, even though her sea communications should be severed.

 h. Formosa-Luzon-Mindanao. The Japanese are busily engaged in strenuous efforts to reinforce this line. They will resist fiercely any penetration of this line, particularly the Luzon-Formosa area. They will accelerate the rate of reinforcement should the Allies occupy the western Carolines.

 i. Central Pacific. In the Bonins, at Palau, and at Halmahera local Japanese ground forces will resist to the maximum extent of their capabilities, but without strong naval and air support.

6. A detailed estimate of enemy order of battle and deployment will be available as Annex "A" when required.

SECRET

APPENDIX "A"

POLITICAL AND PSYCHOLOGICAL FACTORS

1. *External politics.*

   a. General. Japan has propounded two powerful propaganda themes: "Asia for the Asiatics" and "The Co-Prosperity Sphere;" and has adopted such relations with neighboring peoples as she believes will contribute to the fulfillment of her plans. Following are the steps which have been taken, but they represent changes in form rather than in substance.

   (1) *Relations with China.* Japan has recognized the "independence" of China, as represented by the Nanking puppet government, and has sought to enlist Chinese nationalism in support of that regime by surrendering to it various foreign concessions, notably those at Shanghai.

   (2) *Relations with subject peoples.* Japan has granted "independence" to Burma and the Philippines, seeking to enlist the relatively developed nationalism of those countries in her favor; she has hinted that other occupied areas (e.g., Java) may receive similar grants of "independence;" and she has rewarded Thailand for cooperation by the cession of certain neighboring territory to which Thailand had some pretensions.

   b. Relations with the U.S.S.R. There exists between Japan and the U.S.S.R. a basic conflict of interest. Japan's concept of strategic security cannot be satisfied without gaining control of the eastern region of Siberia. For the present, however, Japan desires to avoid war with the U.S.S.R. in order to be free to direct all her efforts against her enemies.

   c. Relations with the Axis. Japan's connection with the Axis is a matter of expediency only. Her action will be coordinated with that of Germany only insofar as she believes that such coordination will contribute to the realization of her basic aims.

2. *Psychology and morale.* The Japanese, traditionally, are an intensely nationalistic and close knit family whose broad characteristics are a toughness of fiber and a fatalistic singleness of purpose. They have been taught that they are of divine origin, that the Emperor is directly descended from the god-founder of the nation and that the Japanese are divinely and infallibly guided towards the establishment of a new world order. The Japanese soldier is taught

Appendix "A"

to give blind obedience and to regard death in the service of the Emperor as an honor. He is told that he is invincible and that to show weakness or to surrender is to accept disgrace.

As a result of these teachings, the morale of the Japanese populace, and especially of the armed forces, has remained high, but the unfavorable course of the war has caused some disillusionment. Moreover, since much of popular morale is based upon the theory of invincibility, a series of sharp defeats, as they are brought home to them, will tend further to confuse and bewilder the people as a whole.

Real power in Japan rests in the hands of small groups of leaders capable of exploiting the position of the Emperor. The collapse of Germany will have a tremendously depressing effect upon such leaders. This, combined with ever increasing United Nations pressure and approach to the homeland, might conceivably bring about a reshuffle of the ruling cliques followed by an attempt to secure a negotiated peace.

Official propaganda on the home front has lost its self-assured tone and determination to fight for existence is replacing exaltation in victory. The potential of the United Nations is admitted to be high, and the government has announced its intention to prepare for the defense of the homeland. Japanese withdrawals are admitted. It is implied that the Japanese have finished winning independence for other Asiatic countries and now must prepare to defend their own islands from frontal attack. The government is also preparing the Japanese people for more serious German reverses in Europe.

Appendix "A"

SECRET

APPENDIX "B"

ECONOMIC FACTORS

1. *General.* Though Japan may still be able to increase production of certain high priority armament items, e.g. aircraft, the expansion of her basic industry, which had ceased by the end of 1943, almost certainly cannot be resumed during this war. Lack of shipping is the most important limiting factor on the expansion of basic industry. Japan still depends on the Outer Zone for certain essential raw materials, especially oil. The Japanese have partially succeeded in reducing this dependence by stockpiling materials in the Inner Zone where nearly all Japanese industry is concentrated. The stockpiling program has fallen short because of lack of shipping.

2. *Shipping.* Japan's shipping position is her most critical weakness and is deteriorating rapidly. We estimate that Japan now has much less shipping than she needs to carry out military commitments and at the same time to utilize her industrial capacity to the full. This condition will grow progressively worse. We believe, however, that Japan will not voluntarily abandon any strategic outpost because of a shipping stringency alone, but will accept a curtailment in her basic over-all industrial production by reducing the import of raw materials. Should the sinking rate increase, as it has increased in recent months, the Japanese would be forced to accept this import reduction proportionately sooner. Sufficient shipping should be available, if necessary, by diversion from trade, for essential troop movements.

We estimate that Japan will be unable to build more than 800,000 gross tons of steel merchant vessels in 1944, which is far behind the rate required to replace losses, and that her ship repair facilities are heavily overburdened. Great emphasis has been placed on wooden shipbuilding, but this program is not believed to be progressing as well as planned and could not, in any event, offset the discrepancy between losses and construction of steel ships. Japan's shipping position would be relatively easier were she cut off from the Outer Zone.

3. *Petroleum and other raw materials.* In general, Japan's industrial machine is dependent upon raw materials which must come from outside Japan Proper and thus the continuance of supply depends upon transportation. The most essential raw material contribution from the Outer Zone is oil. Other critical materials which Japan obtains from the Outer Zone include nickel,

Appendix "B"

chrome, iron ore, manganese, lead, copper, zinc, bauxite and phosphates. Her dependence on the Outer Zone for these materials is however less than in the case of oil either because of the existence of relatively large stockpiles or the possibility in some cases of increasing Inner Zone supplies or of substituting other materials.

Among *petroleum products*, Japan's position is weakest in fuel oil. Inner Zone production and stocks are believed sufficient for about nine months and estimated present over-all production roughly balances consumption at the present calculated scale. Furthermore, about 75 percent of production is in the East Indies. Japan is developing new synthetic facilities in the Inner Zone, but present fuel oil output there would, we estimate, operate her naval fleet and merchant marine at less than one-third their present rate of activity, if stocks are not drawn upon. In aviation gasoline, Japan is similarly dependent upon the East Indies, 80 percent coming from there, but stocks, chiefly in the Inner Zone, are believed sufficient for somewhat more than a year at the present rate of consumption.

Japan's *tanker fleet* has been reduced far below the minimum tonnage required to move fuel oil and aviation gas out of the East Indies to all consumption centers, and the deficit has been only partially offset by diversion of dry cargo vessels to oil-carrying. We believe that Japan will continue this diversion at the expense of other cargoes in order to keep the oil line full and moving.

Although about 20 percent of Japan's *iron ore* is now derived from Outer Zone areas, we believe that Inner Zone production, most of which is outside Japan Proper, could fill all essential needs. Nearly all of Japan's *coal* supply is in the Inner Zone, but more than 50 percent of it lies outside of Japan Proper. Thus iron ore and coal constitute the greatest burden of Japanese shipping. Japan is almost completely dependent on north China and Manchuria for coking coal since the supplies available to her elsewhere are generally of too poor quality to make high grade coke without the admixture of the coal from north China.

Stockpiles of *bauxite* and the possibility of producing alumina from inferior ores in the Inner Zone reduce Japan's dependence on bauxite supplies from Bintan Island (Malaya) and Indochina. Though Japan's *copper* stockpile is relatively small, she produces more than half her requirements at home. The *lead* stockpile, supplemented by Inner Zone production, would last at least a year. Japan's *zinc* position is more stringent; the Inner Zone produces not

Appendix "B"

more than two-thirds of Japan's requirements and stocks are believed to be low.

Japan's major source of *nickel* is Celebes and if this source were cut off her position would be difficult. A conservative use pattern probably has been observed, however, and we believe that the full effects would not be felt in less than a year. The first results of a sharp reduction in use of nickel would be impairment of the quality of war material.

In *chromium* and *manganese*, Japan's position is believed to be somewhat better. For both, Inner Zone production, plus stocks is believed sufficient for more than a year's consumption. The Philippines are the major source of both, contributing a large portion of new chromium and nearly 40 percent of the new manganese.

The comparative dependence of Japan on specific Outer Zone areas is in the following order:

Sumatra:	Fuel oil and aviation gasoline.
Borneo:	Fuel oil.
Philippine Islands:	Chrome, manganese, copper.
Celebes:	Nickel.
Bintan Island:	Bauxite.

4. *Industry*. Japanese industrial production expanded generally up to the beginning of 1944, when it levelled off because of basically restrictive factors (e.g., lack of shipping) which the Japanese are not expected to overcome during this war. However, production of certain high priority finished products, such as aircraft, continues to increase. Japan will attempt to increase the production of such instruments as fire control gear, radar, and other types of precision electrical equipment, but because of technical and organizational difficulties, we believe that she will not be able to accomplish any great expansion in this field. There is still a slight cushion in consumer and civilian goods which can be sacrificed in all out efforts to increase the production of military armaments. Japanese industry is almost wholly concentrated in Inner Zone areas (southern Hokkaido, central Honshu, northern Kyushu, northern Korea, southern Manchuria and Formosa). Finished munitions production is heavily concentrated in Honshu, although Manchurian industry, with help from Japan Proper, largely supports the Japanese Army in Manchuria.

Appendix "B"

SECRET

5. *Food.* The 1944 rice consumption in the Inner Zone is higher than anticipated because of reduced wheat and barley crops. For this and other reasons, we now believe that Japanese rice reserves are uncomfortably low and that Japan must next year depend upon shipments from Indochina and Thailand for an essential portion of rice supplies. Food rations can be reduced without causing actual starvation or serious political consequences, but any reduction will result in decreased industrial efficiency and further deterioration of public health.

Appendix "B"

APPENDIX "C"

MILITARY FACTORS

1. *General.* The rapid build-up and advance of Allied forces in the Central and South Pacific have brought home to Japan the realization that she must prepare to meet steadily increasing Allied strength. In addition, Japan's relations with the U.S.S.R. are uneasy because of the ever present fear that one day that country may join the forces arrayed against her. Forced to accept the strategic defensive, Japan is attempting to consolidate and make secure her greatly expanded empire. She is developing successive defense lines to hold off her enemies in the hope that they, wearied by the war in Europe and perhaps divided among themselves, will attack her ineffectively or compromise to her advantage.

2. *Air forces.* The Japanese Air Force finds itself totally unable to match the constantly growing strength of our opposing air forces and is irrevocably committed to a strategic defensive role. Strictly offensive operations have become progressively more limited in scope and less frequent. Meanwhile, the highest priority is being given to aircraft production, and latest estimates suggest that at least 1200 combat aircraft are now being produced each month. A strenuous effort is being made to overcome qualitative inferiority by better protective armament, greater fire power, self-sealing fuel tanks, and engines of increased power. Already there has been a marked improvement in the quality of Japanese fighter aircraft. All available indications show that the combat efficiency of the Japanese Air Force is at present suffering seriously from a shortage of fully trained and experienced pilots and crews. Currently expanded facilities for individual and group training are being completed, but in periods of high attrition the Japanese will find it difficult to provide replacement of effectively trained personnel. We believe that a combination of difficulties will make it impossible for Japan's air forces to improve materially their present qualitative inferiority so long as continued and heavy pressure is brought against her.

Although the Allies will probably meet increasingly strong numerical air resistance as they attack successive lines of defense, the scale and duration encountered at each point of attack is likely to be conditioned by Japan's intention to preserve air strength for the final defense of those areas which she considers vital to the defense of the homeland and its critical supply lines.

Appendix "C"

SECRET

3. *Naval forces.* Japan's naval strength is inadequate for the defense of her outer perimeter. She is only able to concentrate portions of her fleet at a few strategic bases to parry thrusts at key points of her defense line. Allied strength is denying the Japanese Fleet the use of all but a small part of the Pacific Ocean. With her present relatively small operational fleet, Japan does not dare risk possible heavy attrition by launching any major offensives. Although she is striving to increase her fleet strength by new units, the appearance of such new ships has been so rare as to suggest difficulties in the outfitting of such forces. We believe that Japan is primarily engaged in building small escort vessels to counter the heavy toll of merchant ships taken by our submarines.

We believe that in the future the Japanese will deploy their fleet so as to be able better to meet readily the next estimated Allied blow. With their fleet concentrated in the Celebes Sea the Japanese had hoped to counter vigorously Allied thrusts at the Philippines. Subsequent to the battle of the eastern Philippines the main elements of the fleet were obliged to retire for reequipping and reorganization. As a result of the threat to the Bonins and the homeland, developed by our advance to the Marianas, the Japanese are likely to dispose their heavy surface units along the Kyushu-Formosa line. However, the fuel oil situation, the shipping stringency and Allied air power will have a bearing on ultimate fleet deployment.

While the Japanese Fleet suffered a heavy loss of aircraft and some carrier units in the recent battle of the eastern Philippines, Japan still retains a battle fleet of considerable power. Despite recent actions we believe that while the Japanese High Command will be cautious in the use of their battle fleet, they will continue to make vigorous efforts to oppose any Allied penetrations of the line Japan-Formosa-Luzon-Mindanao. The main considerations governing the strength, disposition, and employment of Japanese naval units opposing our advance are: local control of the air, strength of Allied forces, and the time factor. If, at any time, the Japanese should gain local control of the air, which is unlikely, we must expect heavy attacks upon our units by task forces composed of carriers, battleships, cruisers, etc. Lacking such air control or strong land-based air cover, the Japanese would use some carriers to attempt attacks on our flanks, and also light task forces might attempt night surface torpedo attacks. We can expect the Japanese to be cautious in all-out attacks on a vastly superior force, such attacks only materializing if local control of the air has been established. The element of timing will be affected by the rapidity with which the High Command reaches the conclusion that an actual occupation is threatened. In any event, our carriers will be the primary

Appendix "C"

SECRET

target for enemy aircraft, with our transports as secondary. Our transports will be the primary target for enemy surface forces, with our own striking forces as secondary.

4. *Ground forces.* Japan's greatest armed strength lies in her large, fairly equipped and very well trained army. Because of the nature of the war in the Pacific to date, the United Nations have been unable to inflict any serious attrition on the over-all strength of the Japanese ground forces, which are as strong or stronger than in 1941.

At the present time the Japanese army ground forces total approximately 3,500,000 men. These troops are organized into about 85 divisions plus many independent units and garrisons, which have been so deployed that Japan now maintains a strong strategically defensive position. In addition, Japan has organized in Manchuria and China puppet units totaling approximately 300,000 and 400,000 men respectively. The strongest concentrations of forces are in Japan Proper, Manchuria and China. Since United Nations forces have begun to threaten seriously Japan's position in the Central and Southwestern Pacific areas, Japan has accelerated her preparations for the defense of the vital East Indies and has reinforced her southern forces, particularly in the Philippines area.

The formation of puppet units has been general throughout Japanese occupied territory, but only on a large scale in Manchuria and China. Puppet troops in other areas have been formed primarily for purposes of political propaganda, and their military value to Japan has been negligible. The actual value of the Manchurian and Chinese puppet troops to Japan cannot be accurately assessed. They are only lightly equipped and, although some have been used in combat against the Chinese, the majority of them have had relatively little training. They are at present being used mainly as garrison units and for the maintenance of order in Japanese occupied territory. Because their loyalty is doubtful, it is unlikely that the Japanese would use them in a major engagement against well trained and equipped troops.

We believe that Japan intends to maintain generally the present strategic disposition of her ground forces after further substantial reinforcement of Formosa and the Philippines.

Appendix "C"

APPENDIX "D"

MILITARY INTENTIONS IN SPECIFIC AREAS

1. *Japan Proper*. As the war draws nearer to Japan, we may expect to find an increasingly large percentage of Japan's heavy naval forces based in contiguous waters to protect the home islands and the essential transport routes between the home islands and the rest of the Inner Zone. Similarly, a large percentage of Japan's total combat aircraft, particularly fighters, will be kept at bases in the homeland to protect against bombing of the concentrations of Japanese armaments production there. Also the formation of new divisions will be expedited and Japanese home defenses strengthened.

2. *Northern Pacific*. In view of the American position in the Aleutian Islands and the possibility of eventual Allied air and naval action from Soviet bases in Kamchatka and Soviet Sakhalin, Japan will continue her present policy of strengthening her defenses in the Kuriles and Japanese Sakhalin.

3. *Manchuria*. Japan has built up in Manchuria a large and highly developed army. It is largely sustained by Manchurian agricultural and industrial production, which is developing more rapidly than any other section of the Japanese Empire. The purpose of this army is to provide a force of sufficient strength to protect Manchuria from any Soviet threat and also to provide a striking force powerful enough to attack Siberia and the Maritime Provinces should Japan consider the latter course to be necessary. The Japanese High Command has abandoned hope of any German victory. Japan must appreciate that following peace with Germany, Soviet military capabilities in the Far East will increase progressively and, in fact, the initiative along the Manchurian border will eventually pass to the U.S.S.R. In view of the Soviet threat, Japan is unlikely to release any appreciable forces from Manchuria unless they can be quickly restored. She will continue to maintain a strong defensive position there, but is unlikely to undertake any offensive action unless she becomes convinced that the U.S.S.R. is about to enter the war against her.

4. *China*. Allied air action from China is increasingly menacing Japan's present economic and defensive position, and the Japanese are taking stronger counter measures by the occupation and neutralization of some of the more accessible Allied bases.

The Japanese have now completed military operations between the Yangtze and Yellow Rivers and are in process of consolidating their position in this newly captured territory while reconstructing the railroad line linking Hankow with Peking. The primary objective of current operations south of the Yangtze is to deny to the Allies air bases in southeastern China. In order to accomplish this we believe that they intend to occupy the railway line between Hengyang and Kweilin and also eventually to establish overland communications between their forces in central and south China by occupation of the railroad line between Hengyang and Canton.

The Japanese have the capability of successfully carrying out these intentions. Whether or not they will commit sufficient forces for the final completion of such operations may however be influenced by the rapidly increasing threat from the Pacific. We believe that the Japanese do not intend to weaken the ground forces they now have based in China unless in due course some of these divisions are urgently required for the defense of Japan Proper or Formosa.

5. *Burma*. The main object of Japanese operations in Burma will be to contain large Allied forces in terrain favorable to the Japanese and to prevent the reopening of the land route to China. The Japanese will, when possible, continue to undertake limited offensive action designed to break up Allied offensive preparations and to divert as large a part as possible of the forces of the Southeast Asia Command.

6. *Malaya-Sumatra*. This area is of great importance to the Japanese, both for its own resources and as a barrier on the approaches to the South China Sea from the west and south. The Japanese, however, presumably consider their present strength there adequate to meet any threat likely to arise during 1944. In view of their preoccupation with more immediate threats to Japan Proper, Formosa, and the Philippines from the Pacific and by air from China, as well as the potential threat from Siberia, we anticipate no substantial reinforcement of Malaya-Sumatra until a threat to that area is more clearly apparent, and then only as may be warranted by the then existing over-all situation.

7. *East Indies*. We believe that Japan will not in any circumstances voluntarily relinquish her hold upon the East Indies, but will continue to maintain in the area the strong ground forces which already have been deployed for their defense. Although the Japanese in due time will appreciate that their

Appendix "D"

SECRET

sea communications to the Indies may be severed, they will consider the continued denial of the area to the United Nations forces as of such strategic importance as to warrant the sacrifice of forces stationed there.

8. *Formosa-Luzon-Mindanao.* Currently the Japanese are engaged in strenuous efforts to reinforce and build up ground, air and naval defenses in these areas. Allied attack upon any part of the line will be fiercely resisted by all forces immediately available, the scale and intensity of such resistance progressively increasing from the southern to the northern part of this strong eastern defense to the vital line of sea communications with the East Indies. Although Allied occupation of Mindanao would greatly increase the threat to Japan's position, the occupation of Luzon would make the passage of shipping through the South China Sea highly precarious, while the capture of Formosa would substantially sever all sea communications to the south and in addition offer a strong base for direct assault upon Japan Proper. We believe that the Japanese intend to have deployed in the immediate future all forces which they consider can be spared for the defense of the southern Philippines, whereas land and air strength in Luzon and Formosa will continue to build up at an accelerated rate should the Allies occupy the Palaus.

9. *Central Pacific.* In the Bonins, at Palau, and at Halmahera local Japanese ground forces will resist to the maximum extent of their capabilities, but without strong naval and air support. The scale of naval resistance will be governed by the number of their own land-based aircraft immediately available, the strength and dispositions of our own forces, and the time at which they determine that further occupation is threatened.

Appendix "D"

TOP SECRET

C.C.S. 654/7   12 September 1944

COMBINED CHIEFS OF STAFF

PROGRAM FOR THE "OCTAGON" CONFERENCE

Reference:

CCS 172d Meeting, Item 3

Note by the Secretaries

In their 172d Meeting the Combined Chiefs of Staff approved the following program for the *OCTAGON* Conference:

I. *Tuesday, 12th September*

    a. Control of Strategic Bomber Force.

    b. Zones of occupation — provision of forces.

    c. Machinery for Inter-Allied coordination in Moscow.

    d. Situation report from SHAEF and SACMED.

    e. C.I.C. report on the enemy situation in Europe.

    f. General Eisenhower's future plan of campaign.

    g. General Wilson's plan of campaign.

II. *Wednesday, 13th September*

    h. Prospect of redeployment of forces from European Theater for war against Japan.

    i. C.I.C. report on enemy situation in the Pacific.

    j. Situation report on the Pacific and from SACSEA.

    k. Strategy for the defeat of Japan.

TOP SECRET

III. *Thursday, 14th September*

    l. British participation in the Pacific in the war against Japan.

    m. Future operations in Southeast Asia.

IV. *Friday, 15th September*

    n. Continuation of discussion of items listed in III above.

    o. Further consideration of the redeployment of forces from the European Theater for the war against Japan.

    p. Possible Russian participation the war against Japan.

A. J. McFARLAND,
A. T. CORNWALL-JONES,
Combined Secretariat.

TOP SECRET

C.C.S. 654/8

BASIC POLICIES FOR THE "OCTAGON" CONFERENCE

References:

CCS 173d Meeting, Item 7
CCS 680/2

By action taken informally and in their 171st Meeting, the Combined Chiefs of Staff, by 8 September 1944, had approved all of the "Basic Policies for the *OCTAGON* Conference" with the exception of paragraph 6 (i). Two proposals for the wording of paragraph 6 (i) were presented for consideration at *OCTAGON* on 12 September (C.C.S. 654/8).

The Combined Chiefs of Staff in their 173d Meeting accepted the wording proposed during the discussion. The agreed basic policies for the *OCTAGON* Conference are included in C.C.S. 680/2.

TOP SECRET

C.C.S. 654/8   12 September 1944

COMBINED CHIEFS OF STAFF

BASIC POLICIES FOR THE "OCTAGON" CONFERENCE

Note by the Secretaries

1. The Combined Chiefs of Staff have agreed on all the basic policies for inclusion in the final *OCTAGON* report to the President and the Prime Minister, with one exception.

2. This exception is as follows:

a. The British Chiefs of Staff have proposed the following as paragraph 6 (i) of C.C.S. 654:

"Reorient forces from the European Theater to the Pacific and Far East as a matter of highest priority, *having regard to other inescapable commitments*, as soon as the German situation allows."

b. The United States Chiefs of Staff have proposed that this paragraph should read as follows:

"Reorient forces from the European Theater to the Pacific and Far East, as a matter of highest priority, *having regard to other agreed commitments,* as soon as the German situation allows."

3. The decision of the Combined Chiefs of Staff on this wording is requested.

A. J. McFARLAND,
A. T. CORNWALL-JONES,
Combined Secretariat.

SECRET

C.C.S. 660/1

PROSPECTS OF A GERMAN COLLAPSE OR SURRENDER
(as of 8 September 1944)

Reference:

CCS 172d Meeting, Item 6

The Combined Chiefs of Staff in their 172d Meeting took note of the report by the Combined Intelligence Committee (C.C.S. 660/1).

SECRET

C.C.S. 660/1 9 September 1944

COMBINED CHIEFS OF STAFF

PROSPECTS OF A GERMAN COLLAPSE OR SURRENDER
(as of 8 September 1944)

References:

a. CCS 660
b. CCS 506/2

Note by the Secretaries

1. The Combined Chiefs of Staff in paragraph 4 *f* of the Enclosure to C.C.S. 506/2, as amended by "Decision Amending C.C.S. 506/2," dated 9 June 1944, directed the Combined Intelligence Committee to prepare estimates of the enemy situation in the Pacific and Far East and European Theater, and keep such estimates up to date. It was further directed that these estimates, with subsequent amendments when necessary, should be circulated to the Combined Chiefs of Staff for information.

2. The estimate of the enemy situation in the Pacific and the Far East is contained in C.C.S. 643/1.

3. The enclosed report of the Combined Intelligence Committee, an estimate of the enemy situation in the European Theater, is submitted for consideration by the Combined Chiefs of Staff.

A. J. McFARLAND,
A. T. CORNWALL-JONES,
Combined Secretariat.

SECRET

ENCLOSURE

PROSPECTS OF A GERMAN COLLAPSE OR SURRENDER
(as of 8 September 1944)

Report by the Combined Intelligence Committee

THE PROBLEM

1. To review the principal factors bearing on German surrender or the collapse of German resistance and to estimate the form which such an event is likely to take and the time when it is likely to occur.

DISCUSSION

2. See Appendix.

SUMMARY AND CONCLUSIONS

3. The German strategic situation has deteriorated to such a degree that no recovery is now possible. In addition to the disintegration of the German front in the West, the crumbling of the German position in the Balkans, and the penetration of German defenses in Italy, the general decline in Germany's war potential brought about mainly by Allied bombing and by German losses of manpower has contributed largely to this situation.

4. The present German Government, or any Nazi successor, is unlikely to surrender. Control by the Party appears strong enough to prevent governmental overthrow or internal disintegration prior to an extensive collapse of military resistance.

5. Although causes for collapse are undoubtedly present, the lack of visible symptoms indicates that German national life is still mobilized behind the war effort. This support is not likely to break down until the final military debacle has reached its final stage.

6. The collapse will probably take the form of piecemeal surrenders by field commanders, who will be influenced both by the tactical pressure on them and

SECRET

by their individual appreciation of the hopeless strategic situation, and possibly by their disagreement with the policy of the Central Government.

7. Unmistakable signs of the imminence of collapse are unlikely to be apparent until the end of resistance is close at hand, but collapse, once begun, is likely to spread rapidly. We consider that organized resistance under the effective control of the German High Command (Oberkommando der Wehrmacht) is unlikely to continue beyond 1 December 1944, and that it may end even sooner.

SECRET

APPENDIX

1. *Strategic Situation*

   a. Ground. Prior to the opening of the summer offensives, German strategy had as its primary goal the crushing of any Allied attempt to establish a front in western Europe. In order to accomplish this, Germany was prepared to yield ground elsewhere under pressure in the hope that, after defeating Allied operations in the West, she might be able to retrieve such situations as had worsened in the meantime.

   This strategy failed to produce the desired results. In France the German front has virtually ceased to exist. Since the break through in Normandy, the Germans have been unable to hold any line and the Allies are advancing against very light resistance to the German Frontier. In Italy, the German defenses based on the Gothic position have been penetrated. In the Balkans, the whole German position is crumbling. In the East, although the Germans have, at the moment, an organized front between the Russian and the German Frontier, they cannot be confident of holding their present line in Poland against a renewal of the Russian offensive.

   The aim of German strategy must be to prolong the war and to prevent, for as long as possible, the invasion of the Reich itself; but the speed of recent events has taken Germany completely by surprise and has left her without the resources and apparently without any coordinated plan to meet her radically altered strategic position.

   Sound military strategy would long ago have seemed to dictate territorial retrenchment in order to concentrate additional forces in the decisive areas. This, however, would have involved grave political dangers, the very weakness of Germany's position making it imperative for her to disguise the true state of affairs as long as possible, not only from her enemies, but from the wavering satellites and neutrals, the restive populations in occupied territories, and her own people.

   We believe that Hitler may now have realized that his only hope of using some of his troops, now in outlying parts of Europe, for the prolongation of the war and the defense of the Reich, lies in withdrawing them immediately. There is evidence that this process has already started from the most outlying areas. Even so, he has waited too long. During September he might be able to make available for the defense of the West Wall, in addition to the divisions he is able to extricate from France, the equivalent of 10-15 full divisions from elsewhere, excluding the Eastern Front. These would include some ten low category divisions at present forming in Germany, but they are generally under strength, inadequately trained, short of artillery, and fitted only for static defense, and are considered equivalent to about five full-strength divisions. We are also unable to exclude the possibility that some divisions might even be transferred from the Eastern to the Western Front. Any divisions which Germany can make available will be sent to the West so long as this front presents the most immediate threat. However, if these transfers do take place, they will not be sufficient to hold the Allied attack in the West.

b. Air. The offensive strength of the German Air Force has declined to negligible proportions. In view of Germany's increasing shortage of oil and air crews no revival of effort on an intensive or sustained scale is possible.

In order to provide for the defense of vital strategic objectives in the Reich against Allied bombing operations, the Germans have already found it necessary to curtail drastically air support of their military operations on all fronts and the air defense of occupied territories. Nevertheless, the German Air Force is unable to prevent heavy and systematic destruction of high priority objectives by Allied bombing attacks, nor will it be able to prevent the invasion of the Reich or exert any important influence on the final outcome of that invasion. Although some temporary increase in fighter strength may be achieved by the avoidance of combat, the shortages of fuel and of trained pilots probably preclude any substantial improvement in defensive capabilities.

Jet propelled aircraft have now appeared operationally in relatively small numbers. Although this may necessitate some slight revision of Allied air tactics, it is highly unlikely that a sufficient number of this type will become operational before the end of the war to change substantially the present over-all ineffectiveness of the German Air Force.

c. Sea. The German operations against Allied shipping and against Allied supply lines to the Continent have degenerated into harassing activities owing principally to the success of Allied anti-submarine measures and, to some extent, to the impotence of the German Air Force.

The enemy still disposes of a large U-boat fleet and is now constructing improved types. An increase of activity may be expected in the autumn. When these new types become operational, it is likely that these operations may temporarily meet with more success than has been the case for some months past. Operations will, however, be seriously hampered by the loss of bases in the Biscay and consequently by the disadvantages of being forced to

SECRET

use Norwegian ports. Such operations are, therefore, unlikely to achieve a sufficient degree of success to exert any important influence on the course of the war.

The German surface forces may still be able to delay further deterioration of the situation in the Baltic, where all the major units except the *TIRPITZ* are now concentrated, but it is very unlikely that they will be able to influence appreciably developments in any other theater. No forces remain in areas south of the Straits of Dover.

New technical developments in U-boat equipment and in such weapons as torpedoes, bombs and mines may, as in the past, prove of material value to the enemy. The operation of "Small Battle Units," comprising one-man torpedoes, explosive motor boats, and such weapons, may be intensified. It is very unlikely, however, that the enemy will be able by these means to exert any important influence on the course of the war.

d. Manpower. Lack of combat-fit manpower constitutes one of the most critical over-all weaknesses in the German situation. The number of physically fit young men remaining in the entire German population is already substantially less than the minimum requirements of the armed forces. German losses in manpower have already been enormous. These can no longer be replaced nor can the fighting effectiveness of her combat units be maintained in the face of this heavy attrition. Mobilization of the civilian labor forces is already virtually complete and the importation of more foreign workers is not now possible on any substantial scale and would increase the already grave potential source of danger they represent. Announced German measures for "full mobilization" of the home front therefore cannot have any substantial effect in alleviating the manpower crisis.

e. Political and Psychological Factors. The strongest elements in the German strategic situation are the political and psychological forces which maintain the German will to resist in spite of the overwhelming pressure exerted by the adverse military situation. Nazi controls governing every aspect of German life continue to be outwardly effective. As a result of the attempted *coup d'état* of 20 July, Nazi control has been further extended into the Wehrmacht. Undoubtedly, the extent of the plot, which came to light on 20 July after brewing for months, indicates serious discontent in the armed forces, especially in the officer corps. This discontent is being kept in check only at the expense of further weakening the fighting power of the army through the replacement of disaffected officers by Nazi officers of less ability and experience.

SECRET

The attitude of the civilian population continues to oscillate between apathy and hopes for a negotiated peace. The complete Party control of the home front, in any case, renders the likelihood of purely civilian revolt extremely remote.

f. Economic. There is evidence that the Allied attacks on Germany's oil production, stocks, etc., are now confronting her with disaster. This is the most serious shortage of material with which Germany is at present faced, and seriously reduces her capacity to deal with the catastrophic developments in her strategic situation. Other shortages, especially in ferro-alloys, will become increasingly acute.

The German war economy is now clearly unable to meet Germany's military requirements. Shortage of tanks, military vehicles, and even ammunition is now seriously affecting operations on the fighting fronts. Losses in equipment have been enormous and cannot possibly be replaced.

The civilian supply position, although increasingly tight, is unlikely directly to cause military difficulties or to precipitate a civil revolt. Lack of civilian goods may cause some political difficulties and may reduce labor efficiency.

g. Occupied and Satellite Countries. The satellite states are increasingly concerned to save themselves from the effects of a German defeat. Rumania has already proclaimed her surrender and declared war on Germany. Bulgaria has asked for an armistice and is reported to have declared war on Germany. Finland has accepted Soviet conditions for the opening of armistice negotiations and claims to have received Germany's agreement to the withdrawal of German forces from her territory. Hungary still remains in the war because she is unwilling to restore to Rumania the ceded territories in Transylvania and because she fears the U. S. S. R.

The Germans are reported to be already withdrawing from Finland, but it is unlikely that more than one-half of the total force can be withdrawn sufficiently rapid to be effective as reinforcements. German withdrawal from southern Greece and the Aegean Islands may have begun already. The only area from which German withdrawal is unlikely is Norway which now provides the only bases from which German U-boats can hope to operate in the Atlantic.

h. Relations with Neutrals. The remaining European neutrals may be expected to cling to their neutrality; they will nevertheless give greater assistance to the United States and Great Britain at Germany's expense despite the apprehensions of some of these neutrals over the increase of Soviet influence on the Continent. As her position deteriorates, Germany will get less and less economic aid from the neutrals.

SECRET

i. German Hopes. For many months the only bases for German hopes of avoiding unconditional surrender have been the possibility of division among the United Nations, the possibility of new weapons that would affect fundamentally the course of the war, and the possibility of war weariness or discouragement in one or more of the United Nations. At present the relations of the three major United Nations are more harmonious than ever. Secret weapons cannot, of course, be evaluated precisely in advance, but the overwhelming weight of scientific and military conjecture holds that the Germans are not likely to produce a new weapon that can fundamentally alter the course of the war. The Allied advance in the West has already occupied or cut off all the main areas from which ground-launched flying bombs or long-range rockets can be operated against England and has thus destroyed German hopes of influencing the course of the war by the use of these weapons. War weariness among the United Nations can scarcely be expected to become critical at a time when their military progress is more rapid than in any former period. Thus, the virtual hopelessness of the German situation is driven home more forcefully week by week as the hope of being able to prolong the war recedes.

2. *Explanation of Continued German Resistance.*

The preceding paragraphs indicate that the factors which should produce a collapse or surrender are already present in the German situation. Continued German resistance is chiefly due to the fanatical determination of the Nazi Party leaders to fight to the end and to their possession of the necessary political and psychological control within Germany. This determination is based on the doctrine held by the Nazis that Germany surrendered too quickly in 1918; their fear for their own safety; a fanatical belief in their own capabilities which prevents them from accurately appraising the situation; and the lack of any alternative to continued resistance which would seem to offer opportunities for a later revival of their power. It is possible that preparations are being perfected to maintain, even after defeat, an underground organization. The failure of the *coup d'état* of 20 July has given the Party still more complete control of both the home front and the Wehrmacht. The civilian population alone has neither the courage nor the capacity to risk revolt, even if it is beginning to appreciate the hopelessness of continued resistance. In the Army, discipline remains reasonably firm although the confidence of the rank and file is being undermined by the shortage of men, munitions, motor transport, and liquid fuels and by the inescapable contrast between German and Allied artillery and air power. Therefore although the strategic situation indicates certain defeat, German resistance is likely to continue beyond the time when any rational objectives within the immediate or distant future seems to be served by doing so.

SECRET

3. *Symptoms of German Collapse or Surrender.*

There are still no certain indications that German groups are acting as though collapse or surrender is imminent. Despite the plot of 20 July and the fact that the promotion of SS officers had a bad effect on the morale of officers of the Army proper, there is no evidence that the officer corps or the rank and file of the Army has been generally and seriously demoralized. Although surrenders are occurring more readily than formerly, large scale mutinies or desertions have not yet developed. In certain areas German soldiers continue to fight tenaciously but elsewhere they have lost the will to resist and only discipline prevents a complete collapse of morale. On the home front, strikes and demonstrations have apparently not yet assumed dangerous proportions. Serious peace feelers have not been put forth by the Germans, but the satellite states, which might be expected to break away from a defeated Germany before final collapse, have already begun to do so.

4. *Form of Surrender.*

Since it is unlikely that the present German Government or any Nazi successor will surrender, the end of German resistance is most likely to come through a series of piecemeal surrenders by German armed forces in the field. Individual commanders who find themselves in difficult situations will be influenced to surrender by their own appraisal of the general strategic situation and possibly by their disagreement with the policy of the Central Government. Once the tendency toward piecemeal surrender gathers momentum, elements of the Wehrmacht which have retreated into Germany under arms may even carry out the actual final expulsion of the Nazi regime. But this possibility cannot be envisaged until one or more of the main fighting fronts has collapsed.

5. *Time of Surrender.*

We believe that organized German resistance under the effective control of the German High Command (Oberkommando der Wehrmacht) is unlikely to continue beyond 1 December 1944. In reaching this conclusion we consider the collapse of the German front in the West, the rapid deterioration of the position in the East, especially in the Balkans, the impotence of the German Air Force, and increasing shortages of oil and weapons of war which will have become most critical by that date. The military situation therefore is ripe for a collapse. It is impossible to forecast the date at which this collapse might begin, but once begun it is likely to spread rapidly. We therefore believe that organized resistance may end even sooner than 1 December.

TOP SECRET

C.C.S. 674
C.C.S. 674/1

ASSUMPTION OF COMMAND OF "DRAGOON" FORCES BY SUPREME COMMANDER, ALLIED EXPEDITIONARY FORCE

References:

CCS 172d Meeting, Item 7
CCS 680/2, Paragraphs 14 - 16

A message from the Supreme Commander, Allied Expeditionary Force, SCAF 77, proposing certain recommendations relative to the assumption of command of *DRAGOON* forces, was circulated in C.C.S. 674 on 11 September 1944.

The recommendation of the United States Chiefs of Staff that the message contained in C.C.S. 674/1 be dispatched was approved by the Combined Chiefs of Staff in their 172d Meeting.

TOP SECRET

C.C.S. 674　　　　　　　　　　　　　　　　　　　　11 September 1944

COMBINED CHIEFS OF STAFF

ASSUMPTION OF COMMAND OF "DRAGOON" FORCES BY SUPREME COMMANDER, ALLIED EXPEDITIONARY FORCE

References:

a. CCS 304/12
b. CCS 145th Meeting, Item 3

Note by the Secretaries

The enclosed message (SCAF 77) from the Supreme Commander, Allied Expeditionary Force is submitted for consideration by the Combined Chiefs of Staff.

A. J. McFARLAND,

A. T. CORNWALL-JONES,

Combined Secretariat.

TOP SECRET

ENCLOSURE

From: CG, Supreme Headquarters, Allied Expeditionary Forces, Forward on Continent

To: Combined Chiefs of Staff

Nr: FWD 14276   SCAF 77   9 September 1944

1. Following are my recommendations relative to assumption of command of *DRAGOON* forces.

2. It is estimated that by 15 September the *DRAGOON* forces will be located in strength in the Dijon area, that Seventh Army Headquarters will be north of Lyons and that an advance echelon of General Devers' Army Group Headquarters will be near Lyons. At that time, therefore, operational control should pass to me and I will transmit operational directives direct to General Devers with copies to SACMED and the Commanding General, Seventh Army.

3. Coincident with my taking operational control of the *DRAGOON* forces, the Commanding General, Ninth Air Force will assume operational control of the XII Tactical Air Command of 1st Fighter Group and auxiliary units which is actually with the Seventh Army. The Ninth Air Force will augment the XII Tactical Air Command as now constituted as necessary in order to support the Army Group adequately. The Twelfth Air Force in support of the Allied Armies in Italy will continue to support the *DRAGOON* forces until the Ninth Air Force can assume this responsibility.

Subsequently when General Devers' Army Group comprises the French Army and at least 1 United States Army and provided the Twelfth Air Force can be spared from Italy, it should be transferred to *DRAGOON*. Alternately should existing conditions in Italy make such a transfer undesirable, in the opinion of the Combined Chiefs of Staff, the Twelfth Air Force will furnish a command and staff echelon to General Devers' Army Group for the necessary coordination of air operations and for complete air liaison with SHAEF. Under this alternative it may be that we shall have to obtain at least 1 more fighter-bomber group from the Twelfth Air Force.

4. The exact date when administrative control should pass to me cannot be stated at the present time. Logistical support and maintenance for the

TOP SECRET

DRAGOON forces should continue from the Mediterranean Theater so long as United States supplies are in excess of reserves needed for other United States units in that theater. Thereafter maintenance may continue through southern France ports or be shipped to other routes if the latter prove more advantageous. Close coordination with the Mediterranean Command will be essential while resources are being shipped through the ports of southern France, whether from the United States or from North Africa or a combination of the two. I recommend that the terminating date of this responsibility be arranged by mutual agreement between Generals Wilson and Devers.

5. It is suggested that the Combined Chiefs of Staff directive to General Wilson and me regarding my assumption of command of the *DRAGOON* forces be based upon the recommendations presented in the foregoing paragraphs.

End

TOP SECRET

C.C.S. 674/1   12 September 1944

COMBINED CHIEFS OF STAFF

ASSUMPTION OF COMMAND OF "DRAGOON" FORCES BY SUPREME COMMANDER, ALLIED EXPEDITIONARY FORCE

Memorandum by the United States Chiefs of Staff

The United States Chiefs of Staff recommend that the following message be sent to SCAEF and SACMED at once:

"Effective 15 September SCAEF will assume command of *DRAGOON* forces according to plan recommended in SCAF 77."

TOP SECRET

C.C.S. 675
C.C.S. 675/1
C.C.S. 675/2

COMBINED PERSONNEL MOVEMENT PROBLEM ARISING DURING THE FIRST YEAR AFTER THE DEFEAT OF GERMANY

References:

CCS 172d Meeting, Item 2
CCS 175th Meeting, Item 5
CCS 679

On 12 September 1944, C.C.S. 675 circulated a memorandum in which the British Chiefs of Staff recommended that an examination be made of the scope of the movement problems involved immediately before and following the termination of hostilities in Europe and the availability of the shipping resources with which to meet the requirements.

The Combined Chiefs of Staff in their 172d Meeting invited General Somervell to confer with Lord Leathers on this matter. As a result of this invitation a report prepared by the Representatives of United States and British Military Services in conjunction with appropriate shipping authorities was circulated as C.C.S. 675/1 (13 September 1944).

An additional report, from General Somervell and Lord Leathers, was circulated on 15 September (C.C.S. 675/2) and was noted by the Combined Chiefs of Staff in their 175th Meeting.

TOP SECRET

C.C.S. 675　　　　　　　　　　　　　　　　　　　　　　　　12 September 1944

COMBINED CHIEFS OF STAFF

PRIORITIES FOR PERSONNEL SHIPPING SUBSEQUENT TO TERMINATION OF HOSTILITIES IN EUROPE

Memorandum by the British Chiefs of Staff

1. It is clear that the global personnel movement problems which will arise immediately before and following on the termination of hostilities in Europe will be of considerable magnitude and complexity, and that decisions will be necessary as to the priorities to be afforded to the various movements involved.

2. In order that consideration may be given to this matter, it is recommended that the Combined Chiefs of Staff instruct the representatives of the United States Service Departments and the British Service Departments to undertake immediately, in conjunction with the appropriate shipping authorities, an examination of the scope of the movement problems involved and of the availability of shipping resources with which to meet the requirements.

TOP SECRET

C.C.S. 675/1 13 September 1944

COMBINED CHIEFS OF STAFF

A COMBINED MEMORANDUM ON TROOP MOVEMENTS, COVERING THE PERIOD OCTOBER 1944 TO MARCH 1945

Note by the Secretaries

The Representatives of United States and British military services in conjunction with appropriate shipping authorities submit the attached report of the examination of troop shipping requirements suggested by the Combined Chiefs of Staff in their 172d Meeting of 12 September.

A. J. McFARLAND,
A. T. CORNWALL-JONES,
Combined Secretariat.

TOP SECRET

COMBINED MEMORANDUM ON TROOP MOVEMENTS
COVERING THE PERIOD OCTOBER 1944 TO MARCH 1945

A. *Assumptions.*

1. The state of war in Europe is such that the Combined Chiefs of Staff agree:

   a. That it is feasible to release British troops from Europe for Operation *DRACULA.*

   b. No further U.S. troops need be transported to European theaters.

2. If the decision with regard to the two conditions in 1 above is not made by 1 October the necessary transfer of British forces to India cannot be accomplished in time to execute the operation before the monsoon.

B. *Statement of the Problem.*

1. The problem therefore is to determine the effect of employment of troop shipping for *DRACULA* on U.S. and British deployments subsequent to the defeat of Germany.

C. *Facts Bearing on the Problem.*

1. The build-up of a British task force in India for *DRACULA* involves the movement of six British divisions or 370,000 personnel from Europe to India prior to 1 March 1945.

2. It is estimated that this movement will during its peak period involve virtually the entire British trooping lift.

3. This requirement will limit British assistance to the United States in the Atlantic to a trooplift of about 25,000 per month from November 1944 to April 1945 by leaving only the two Queens on this run. However in the event of any unforeseen difficulties in meeting the *DRACULA* program it might prove necessary to withdraw one or both of the Queens from the Atlantic service.

4. A further effect will be the withdrawal of all British ocean-going troopships now employed in cross-Channel movements. This amounts to a capacity of 25-30,000 troop spaces for combined cross-Channel troop movements. It is

TOP SECRET

estimated that British cross-Channel troop movements can be accomplished in other type vessels. The scale of U.S. cross-Channel troop movements cannot be determined but should be relatively light in proportion to total U.S. withdrawals from the Continent. To the extent required such movement must be accomplished in U.S. shipping.

5. The *DRACULA* movement of British troops absorbs the full capacity of Indian ports with the exception of such U.S. troops as can be received through the port of Calcutta. India has stated that they can disembark two "General" class ships off Calcutta simultaneously by the use of Indian Ocean shipping.

D. *Discussion.*

1. *Effect on British movement up to approximately mid-March 1945.*

a. After 30 September it will not be possible to carry out any normal trooping from the United Kingdom to theaters abroad other than any replacements included in the *DRACULA* program. Allowance has been made for 4,500 a month between Canada and the United Kingdom.

b. No non-operational movement can take place except those which might be capable of being effected in ships returning empty from operational voyages.

c. No troop ships could be spared for conversion to other tasks, viz: fleet train, hospital ships, etc.

d. It will only be possible to carry out movement already planned between theaters abroad, mainly reinforcements from West and East Africa to India and New Zealanders to Italy which are small in relation to the total fleet and for which shipping is being positioned. Internal movement in the Mediterranean will be reduced to a local lift of some 15,000.

2. *Effect on U.S. movements up to approximately end of March 1945.*

a. U.S. shipping schedules for redeployment have included the movement of 70,000 U.S. troops per month from Europe to the United States in British ships. Under this assumption the strength of U.S. forces in Europe will be:

1 Oct 44	2,760,000
1 Apr 45	1,535,000
6 months withdrawals from Europe	1,225,000

b. The reduction of British assistance in the Atlantic to 25,000 troops monthly would result in the following European position:

1 Oct 44	2,760,000
1 Apr 45	<u>1,805,000</u>
6 months withdrawals from Europe	955,000

In other words a reduction in the rate of return of U.S. troops from the European Theater will be required amounting to 270,000 in six months.

c. Troop movements to Pacific theaters in accordance with redeployment plans tentatively set up, but now under review, would be possible.

E. *Conclusion.*

1. Until the strategic requirements for the furtherance of the war against Japan subsequent to the defeat of Germany have been determined and until shipping priorities have been established as between operational and non-operational moves, it is not possible to present more detailed shipping implications during and after the period 1 October 1944 to 1 April 1945.

TOP SECRET

C.C.S. 675/2   15 September 1944

COMBINED CHIEFS OF STAFF

COMBINED PERSONNEL MOVEMENT PROBLEM ARISING DURING THE FIRST YEAR AFTER THE DEFEAT OF GERMANY

Note by the Secretaries

The enclosure has been presented by Lord Leathers and General Somervell.

A. J. McFARLAND,
A. T. CORNWALL-JONES,
Combined Secretariat.

TOP SECRET

ENCLOSURE

MEMORANDUM BY THE U.S. TRANSPORTATION, BRITISH MOVEMENT, AND COMBINED SHIPPING AUTHORITIES

1. The attached Appendix "A" indicates the magnitude of the combined personnel movements which may be required during the first year after the defeat of Germany (assumed at 1 Oct. 1944) on the basis of tentative redeployment plans.

2. The attached Appendix "B" indicates the probable combined resources estimated to be available during the period under consideration.

3. Owing to changes in plans under way and in prospect a precise analysis of this problem cannot be made until the entire matter has been studied by combined agencies based on decisions by the Combined Chiefs of Staff on strategy and priorities.

4. It is therefore recommended that the Combined Administrative Committee, in collaboration with the Combined Staff Planners, the Combined Military Transportation Committee, and the combined shipping authorities, study and report on this problem in the light of decisions to be made by the Combined Chiefs of Staff.

TOP SECRET

APPENDIX "A"

ANALYSIS OF THE COMBINED PERSONNEL MOVEMENT PROBLEM

*Subsequent to a 1 October Defeat of Germany
and for 1 year thereafter*

	British	U.S.
1. OPERATIONAL REQUIREMENTS		
a. Replacements (reinforcements) for forces already engaged in the war against Japan on 1 October.	(a)	693,000
b. Build-up *from U.S.* for war against Japan.	—	826,000
c. *Redeployment* for war against Japan.	1,052,000	804,000
d. Additional replacements (reinforcements) to support increased strength due to *b* and/or *c*.	385,000	213,000
e. Replacements or readjustments in garrisons, of non-operational areas.	265,000	10,000
f. Rotational programs for forces engaged in the war against Japan.	150,000	280,000
g. Intra-Area movement accomplished by retained ships.	250,000	768,000
Subtotal	2,102,000	3,594,000
2. DEMOBILIZATION AND REPATRIATION WITHOUT REPLACEMENT		
a. British and U.S. Forces.	678,000	1,720,000(b)
b. Dominion, Colonial and other personnel.	251,000	28,000
Subtotal	929,000	1,748,000

Appendix "A"

TOP SECRET

		British	U.S.
3. *PRISONERS OF WAR*			
a. Allied prisoners of war.		53,000	102,000
b. Enemy prisoners of war.		466,000	243,000
	Subtotal	519,000	345,000
4. TOTAL REQUIREMENTS FOR THE SERVICES (c)		3,550,000	5,687,000

Notes:

(a) This figure is included under other headings in item 1.

(b) To the extent that the defeat of Germany is delayed beyond 1 October 1944 this figure will be increased.

(c) To this requirement must be added an unknown number for essential civilian movements.

Appendix "A"

TOP SECRET

APPENDIX "B"

TOTAL AVAILABILITY OF PERSONNEL SHIPPING BY CATEGORIES
(as of 1 Oct 1944)

	British		U.S.	
CATEGORIES	No. of Ships	Capacity	No. of Ships	Capacity
1. OCEAN GOING	84	302,000	220	492,000
2. LIMITED CAPABILITY				
(a) Indian Ocean type	31	48,000	—	—
(b) Miscellaneous	6	6,000	45	35,000
Subtotal	37	54,000	45	35,000
TOTAL TROOPSHIP LIFT	121	356,000	265	527,000

Notes:

	British	U.S.
1. Estimated lift on 1 October 1945, after allowing for additions and losses based on current C.C.S. rates	376,000	708,000

2. Additional trooplift may be realized by use of cargo ships temporarily fitted to carry a few hundred troops each.

3. An indeterminable lift may be obtained from captured enemy vessels.

4. Lift of LSI's and APA's is not included in above inventories but advantage will be taken of their lift whenever operational schedules permit.

5. Lift in U.S. Navy vessels as estimated and included in the above table for normal troop movement is subject to wide variation dependent upon possible utilization of Navy troopships for operational requirements.

6. No British cross-Channel type of shipping is included nor has any allowance been made for possible conversions for the naval fleet train or hospital ships.

Appendix "B"

TOP SECRET

C.C.S. 676

GENERAL PROGRESS REPORT ON RECENT OPERATIONS
IN THE PACIFIC

Reference:

CCS 173d Meeting, Item 5

The Combined Chiefs of Staff in their 173d Meeting took note of the progress report by the United States Chiefs of Staff on recent operations in the Pacific (C.C.S. 676).

TOP SECRET

C.C.S. 676   12 September 1944

COMBINED CHIEFS OF STAFF

GENERAL PROGRESS REPORT ON RECENT OPERATIONS IN THE PACIFIC

Memorandum by the United States Chiefs of Staff

The enclosure, compiled from reports of the area commanders in the Pacific, is presented for the information of the Combined Chiefs of Staff.

TOP SECRET

ENCLOSURE

GENERAL PROGRESS REPORT ON RECENT OPERATIONS
IN THE PACIFIC

PROGRESS OF PACIFIC AND SOUTHWEST PACIFIC OPERATIONS
15 NOVEMBER 1943 — 15 SEPTEMBER 1944

North Pacific

1. Operations in the North Pacific have been limited to periodic air raids and surface ship bombardment of *Paramushiru* and *Shimushu* and other islands in the northern *Kuriles*. Concurrently the establishment of bases to support future operations in the *North Pacific* is being carried to completion.

Central Pacific

2. In furtherance of the approved strategic concept of the war against Japan, the amphibious forces of the Pacific Ocean Areas, supported tactically and strategically by combatant units of the U. S. Pacific Fleet, have successively occupied principal objectives in the *Gilbert, Marshall* and *Marianas Islands*.

3. The *Gilbert Islands* operations were initiated on 17 November 1943, and resulted in the occupation of *Tarawa, Makin,* and *Apamama. Tarawa* was well defended. In particular the beach defenses were extensive and difficult to overcome.

4. The *Marshall Islands* operations were initiated the 31st of January and resulted in the occupation of *Kwajalein* and *Majuro Atolls*. This was followed by the occupation in mid-February of *Eniwetok*.

5. Operations for the seizure of *Saipan* were initiated on the 15th of June. This was followed by the occupation of *Tinian* and *Guam* in late July.

6. The next operation scheduled in this area is the occupation of the *Palaus*. The target date is 15 September 1944.

TOP SECRET

7. From bases established in the *Marshalls* and *Gilberts* continuous air raids have been conducted against isolated Japanese held islands. Particular attention has been given to neutralization of *Truk*. These operations have been coordinated with similar operations conducted from bases in the Southwest Pacific.

8. During the operations for the occupation of the *Marianas* strong units of the Japanese Fleet were engaged by air action from our carriers in the Philippine Seas. Severe damage was inflicted on the Japanese in this engagement.

9. The submarine campaign in the Western Pacific has been prosecuted with vigor and the results attained have been most gratifying. Heavy toll has been taken of Japanese shipping as well as of escorting forces.

10. The occupation of the *Marianas* has presented the opportunity for development of bases for VLR bombers for operations against Japan Proper. Preparations for conducting these operations are underway with all speed.

South Pacific

11. Operations in the South Pacific have been principally harassing operations against the isolated Japanese garrisons by air forces. The Royal New Zealand Air Force participated in combat missions with U.S. Army and Navy air units from bases in the South Pacific. The South Pacific area is being progressively "rolled-up." Bases developed in that area are currently being used for rehabilitation of troops for further operations in the Western Pacific. The naval base at *Espiritu Santo* has proved very useful in repairing battle damage. Repairs have been successfully accomplished on all classes of ships.

12. On 15 February, the 3rd New Zealand Division (less one brigade) seized *Green Island*.

Southwest Pacific

13. A U.S. task force landed in the *Arawe* area of New Britain on 15 December 1943 and terminated organized enemy resistance on 16 January 1944.

14. One U.S. marine division, supported by Allied air and naval forces, landed in the *Gloucester* area on 26 December 1943 and succeeded in capturing

TOP SECRET

the airfields by 30 December. Japanese killed were 3,686 as against our losses of 326. As a result of the *Arawe* and *Cape Gloucester* operations, western New Britain was secured by the middle of March.

15. Preceded by heavy naval and air bombardment, a successful, unopposed landing was made near *Saidor* on 2 January 1944. The airstrip was captured and ready for landing of transport aircraft by 7 January. Commencing 16 January, the remainder of the U.S. division employed reinforced the original landing. In expanding the beachhead, only weak resistance was encountered.

16. One U.S. cavalry division, supported by naval and air force units, made initial landings in the *Admiralty Islands* on 29 February 1944. The landing was made in *Hayne Harbor, Los Negros Island*, against little resistance and *Momote* airdrome was seized on D-day. Several enemy counterattacks were repulsed resulting in large Japanese casualties and by 23 March enemy forces on *Los Negros* were completely surrounded. Adjacent islands in the group were reduced and occupied and by the middle of April complete control of the *Admiralty Islands* had been obtained.

17. Two independent task forces, under the command of the Sixth Army, made simultaneous landings at *Aitape* and *Hollandia* on 22 April 1944. Landings were preceded by heavy naval bombardment and air strafing attacks.

a. The Hollandia Task Force made landings in the *Humboldt Bay* and *Tanahmerah Bay* areas respectively and formed a pincers movement in attacking the three airstrips. Only slight enemy resistance was encountered and by 1 May control of the area had been definitely established.

b. The Aitape Task Force established landings against practically no opposition and the airdrome was reported operational by 25 April.

c. The element of surprise played an important part in the success of both operations resulting in an estimated 54,000 troops to the eastward being cut off.

18. A U.S. task force, supported by air and naval forces, made unopposed landings on *Wakde Island* and near *Arara* on 17 May 1944. All enemy resistance on *Wakde* was overcome by 18 May. The *Arara* perimeter was extended between the *Tementoe River* and the *Tor River* on 17 May with increasing enemy resistance west of the *Tor River*. Strong enemy attacks failed to penetrate the perimeter and were repulsed. The task force perimeter was extended and by 3 July included the *Maffin* airdrome. Casualties suffered by the Japanese are 3,650 killed and 70 prisoners. Active patrolling is continuing.

19. On 27 May 1944 one U.S. infantry division, with the support of air and naval forces, made landings in the *Biak Island* areas and encountered little opposition initially. Enemy strength developed on 5 June and the *Mokmer* airstrip was crossed on 7 June under artillery, mortar and machine gun fire. Artillery fire prevented work on the *Mokmer* airdrome until 11 June and the enemy launched several unsuccessful counterattacks in an effort to regain the field. *Boroke, Sorido* and *Mokmer* dromes were entirely cleared of enemy artillery and small arms fire by 22 June. General patrolling and mopping up operations continue.

20. One U.S. regimental combat team, closely supported by air and naval forces, landed unopposed near the *Kamiri* drome on *Noemfoor Island* on 2 July 1944. On 3 July and 4 July three U.S. parachute battalions were dropped on the *Kamiri* strip, assisting the infantry. By 6 July enemy resistance had been overcome and the *Kamiri, Koransoren* and *Namber* dromes were firmly held.

21. A U.S. infantry task force made an unopposed landing near *Cape Opmarai* in the *Cape Sansapor* area on 30 July 1944. No opposition other than patrol skirmishes has been encountered and active patrolling continues. Japanese dead for the period 30 July to 10 August numbered 92.

22. Air operations conducted in the Southwest Pacific Area have been especially effective in neutralizing Japanese forces and enabling the Allies to conduct further offensive actions aimed at gaining complete control. In all advances, their mission in each case called for securing airfields and other bases from which to conduct further operations. Air supremacy has been achieved to such an extent that only in isolated instances are the Japanese offering any determined air resistance.

23. Australian land force activity in the Southwest Pacific Area consisted primarily of participation in the *Finschhafen* and *Kaiapit-Dumpu* operations and the occupation of the *Madang-Sepik River* coast line. The 9th Australian Division captured *Finschhafen* on 2 October 1943 and drove the remaining Jap troops to *Satelberg*. *Satelberg* fell on 29 November. Elements of the 9th Australian Division, utilizing armor to great advantage, then advanced up *Huon Peninsula* coast line to contact U.S. Saidor Task Force at *Yaut River*, southeast of *Saidor* to complete occupation of *Huon Peninsula* on 10 February.

Simultaneously, the 7th Australian Division was deployed into the *Ramu Valley* to reinforce independent Australian units and to stop the threatened Jap drive overland through the *Ramu-Markham Valley* from *Madang*. The 11th

TOP SECRET

Australian Division relieved the 7th Australian Division 8 January and continued the Australian advance to a final juncture with U.S. troops near *Yalua* on 13 April. Subsequently, U.S. troops were withdrawn and the Australian units continued pressure on the Jap forces which withdrew up the *New Guinea* coast toward *Wewak*. By 6 June Australian troops had reached *Hansa Bay* and are now in contact along the *Sepik River*.

During this period, the RAAF carried on continued attacks from the *Darwin* area. Australian fighter units attached to U.S. task forces were used in each of the landings along the *New Guinea* coast as the initial occupation forces with their light P-40's.

They operated in the advance airdromes before the airdromes were suitable for the operation of U.S. units equipped with heavier aircraft.

The Netherlands East Indies Air Forces operating in the Southwest Pacific Area consists of the 18th Medium Bomber Squadron and the 120th Fighter Squadron. Elements of these forces participated in daily bombing and strafing strikes against enemy shipping and installations in the *Aroe-Tanimbar-Kai* and *Timor* areas.

24. Future operations in this area will advance our forces into the southern and central Philippines via *Morotai, Talaud, Sarangani* and the *Leyte-Samar* area, with a target date of 20 December for *Leyte-Samar*.

TOP SECRET

LOCATIVE MAP FOR

OPERATIONS IN THE PACIFIC

TOP SECRET

C.C.S. 677
C.C.S. 677/1

FUTURE OPERATIONS IN THE MEDITERRANEAN

References:

NAF 774
MEDCOS 181
CCS 172d Meeting, Item 5
CCS 173d Meeting, Item 8
2d Plenary Meeting,
   Item 1 *a*, *b*, and *c*.

In C.C.S. 677, dated 12 September 1944, the United States Chiefs of Staff present their views with regard to General Wilson's progress report as submitted in NAF 774 and MEDCOS 181.

The Combined Chiefs of Staff considered these views in their 172d Meeting. Draft messages to inform the Supreme Allied Commander, Mediterranean of the agreed conclusions on this matter were proposed respectively by the British and United States Chiefs of Staff, Enclosures "A" and "B" to C.C.S. 677/1. The Combined Chiefs of Staff in their 173d Meeting approved the dispatch of the message in Enclosure "B" to C.C.S. 677/1.

TOP SECRET

C.C.S. 677   12 September 1944

COMBINED CHIEFS OF STAFF

FUTURE OPERATIONS IN THE MEDITERRANEAN

Memorandum by the United States Chiefs of Staff

The views of the United States Chiefs of Staff with regard to General Wilson's progress report as submitted in NAF 774 and MEDCOS 181 are as follows:

Part or all of the Fifth Army should be transferred to France, if it can be used effectively in the attack on Germany. The timing of the transfer and the route, whether overland or by sea, is dependent on the progress and outcome of the present offensive in Italy.

If General Eisenhower indicates that he does not require a part or all of the U.S. forces now in Italy, they should then be utilized to clear the Germans from Italy and to assist British forces in operations to the northeastward toward Vienna.

The transfer of part or all of the Twelfth Air Force to France should be dependent on the progress and outcome of the present offensive in Italy, and more particularly on the disposition of the Fifth Army. The Fifteenth Air Force can best perform its mission by remaining at its Foggia bases.

TOP SECRET

C.C.S. 677/1 13 September 1944

COMBINED CHIEFS OF STAFF

FUTURE OPERATIONS IN THE MEDITERRANEAN

Reference:

CCS 172d Meeting, Item 5 c.

Memorandum by the United States Chiefs of Staff

The United States Chiefs of Staff have considered the draft message to General Wilson proposed by the British Chiefs of Staff (Enclosure "A") in connection with item 5 c, C.C.S. 172d Meeting, and recommend that the Combined Chiefs of Staff dispatch the message attached as Enclosure "B" to SACMED in lieu of Enclosure "A."

TOP SECRET

ENCLOSURE "A"

DRAFT

TELEGRAM TO GENERAL WILSON PROPOSED BY THE BRITISH CHIEFS OF STAFF PURSUANT TO ITEM 5 *c*, C.C.S. 172d MEETING

1. The Combined Chiefs of Staff took note of your NAF 774 this morning.

2. The following decisions are sent for your information and guidance in future planning:

    (a) There will be no withdrawals from the Fifth U.S. Army, at any rate until the success of General Alexander's operations is ensured.

    (b) For the capture of the Istrian Peninsula you may count on having the amphibious lift now in the Mediterranean. You should prepare plans for carrying out this operation as soon as possible. You should submit this plan to Combined Chiefs of Staff at the earliest date, and, in any event, not later than 15th October.

Enclosure "A"

TOP SECRET

ENCLOSURE "B"

DRAFT

TELEGRAM TO GENERAL WILSON PROPOSED BY THE UNITED STATES CHIEFS OF STAFF IN CONNECTION WITH ITEM 5 *c*, C.C.S. 172d MEETING

1. The Combined Chiefs of Staff took note of your NAF 774 this morning.

2. The following decisions are sent for your information and guidance in future planning:

- (a) There will be no withdrawals of major units from the Fifth U.S. Army until the outcome of the present Italian offensive is known.

- (b) For planning the capture of the Istrian Peninsula you may count on having the amphibious lift now in the Mediterranean. You should submit this plan to Combined Chiefs of Staff at the earliest date, and, in any event, not later than 10th October.

Enclosure "B"

TOP SECRET

C.C.S. 678
C.C.S. 678/1

PLANNING DATE FOR THE END OF THE WAR AGAINST JAPAN

References:

CCS 174th Meeting, Item 5
CCS 680/2, Paragraphs 31 and 32

The Combined Chiefs of Staff in their 174th Meeting considered C.C.S. 678 and agreed to make certain recommendations to the President and Prime Minister.

The recommendations of the Combined Chiefs of Staff as approved by the President and Prime Minister were subsequently circulated as C.C.S. 678/1.

TOP SECRET

C.C.S. 678   13 September 1944

COMBINED CHIEFS OF STAFF

PLANNING DATE FOR THE END OF THE WAR AGAINST JAPAN

Memorandum by the British Chiefs of Staff

1. The British Chiefs of Staff feel that it is important that the Combined Chiefs of Staff should agree and promulgate a planning date for the end of the war against Japan. The following planning must be related to an estimated date for the end of the war against Japan:—

    a. The redeployment of forces against Japan.

    b. The planning of production.

    c. The allocation of manpower.

2. The British Chiefs of Staff recommend that, in order to make due allowance for contingencies, the Combined Chiefs of Staff should accept as a planning date two years after the defeat of Germany.

TOP SECRET

C.C.S. 678/1   19 September 1944

COMBINED CHIEFS OF STAFF

PLANNING DATE FOR THE END OF THE WAR AGAINST JAPAN

Note by the Secretaries

The President and Prime Minister approved the recommendation of the Combined Chiefs of Staff that the date for the end of the war against Japan, for planning production and for allocation of manpower, should be set at 18 months after the defeat of Germany; this date to be adjusted periodically to conform to the course of the war.

                                             A. J. McFARLAND,
                                             A. T. CORNWALL-JONES,
                                             Combined Secretariat.

TOP SECRET

C.C.S. 679

REDEPLOYMENT OF FORCES AFTER THE END OF THE WAR IN EUROPE

References:

CCS 175th Meeting, Item 4
2d Plenary Meeting, Item 1 *j*.

C.C.S. 679, dated 14 September 1944, circulated a memorandum by the United States Chiefs of Staff. The Combined Chiefs of Staff in their 174th Meeting amended and approved C.C.S. 679 which is published herein as amended.

TOP SECRET

C.C.S. 679   14 September 1944

COMBINED CHIEFS OF STAFF

REDEPLOYMENT OF FORCES AFTER THE END OF THE WAR IN EUROPE

Reference:

CCS 675 Series

Memorandum by the United States Chiefs of Staff

1. We consider that the whole redeployment problem, including repatriation, after the end of the war in Europe needs combined study which cannot be completed at this conference. This study appears to be required in order to assure the optimum use of the resources involved including personnel and cargo shipping and to make certain that forces required for operations against Japan will reach the theater of war at the earliest date.

2. The United States Chiefs of Staff have prepared tentative plans for redeployment which are available to the United States members of the combined agencies concerned. Presumably the British members of these agencies have similar information available.

3. The United States Chiefs of Staff recommend that the Combined Administrative Committee in collaboration with the Combined Military Transportation Committee, Combined Shipping Authorities and Combined Staff Planners study and report on the problem. Questions requiring decision before completion of the study will be submitted to the Combined Chiefs of Staff.

TOP SECRET

C.C.S. 680/2

REPORT TO THE PRESIDENT AND PRIME MINISTER

References:

CCS 175th Meeting, Item 2
2d Plenary Meeting, Item 1

C.C.S. 680, the first draft report to the President and Prime Minister, was amended and approved by the Combined Chiefs of Staff in their 175th Meeting. The amended report was subsequently circulated as C.C.S. 680/1.

In the Second Plenary Meeting with the President and Prime Minister certain amendments to C.C.S. 680/1 were agreed upon. The final report as approved by the President and Prime Minister was circulated as C.C.S. 680/2.

TOP SECRET

C.C.S. 680/2   16 September 1944

COMBINED CHIEFS OF STAFF

REPORT TO THE PRESIDENT AND PRIME MINISTER

Note by the Secretaries

The final report of the Combined Chiefs of Staff on the *OCTAGON* Conference as approved by the President and Prime Minister is enclosed.

                                                     A. J. McFARLAND,
                                                     A. T. CORNWALL-JONES,
                                                     Combined Secretariat.

TOP SECRET

ENCLOSURE

REPORT TO THE PRESIDENT AND PRIME MINISTER
OF THE AGREED SUMMARY OF CONCLUSIONS REACHED
BY THE COMBINED CHIEFS OF STAFF
AT THE "OCTAGON" CONFERENCE

1. The agreed summary of the conclusions reached at OCTAGON Conference is submitted herewith:—

I. *OVER-ALL OBJECTIVE*

2. In conjunction with Russia and other Allies, to bring about at the earliest possible date the unconditional surrender of Germany and Japan.

II. *OVER-ALL STRATEGIC CONCEPT FOR THE PROSECUTION OF THE WAR*

3. In cooperation with Russia and other Allies, to bring about at the earliest possible date the unconditional surrender of Germany.

4. Simultaneously, in cooperation with other Pacific Powers concerned, to maintain and extend unremitting pressure against Japan with the purpose of continually reducing her military power and attaining positions from which her ultimate surrender can be forced. The effect of any such extension on the over-all objective to be given consideration by the Combined Chiefs of Staff before action is taken.

5. Upon the defeat of Germany, in cooperation with other Pacific Powers and with Russia, to direct the full resources of the United States and Great Britain to bring about at the earliest possible date the unconditional surrender of Japan.

III. *BASIC UNDERTAKINGS IN SUPPORT OF OVER-ALL STRATEGIC CONCEPT*

6. Whatever operations are decided on in support of the over-all strategic concept, the following established undertakings will be a first charge against our resources, subject to review by the Combined Chiefs of Staff in keeping with the changing situation:

a. Maintain the security and war-making capacity of the Western Hemisphere and the British Isles.

b. Support the war-making capacity of our forces in all areas.

c. Maintain vital overseas lines of communication.

d. Continue the disruption of enemy sea communications.

e. Continue the offensive against Germany.

f. Undertake such measures as may be necessary and practicable to aid the war effort of Russia to include coordinating the action of forces.

g. Undertake such measures as may be necessary and practicable in order to aid the war effort of China as an effective ally and as a base for operations against Japan.

h. Continue assistance to the French and Italian forces to enable them to fulfill an active role in the war against Germany and/or Japan. Within the limits of our available resources, to assist other co-belligerents to the extent they are able effectively to employ this assistance against the enemy Powers in the present war.

i. Reorient forces from the European Theater to the Pacific and Far East as a matter of highest priority having regard to other agreed and/or inescapable commitments as soon as the German situation allows.

j. Continue operations leading to the earliest practicable invasion of Japan.

IV. EXECUTION OF THE OVER-ALL STRATEGIC CONCEPT

DEFEAT OF GERMANY

CONTROL OF STRATEGIC BOMBER FORCES IN EUROPE

7. Prior to the launching of OVERLORD an air plan was developed by the Supreme Commander in preparation for and in support of OVERLORD, and in April 1944, control of the air operations out of England of all the air forces involved, including the Strategic Air Force and the RAF Bomber Command, passed to the Supreme Commander, Allied Expeditionary Force. We have now decided that the special conditions which made it desirable that the Supreme Commander, Allied Expeditionary Force should control all forces operating

TOP SECRET

out of the United Kingdom no longer carry their original force. We have therefore agreed that the control of the Strategic Bomber Force in Europe shall be exercised by the Deputy Chief of the Air Staff, Royal Air Force and the Commanding General, United States Strategic Air Forces in Europe acting jointly for the Chief of the Air Staff, RAF and the Commanding General, United States Army Air Forces, the latter acting as agents of the Combined Chiefs of Staff. A directive (C.C.S. 520/6) has accordingly been issued to the Deputy Chief of the Air Staff, RAF and the Commanding General, United States Strategic Air Forces in Europe.

OPERATIONS IN NORTHWEST EUROPE

8. The Supreme Commander, Allied Expeditionary Force has reported (SCAF 78) on the course of operations in France and the Low Countries and has given us a review of his future intentions.

9. The Supreme Commander's broad intention is to press on with all speed to destroy the German armed forces and occupy the heart of Germany. He considers his best opportunity of defeating the enemy in the West lies in striking at the Ruhr and Saar since he is convinced that the enemy will concentrate the remainder of his available forces in the defense of these essential areas. The Supreme Commander's first operation will be to break the Siegfried Line and seize crossings over the Rhine. In doing this his main effort will be on the left. He will then prepare logistically and otherwise for a deep thrust into Germany.

10. We have approved General Eisenhower's proposals and drawn his attention (FACS 78):

    a. To the advantages of the northern line of approach into Germany, as opposed to the southern, and,

    b. To the necessity for the opening up of the northwest ports, particularly Antwerp and Rotterdam before bad weather sets in.

OPERATIONS IN ITALY

11. We have examined a report by General Wilson (NAF 774) on operations within his theater. In so far as the battle in Italy is concerned he considers that operations will develop in one of two ways:

a. Either Kesselring's forces will be routed, in which case it should be possible to undertake a rapid regrouping and a pursuit towards the Ljubljana Gap (and across the Alps through the Brenner Pass) leaving a small force to clear up northwest Italy, or,

b. Kesselring's Army will succeed in effecting an orderly withdrawal; in which event it does not seem possible that we can do more than clear the Lombardy Plains this year. Difficult terrain and severe weather in the Alps during winter would prevent another major offensive until spring of 1945.

12. We have agreed:

a. That no major units should be withdrawn from Italy until the outcome of General Alxander's present offensive is known;

b. That the desirability of withdrawing formations of the United States Fifth Army should be reconsidered in the light of the results of General Alexander's present offensive and of a German withdrawal in northern Italy and in the light of the views of General Eisenhower.

c. To inform General Wilson that if he wishes to retain for use in the Istrian Peninsula the amphibious lift at present in the Mediterranean he should submit his plan therefor to the Combined Chiefs of Staff as soon as possible, and not later than 10th October. We have instructed the Supreme Allied Commander accordingly (FAN 415).

OPERATIONS IN THE BALKANS

13. General Wilson considers that a situation can be anticipated in which the bulk of the German forces south of a line, Trieste-Ljubljana-Zagreb and the Danube, will be immobilized and will so remain until their supplies are exhausted, in which case they would be ready to surrender to us or will be liquidated by Partisans or the Russian forces. We have noted that as long as the battle in Italy continues there will be no forces available in the Mediterranean to employ in the Balkans except:

a. The small force of two British brigades from Egypt which is being held ready to occupy the Athens area and so pave the way for the commencement of relief and establishment of law and order and the Greek Government.

b. The small land forces in the Adriatic which are being actively used primarily for commando type operations.

TOP SECRET

COMMAND OF "DRAGOON" FORCES

14. Command of the DRAGOON forces operating from southern France has been transferred as from the 15th September to the Supreme Commander, Allied Expeditionary Force (FACS 76).

15. Adjustments of the ground and air forces on which the decision of the Combined Chiefs of Staff will be required are dependent on the development of the campaign in Italy.

16. Logistic support for the DRAGOON forces will for the present continue to be supplied from the Mediterranean area.

MACHINERY FOR COORDINATION OF UNITED STATES-SOVIET-BRITISH MILITARY EFFORT

17. Some two months ago Marshal Stalin in conversation with the U.S. Ambassador in Moscow suggested that improvement should be made in the system of military coordination between the U.S.S.R., U.S. and the United Kingdom.

18. We have examined the possibility of improving the coordination with the U.S.S.R. and have instructed the heads of the U.S. and British Military Missions in Moscow to initiate action at once with the Soviet General Staff with a view to the setting up in Moscow of a Tripartite Military Committee consisting of senior representatives of the Russian General Staff, of the United States Chiefs of Staff and of the British Chiefs of Staff.

19. We have instructed them to make it clear that this Committee will be purely consultative and advisory, with no power to make decisions without reference to the respective Chiefs of Staff and the Russian General Staff and further, that it must be military in its character and not impinge upon the work at present being done by the European Advisory Commission such as civil affairs, et cetera.

20. In our instructions we have stressed that to eliminate the delays now existent in dealings between the Russians and the United States and British Military Missions, it is essential that the Russian representative on the Committee should be a senior member of the Russian General Staff. On the United States and British sides the heads of the present missions would represent the United States and British Chiefs of Staff respectively, each being responsible to his own Chiefs of Staff.

THE WAR AGAINST JAPAN

OVER-ALL OBJECTIVE IN THE WAR AGAINST JAPAN

21. We have agreed that the over-all objective in the war against Japan should be expressed as follows:

To force the unconditional surrender of Japan by:

a. Lowering Japanese ability and will to resist by establishing sea and air blockades, conducting intensive air bombardment, and destroying Japanese air and naval strength.

b. Ultimately invading and seizing objectives in the industrial heart of Japan.

OPERATIONS IN THE PACIFIC AREA

22. We believe that operations must be devised to accomplish the defeat of Japan at the earliest possible date and to that end our plans should retain flexibility, and provision should be made to take full advantage of possible developments in the strategic situation which may permit taking all manner of short cuts. We propose to exploit to the fullest the Allied superiority of naval and air power and to avoid, wherever possible, commitment to costly land campaigns. Unremitting submarine warfare against the enemy ships will be continued. Very long range bomber operations against Japan Proper will be continued from China bases and will be instituted from bases being established in the Marianas and from those to be seized in the future. The air forces in China will continue to support operations of the Chinese ground forces and will also provide the maximum practical support for the campaign in the Pacific.

23. Pursuant to the above, the operations in the Pacific Theater are being conducted to effect the reconquest of the Philippines and the opening of a seaway to China.

24. We have noted that British operations against Japan, not yet approved, will require the allocation of resources. In planning production these requirements will be borne in mind.

TOP SECRET

BRITISH EMPIRE PARTICIPATION IN THE PACIFIC

25. We have agreed that the British Fleet should participate in the main operations against Japan in the Pacific, with the understanding that this Fleet will be balanced and self-supporting. The method of the employment of the British Fleet in these main operations in the Pacific will be decided from time to time in accordance with the prevailing circumstances.

26. We have invited the British Chiefs of Staff to put forward, as a basis for planning, an estimate in general terms of the contribution the Royal Air Force will be prepared to make in the main operations against Japan.

27. Canadian participation is accepted in principle.

OPERATIONS IN SOUTHEAST ASIA

28. We have agreed that our object in Southeast Asia is the recapture of all Burma at the earliest date, it being understood that operations to achieve this object must not prejudice the security of the existing air supply route to China, including the air staging base at Myitkyina, and the opening of overland communications.

29. We have approved the following operations: —

a. Stages of Operation *CAPITAL* necessary to the security of the air route and the attainment of overland communications with China;

b. Operation *DRACULA*.

We attach the greatest importance to the discharge of the task under paragraph 29 *a* and to the execution of Operation *DRACULA* before the monsoon in 1945 and with a target date of 15 March. If *DRACULA* has to be postponed until after the monsoon of 1945, it is our intention to exploit Operation *CAPITAL* as far as may be possible without prejudice to preparations for the execution of Operation *DRACULA* in November, 1945. Our directive to the Supreme Allied Commander, Southeast Asia is attached. (See Annex)

REDEPLOYMENT AFTER THE END OF THE WAR IN EUROPE

30. We consider that the whole problem of the redeployment of forces after the end of the war in Europe, including repatriation, needs combined study in order to assure the optimum use of the resources involved, including

personnel and cargo shipping, and to make certain that the forces required for operations against Japan will reach the theater of war at the earliest date. We have accordingly instructed the combined staffs in consultation with the combined shipping authorities to study and report on this problem, submitting to the Combined Chiefs of Staff such questions as may require decision before completion of the study.

DURATION OF THE WAR AGAINST JAPAN

31. We feel that it is important to agree and promulgate a planning date for the end of the war against Japan. This date is necessary for the purpose of planning production and the allocation of manpower.

32. We recommend that the planning date for the end of the war against Japan should be set at 18 months after the defeat of Germany; this date to be adjusted periodically to conform to the course of the war.

ALLOCATION OF ZONES OF OCCUPATION IN GERMANY

33. Upon the collapse of organized resistance by the German Army the following subdivision of that part of Germany not allocated to the Soviet Government for disarmament, policing, and the preservation of order is acceptable from a military point of view by the Combined Chiefs of Staff.

34. For disarmament, policing and preservation of order:

a. The British forces under a British Commander will occupy Germany west of the Rhine and east of the Rhine north of the line from Koblenz following the northern border of Hessen and Nassau to the border of the area allocated to the Soviet Government.

b. The forces of the United States under a United States Commander will occupy Germany east of the Rhine, south of the line Koblenz-northern border of Hessen-Nassau and west of the area allocated to the Soviet Government.

c. Control of the ports of Bremen and Bremerhaven, and the necessary staging areas in that immediate vicinity will be vested in the Commander of the American Zone.

d. American area to have in addition access through the western and northwestern seaports and passage through the British controlled area.

e. Accurate delineation of the above outlined British and American areas of control can be made at a later date.

TOP SECRET

ANNEX

DIRECTIVE TO SUPREME ALLIED COMMANDER, SOUTHEAST ASIA COMMAND

1. Your object is the destruction or expulsion of all Japanese forces in Burma at the earliest date. Operations to achieve this object must not, however, prejudice the security of the existing air supply route to China, including the air staging post at Myitkyina, and the opening of overland communications.

2. The following are approved operations:—

   a. The stages of Operation *CAPITAL* necessary to the security of the air route, and the attainment of overland communications with China.

   b. Operation *DRACULA*.

The Combined Chiefs of Staff attach the greatest importance to the effective discharge of the task under paragraph 2 *a* and to the execution of Operation *DRACULA* before the monsoon in 1945, with a target date of 15th March.

3. If *DRACULA* has to be postponed until after the monsoon of 1945, you will continue to exploit Operation *CAPITAL* as far as may be possible without prejudice to preparations for the execution of Operation *DRACULA* in November 1945.

TOP SECRET

C.C.S. 681/2

COMMUNICATION OF THE RESULTS OF "OCTAGON" CONFERENCE TO MARSHAL STALIN AND GENERALISSIMO CHIANG KAI-SHEK

References:

CCS 174th Meeting, Item 7
CCS 175th Meeting, Item 3
2d Plenary Meeting, Item 3

C.C.S. 681 and C.C.S. 681/1 circulated proposed draft messages to Marshal Stalin and Generalissimo Chiang Kai-shek respectively.

The Combined Chiefs of Staff in their 175th Meeting amended and approved the proposed messages and submitted them as C.C.S. 681/2 to the President and Prime Minister, who in their Second Plenary Meeting approved the terms of the communications as set forth therein.

TOP SECRET

C.C.S. 681/2 15 September 1944

COMBINED CHIEFS OF STAFF

COMMUNICATION OF THE RESULTS OF "OCTAGON" CONFERENCE TO MARSHAL STALIN AND GENERALISSIMO CHIANG KAI-SHEK

Note by the Secretaries

The Combined Chiefs of Staff have approved the enclosed draft telegrams to Marshal Stalin and Generalissimo Chiang Kai-shek on the results of the *OCTAGON* Conference.

A. J. McFARLAND,
A. T. CORNWALL-JONES,
Combined Secretariat.

TOP SECRET

ENCLOSURE "A"

September, 1944

To: Alusna, Moscow

From: Naval Aide to the President

My immediately following message is top secret. It should be seen only by Alusna, a decoder appointed by him and the Ambassador who is then requested to deliver it to the British Ambassador. If possible it should then be delivered by the British and American Ambassadors jointly to Marshal Stalin. Message should be carefully paraphrased before delivery. Acknowledge receipt and delivery.

September, 1944

To: Alusna, Moscow

Top secret and personal to Marshal Stalin from the United States Government and His Majesty's Government in the United Kingdom.

1. In our Conference at Quebec just concluded we have arrived at the following decisions as to military operations.

Operations in Northwest Europe

2. It is our intention to press on with all speed to destroy the German armed forces and penetrate into the heart of Germany. The best opportunity to defeat the enemy in the West lies in striking at the Ruhr and Saar since it is there that the enemy will concentrate the remainder of his available forces in the defense of these essential areas. The northern line of approach clearly has advantages over the southern and it is essential that we should open up the northwest ports, particularly Antwerp and Rotterdam, before bad weather sets in. Our main effort will therefore be on the left.

Enclosure "A"

TOP SECRET

Operations in Italy

3. As a result of our present operations in Italy,

   (a) Either Kesselring's forces will be routed, in which case it should be possible to undertake a rapid regrouping and a pursuit towards the Ljubljana Gap; or,

   (b) Kesselring's Army will succeed in effecting an orderly withdrawal, in which event we may have to be content with clearing the Lombardy Plains this year.

Our future action depends on the progress of the battle. Plans are being prepared for an amphibious operation on the Istrian Peninsula to be carried out if the situation so demands.

Operations in the Balkans

4. Operations of our air forces and commando type operations will continue.

Operations against Japan

5. We have agreed on further operations to intensify the offensive against the Japanese in all theaters, with the ultimate objective of invading the Japanese homeland.

6. Plans for the prompt transfer of power to the Pacific Theater after the collapse of Germany were agreed upon.

Enclosure "A"

TOP SECRET

ENCLOSURE "B"

From: Agwar

To: Commanding General, U.S. Army Forces in China-Burma-India, Forward echelon — Chungking, China

From Admiral Leahy, Chief of Staff to the President

My immediately following message is top secret and should be seen only by General Stilwell, a decoder appointed by him, and the Ambassador who is then to deliver it to the British Ambassador upon receipt. If possible it should be delivered by the two Ambassadors at the same time to the Generalissimo. Message should be carefully but closely paraphrased before delivery. Acknowledge receipt and delivery.

From: Agwar

To: Commanding General, U.S. Army Forces in China-Burma-India, Forward echelon — Chungking, China

From Admiral Leahy, Chief of Staff to the President

Top secret and personal to Generalissimo Chiang Kai-shek from President Roosevelt and Prime Minister Churchill.

We have just concluded our conference in Quebec during which we discussed ways and means to bring about the earliest possible defeat of Germany so that we can reorient the entire weight of our forces and resources against Japan. We hasten to inform you of plans for our mutual effort, particularly in Southeast Asia.

First: We are determined fully to employ all available resources toward the earliest practicable invasion of the Japanese homeland. To this end we have devised courses of action and are taking vigorous steps to expedite the redeployment of forces to the war against Japan following the defeat of Germany.

Enclosure "B"

TOP SECRET

  Second: To continue and extend present operations under Admiral Mountbatten in north Burma to provide additional security for intermediate air ferry bases in the Myitkyina area, and at the beginning of favorable weather to launch a determined campaign to open overland communications between India and China. These operations will require continued effective cooperation of the Chinese troops who have already so distinguished themselves in Burma, as well as of your armies that are now engaged west of the Salween. All these operations will be fully supported by our preponderant air strength, and by adequate air supply. Small scale amphibious operations on the Arakan Coast, and activities by long range penetration groups will contribute to our success. We feel that the vigorous prosecution of these operations should result in securing an area by next spring which will permit the extension of the Ledo Road with accompanying pipelines in order to support the heroic effort of your forces.

  Third: Admiral Mountbatten has been further directed to prepare a large scale amphibious operation in the Bay of Bengal to be undertaken as soon as developments in the European Theater will allow the necessary resources to be made available.

  Fourth: We have agreed on further operations to intensify the offensive against the Japanese in the Pacific Theater, including the opening of a seaway into China.

Enclosure "B"

TOP SECRET

C.C.S. 682

OPERATION "HIGHBALL"

Reference:

CCS 175th Meeting, Item 6

The Combined Chiefs of Staff in their 175th Meeting took note of the statement contained in C.C.S. 682.

TOP SECRET

C.C.S. 682 　　　　　　　　　　　　　　　　　　　15 September 1944

COMBINED CHIEFS OF STAFF

OPERATION "HIGHBALL"

Memorandum by the British Chiefs of Staff

The American Chiefs of Staff are asked to take note that Operation *HIGHBALL* will be available in the Eastern Theatre at the end of November, 1944.

TOP SECRET

C.C.S. 684

"RANKIN" PLANNING IN THE MEDITERRANEAN THEATER

Reference:

CCS 176th Meeting, Item 2

The Combined Chiefs of Staff in their 176th Meeting approved the directive to General Wilson contained in C.C.S. 684.

TOP SECRET

C.C.S. 684　　　　　　　　　　　　　　　　　　　　15 September 1944

COMBINED CHIEFS OF STAFF

"RANKIN" PLANNING IN THE MEDITERRANEAN THEATER

Memorandum by the British Chiefs of Staff

1. We have noted the request from General Wilson in his telegram (MEDCOS 181) for a firm directive on his responsibilties for *RANKIN* in the Mediterranean.

2. We ask that the Combined Chiefs of Staff should agree to the immediate dispatch of the enclosed message to General Wilson.

TOP SECRET

ENCLOSURE

From: A.M.S.S.O.

To: A.F.H.Q.

Following for General Wilson from Chiefs of Staff.

Reference MEDCOS 153 and 181.

1. Your planning for *RANKIN* in the Mediterranean Theatre of Operations should proceed on the following basis.

Areas of Occupation

2. You should plan to seize immediate control of countries in the Mediterranean Theatre of Operations as follows:—

(a) Austria with four divisions and small tactical air force. Instructions have already been issued in FAN 410 and FAN 411.

(b) Greece with approximately a division of British troops and small air forces. Instructions have already been issued in FAN 409.

(c) The Dodecanese with approximately 2,400 men.

(d) Venezia Giuilia with approximately one division.

3. It is not intended that you should station forces in Yugoslavia or Albania beyond guards which may be required in connection with distribution of supplies. No immediate action by you will be required in Hungary or Roumania.

4. It is not the present intention to send any British troops to Bulgaria.

5. It is intended in due course to offer British naval assistance in the administration of the Danube and in particular in the clearance of mines. On no account however will any British naval forces enter the Danube except after prior agreement with the Russians.

Availability of Forces

6. In estimating what forces are available for the above operations, you should bear the following considerations in mind:

TOP SECRET

(a) As stated in *COSMED* 127, United States forces will be withdrawn as soon as practicable after the cessation of hostilities.

(b) It will probably be the policy to withdraw Dominion forces as early as possible after the defeat of Germany for repatriation at an early date. Pending repatriation they should not be employed on occupational duties in Austria, Greece or Dodecanese or for internal security duties in Middle East until after discussion with Dominion Governments, which is being initiated forthwith.

(c) The four British Indian divisions in your command will be withdrawn as early as possible and should not be used for *RANKIN* operations.

(d) French and Italian divisions will not be used.

(e) The internal security commitment in the Middle East after the defeat of Germany will require three divisions from forces at present in the Mediterranean and Middle East.

7. After making allowance for the above considerations, we calculate that you should have sufficient forces to meet the commitments in paragraph 2 above and still retain a small reserve for contingencies.

8. All the above applies to *RANKIN* only, i.e., the immediate seizure of control in enemy and enemy occupied territories. Direction upon the final occupation of Europe after the establishment of control will be issued later.

Ends

TOP SECRET

C.C.S. 687

RELEASE OF AMPHIBIOUS CRAFT FROM
"OVERLORD" TO OTHER THEATERS

Reference:

CCS 176th Meeting, Item 3

The Combined Chiefs of Staff in their 176th Meeting approved the dispatch of the message contained in C.C.S. 687.

TOP SECRET

C.C.S. 687   16 September 1944

COMBINED CHIEFS OF STAFF

RELEASE OF AMPHIBIOUS CRAFT FROM
"OVERLORD" TO OTHER THEATERS

Memorandum by the United States Chiefs of Staff

The United States Chiefs of Staff propose the dispatch of the following message to the Supreme Commander, Allied Expeditionary Force:

Accelerated operations in the Pacific and prospective plans for SEAC require earliest practicable withdrawal of amphibious craft especially LST's from European Theater. Having due regard for your requirements for build-up until adequate port facilities become available and considering limitation on the use of these craft in the near future due to weather, Combined Chiefs of Staff desire you review the situation carefully with the object of early release of amphibious craft from *OVERLORD*. Early report in this matter is desired.

MINUTES OF
COMBINED CHIEFS OF STAFF
MEETINGS HELD IN LONDON,
JUNE 1944

TOP SECRET

COMBINED CHIEFS OF STAFF

C.C.S. 162d Meeting

MINUTES OF MEETING HELD IN CONFERENCE ROOM "A"
WAR CABINET OFFICE, LONDON, ENGLAND
ON SATURDAY, 10 JUNE 1944, AT 1130.

PRESENT

United States

General G. C. Marshall, USA
Admiral E. J. King, USN
General H. H. Arnold, USA

British

Field Marshal Sir Alan F. Brooke
Marshal of the Royal Air Force
  Sir Charles F. A. Portal
Admiral of the Fleet
  Sir Andrew B. Cunningham

ALSO PRESENT

General Sir Hastings L. Ismay
Major Gen. R. E. Laycock

SECRETARIAT

Major Gen. L. C. Hollis
Brigadier H. Redman
Colonel A. J. McFarland, USA

TOP SECRET

CURRENT OPERATIONS

First a brief discussion took place on the progress of Operation *NEPTUNE* to date.

SIR ALAN BROOKE outlined briefly the progress of land operations and included reference to Allied build-up and construction of artificial harbors, and to enemy build-up, including panzer divisions, lack of Tiger or Panther tanks, and enemy capacity for counterattack.

SIR ANDREW CUNNINGHAM then reviewed briefly the naval situation with particular reference to enemy submarines and destroyers.

SIR CHARLES PORTAL referred briefly to Allied air activity, to the lack of action by enemy bombers, the enemy build-up of fighters in the battle area, the evident signs of confusion in the enemy air formations, and the probable difficulty the German Air Force would find in supporting the counterattack, with possible resulting delay in that counterattack.

As a result of questions by General Marshall a short discussion then took place on the subject of the enemy counterattacks to be expected.

The discussion then turned to the Italian campaign.

SIR ALAN BROOKE made a brief appreciation of the fighting value of the enemy forces in Italy, of the action likely to be expected of them, and the strength considered necessary to hold the Pisa-Rimini line. He referred to enemy anxiety regarding amphibious operations on their western flank which the operation being staged from Corsica against Elba would be likely to foster.

GENERAL MARSHALL drew from the known location of the five German divisions still untouched in Italy the conclusion that there were no enemy formations on the Pisa-Rimini line, and no other enemy line across Italy.

A very brief discussion then took place on the Balkans including movements of Tito and the raid on his headquarters; effective Allied air action against Germans in Yugoslavia; the air supply to Partisans in Yugoslavia; the thinning out of German air forces in the Adriatic for France; a possible change in German policy in the Balkans as a result of the Russian threat, the Italian

TOP SECRET

fiasco, and now the opening of the Second Front; the big salient that the Balkans now presented, and possibilities of enemy withdrawal from the Dodecanese and the Balkans.

SIR ALAN BROOKE referred briefly to the Hitler mentality as tending possibly to force the Germans to hold on until too late as they had done at Stalingrad, in Tunisia, on the Dnieper bend, and in Italy.

A short discussion then took place on the likely direction of forthcoming Russian offensives.

Turning to the Southeast Asia Command *SIR ALAN BROOKE* referred briefly to the need to open the Imphal Kohima Road, to the problem of maintaining Myitkyina as well as Imphal by air, and to the effect of these operations on the Hump.

GENERAL MARSHALL mentioned the deep concern in the United States at the reaction of the Generalissimo to the recent Japanese advance in central China. He referred to the recent cut by 1500-tons per month of the Hump traffic to Fourteenth Air Force, and of the transport lift of the additional bomber group; also to a request, which had been disapproved, that stores collected at Chengtu for B-29 operations should be allocated to the Fourteenth Air Force.

GENERAL MARSHALL referred briefly to recent operations in New Guinea, to the decision to build an airbase at Biak instead of Hollandia, and to Japanese reinforcements of Mindanao, the Palaus and Halmahera.

ADMIRAL KING spoke briefly concerning the operations about to commence in the Marianas, of the probable acceleration by a week or a fortnight of the Palau operations, the recent directive for redeployment in the South Pacific, of the consideration given to action by escort carriers against Japan, harassing operations from the Kuriles, Japanese shipping losses and loss of amphibious possibilities.

GENERAL MARSHALL and *ADMIRAL KING* then outlined briefly the manpower difficulties with which United States Chiefs of Staff were faced. General Marshall referred particularly to replacements and to the new policy by which divisions at the front were being kept at full strength throughout operations with resultant increase in morale and in the length of the periods possible for units to operate without relief.

TOP SECRET

A brief reference was then made by General Marshall to statements called for by the President regarding Operation *NEPTUNE*.

Future movements and meetings of the Chiefs of Staff were then discussed and the British Chiefs of Staff accepted an invitation to lunch at Stanwell Place on the next day, June 11th, to be followed by a further meeting of the Combined Chiefs of Staff.

TOP SECRET

COMBINED CHIEFS OF STAFF

C.C.S. 163d Meeting

MINUTES OF MEETING HELD IN THE CONFERENCE ROOM OF STANWELL PLACE, STANWELL, MIDDLESEX, ENGLAND ON SUNDAY, 11 JUNE 1944, AT 1415.

PRESENT

United States

General G. C. Marshall, USA
Admiral E. J. King, USN
General H. H. Arnold, USA

British

Field Marshal Sir Alan F. Brooke
Marshal of the Royal Air Force
   Sir Charles F. A. Portal
Admiral of the Fleet
   Sir Andrew B. Cunningham

ALSO PRESENT

General Sir Hastings L. Ismay

SECRETARIAT

Major Gen. L. C. Hollis
Brigadier H. Redman
Colonel A. J. McFarland, USA

TOP SECRET

1. *OPERATIONS IN EUROPE*

The meeting began with a statement of the progress of Operation *NEPTUNE* by Brigadier General F. H. Smith, Jr., USA, of Supreme Headquarters, Allied Expeditionary Force.

SIR CHARLES PORTAL drew attention to the extent to which the enemy build-up was behind schedule.

SIR ALAN BROOKE then made a brief appreciation of future possibilities in Italy with particular reference to the immediate tasks to be undertaken and the tasks that would face the forces in Italy on arrival at the Pisa-Rimini line. He referred to General Alexander's forecast of 15 July as the date likely for that line to be reached; to the planning that had been going on for amphibious operations against the south of France with target date 15 August. He then considered briefly the possible progress by that date of Operation *NEPTUNE*; the kind of amphibious operation most likely to fit in with Operation *NEPTUNE*; and the difficulty of staging another amphibious operation from the United Kingdom.

In answer to a question by General Marshall he outlined the formations likely to be available for future operations in Italy.

SIR ANDREW CUNNINGHAM then spoke briefly of the naval forces of the enemy in the Mediterranean and the Baltic, and of the effect that Allied capture of the Brest Peninsula would have on enemy submarines in the Bay of Biscay and on reduction of the time at sea of Atlantic convoys.

SIR CHARLES PORTAL then spoke of the air situation in Europe and of enemy first-line air strength as reduced by the bombing offensive. He made a brief appreciation of the capacity of the German Air Force to stand up to intensive fighting over a period; also of the steady decline in efficiency of the German bomber force, and the likelihood that it could no longer make an effective contribution. He mentioned the immediate enemy reaction to the attacks that had been made on his synthetic oil plants and refineries and the prospect of good results when bomber effort could be diverted to renew such attacks.

He then discussed briefly the air situation in the Mediterranean; the employment of the Mediterranean air forces once the Pisa-Rimini line had been reached; the importance of remaining flexible, of keeping options open, and at the same time of maintaining a threat to southern France.

TOP SECRET

SIR CHARLES PORTAL also suggested that the possibilities should be examined of an advance northeast via Istria should Russian progress make this attractive. Such an operation might cut off the whole of southeast Europe from the Germans.

Discussion then ensued as to the likely effect of Russian successes, either in the north resulting in the fall of Finland, or in the center.

GENERAL MARSHALL then spoke regarding the Mediterranean. He referred to the desirability of mounting from the Mediterranean the projected amphibious operation to help *NEPTUNE* in order to permit use of existing administrative facilities; the probability that Operation *ANVIL* would be too slow to assist greatly Operation *NEPTUNE*; the importance of advancing as much as possible the target date of amphibious operations in the Mediterranean; the importance of making preparations now for an amphibious operation, leaving until later the decision as to which operation should be undertaken; the resources in landing craft that might be spared from *NEPTUNE* for the operation; the relative desirability of operations against Marseilles or Cette.

A short discussion then ensued as to the length of time necessary to make available the additional shipping, service troops, et cetera, that would be required for such an operation.

ADMIRAL KING stressed the importance of forcing the enemy to hold the Pisa-Rimini line in strength; asked what the enemy would do if they withdrew from that line; stressed the dependence on Russian operations of an advance northeast to Istria; the value of the Pyrenees as left flank protection to an advance from Cette on Bordeaux; the desirability of reserving for the present the decision as to the amphibious operation to be undertaken; and finally the importance of capturing Le Havre.

A brief discussion then ensued as to an appropriate telegram to be sent to Supreme Allied Commander, Mediterranean and Supreme Commander, Allied Expeditionary Force.

GENERAL MARSHALL proceeded to outline the great possibilities of extensive airborne operations in connection with Operation *NEPTUNE*, and the big transport lift likely to be available within the next three months. He

TOP SECRET

stressed the importance of bold decisions and a fresh approach to this problem, particularly if Russian fighting should go as anticipated. A short discussion followed.

GENERAL ARNOLD confirmed the future availability of aircraft and the considerable transport lift that would be made available by temporary diversion of heavy bombers.

He drew attention to the importance of studying the best uses that could be made of the 28,000 aircraft now available for operations in Europe.

The United States Assistant Chiefs of Staff were then called in to discuss what craft might be made available from *NEPTUNE* resources to increase the assault lift in the Mediterranean to three divisions. The time necessary to make available from the United States the additional resources required in the Mediterranean for an amphibious operation was also discussed.

THE COMBINED CHIEFS OF STAFF:—

Agreed:

a. That there would be an amphibious operation to be mounted from the Mediterranean with target date 25 July.

b. That this operation would be of approximately three-division assault lift.

c. That the objective for the operation would be determined later.

d. That plans for the following alternate objectives should be prepared:
   (1) Cette.
   (2) Istria.
   (3) Bay of Biscay with particular attention to the mouth of the Loire and Bordeaux.

   SACMED to be responsible for the coordination of the planning for (1) and (2) and SCAEF for (3).

e. That planning representatives should be instructed to examine with SHAEF the possibility of release from Operation *NEPTUNE* by 1 July 1944 of 15 combat loaders (APA's, XAP's LSI(L)'s) and 24 LST's for use in the proposed operation.

TOP SECRET

f. To invite General Ismay to prepare and circulate for consideration an appropriate telegram to SACMED and SCAEF.

2. OPERATIONS IN THE PACIFIC AND THE FAR EAST

At the request of Admiral King, *SIR ALAN BROOKE* then outlined briefly the possible alternative ways in which the British might assist United States forces in the defeat of Japan. In doing so, he explained that British views on this subject were still unsettled. He gave a brief forecast of availability of naval, land and air forces, with particular reference to the difficulty of timing in view of the acceleration of operations by United States forces in the Pacific. He mentioned the need to replace long-service men now serving in the East and the intention to reorganize units on a lighter basis as recommended in the Lethbridge Report. He referred to studies in progress as to the possibilities of Australia as a base, and to the task that would continue in Southeast Asia Command of keeping the air supply route open to China.

ADMIRAL KING then referred to the great logistic difficulties in the Pacific and said that the United States Chiefs of Staff were anxious for an outline of British ideas as to how they might best assist United States forces in the war against Japan, in order to be able to examine to what degree the United States could lend a hand.

At the request of General Marshall, discussion then turned again to the Southeast Asia Command and covered the following points: The extent to which British troops in Southeast Asia Command were locked up in operations in Burma; the problem of holding Myitkyina; the great importance to the Formosa operations of an effective Fourteenth Air Force and of an additional lift to get Chinese ground forces operating effectively in China against the Japanese, the danger of an indefinite postponement to the ultimate defeat of Japan if the Japanese should withdraw from the Philippines, et cetera, and concentrate on effective action in China; the fact that the Japanese could, by threatening Assam, force us to fight there; and that air superiority in Burma, excepting for transport aircraft, was relatively of little value compared with other theaters.

GENERAL MARSHALL then referred to the drastic changes that had been effected as a result of stepping up the tempo of operations in the Pacific. This, added to Japanese shipping losses and the Marianas operations, which promised to be a surprise, would face the Japanese with a real dilemma by November 1944.

TOP SECRET

A brief discussion then ensued as to the possibilities of British assistance should Mindanao be captured by the United States forces in November 1944, or Formosa in December 1944; the possibilities of an operation from the Indian Ocean, possibly airborne, to take Rangoon and Bangkok; finally, as to the need for an early decision as to whether British assistance to the United States in the war against Japan should be based on India, or on Australia operating from the Southeast on the left flank of the United States forces.

3. *RECORD OF DISCUSSION*

After consideration the Combined Chiefs of Staff agreed that the minutes of their present meetings in London should contain only an outline of their discussion.

TOP SECRET

COMBINED CHIEFS OF STAFF

C.C.S. 164th Meeting

MINUTES OF MEETING HELD IN CONFERENCE ROOM "A"
WAR CABINET OFFICE, LONDON, ENGLAND
ON TUESDAY, 13 JUNE 1944, AT 1130.

PRESENT

United States

General G. C. Marshall, USA
Admiral E. J. King, USN
General H. H. Arnold, USA

British

Field Marshal Sir Alan F. Brooke
Marshal of the Royal Air Force
  Sir Charles F. A. Portal
Admiral of the Fleet
  Sir Andrew B. Cunningham

ALSO PRESENT

General Sir Hastings L. Ismay
Major Gen. R. E. Laycock

SECRETARIAT

Major Gen. L. C. Hollis
Brigadier H. Redman
Colonel A. J. McFarland, USA

TOP SECRET

1. *OPERATIONS TO ASSIST "OVERLORD"*

The Combined Chiefs of Staff considered two memoranda from Supreme Headquarters, Allied Expeditionary Force (Annexes "A" and "B" to these minutes). It was made clear during the discussion that while the 17th Airborne Division could be made available from the United States so far as logistic considerations were concerned, it was being counted upon by the Supreme Commander, Allied Expeditionary Force for Operation *OVERLORD* and, as far as could be seen, could not be spared for an operation from the Mediterranean. It was deemed possible, however, for SHAEF to spare sufficient transport aircraft to bring the airborne lift available for such an operation up to a full division.

The Combined Chiefs of Staff discussed at some length the alternative objectives possible for the amphibious operation to be mounted from the Mediterranean. They considered in this connection the possibility of employing long range penetration groups, similar to those used in the Burma campaign, to foster and support the underground movement in France.

The Combined Chiefs of Staff then considered the draft telegram to SACMED and SCAEF prepared by General Ismay, and amended it in several particulars.

THE COMBINED CHIEFS OF STAFF:—

Approved the telegram to SACMED and SCAEF as amended during the discussion (See Annex "C" to these minutes), and directed that it be dispatched subject to the approval which the British Chiefs of Staff undertook to obtain from the Prime Minister.

2. *OPERATIONS*

An account of the first *CROSSBOW* attack was given by *SIR CHARLES PORTAL*. General satisfaction was expressed at the lack of success that had attended the introduction of this new weapon.

SIR CHARLES PORTAL also referred to the encouraging results of the attack on the synthetic oil plants at Gelsenkirchen.

TOP SECRET

    ADMIRAL KING gave a brief account of the very good beginning of the operation against the Marianas by United States forces in the Pacific.

3. *FUTURE MEETINGS*

After discussion,

THE COMBINED CHIEFS OF STAFF:—

Agreed to meet at 1430 on Wednesday, 14 June 1944, at the War Cabinet Offices, London.

TOP SECRET

ANNEX "A"

SHAEF/17101/1/Plans (A)   12th June, 1944

SUPREME HEADQUARTERS
ALLIED EXPEDITIONARY FORCE

MEMORANDUM

RELEASE OF SHIPPING AND CRAFT FROM OPERATION "NEPTUNE"

1. The possibility has been examined of releasing a proportion of the shipping and craft allotted to *NEPTUNE* for use in an amphibious operation to be mounted from the *Mediterranean*.

COMBAT LOADERS

2. Examination shows that it should be possible to release six APA's, three XAP's and up to six LSI(L)'s forthwith, provided the six LSI(L)'s are replaced by equivalent personnel shipping in order to maintain the planned rate of build-up.

LST

3. We are informed that the release of twenty-four LST's in time to sail from *United Kingdom* by 1st July, 1944, is essential to the operation, and that if possible thirty-six should be released. If these craft are to sail on 1st July, 1944, they would have to be released by us at least one week earlier to allow for refit.

While, on the original planning figures, it would have been possible to release thirty-six LST's by 13th July (D plus 37), none of these could have been released earlier if the planned build-up was to be maintained.

Annex "A"

TOP SECRET

However, losses so far have been considerably below estimates. The losses up to 11th June are:—

LST: 3 sunk; 18 damaged; Total 21

On our original estimate, losses by this date would have been:—

LST: 30 sunk; 55 damaged; Total 85

Accordingly, we are at least twenty-seven LST's better off than we expected to be by 11th June. Therefore, provided that there is no increase in the rate of losses above the planning figures, we will be able to release twenty-four LST's in time to enable them to sail by 1st July.

In fairness to this Headquarters and to those planning operations in the *Mediterranean,* however, it must be pointed out that the possible effects of a spell of bad weather, increased enemy naval activity in the Channel, an increased tempo in air attacks, or a combination of all of these may militate against a firm commitment.

OTHER CRAFT

4. The possibility of supplying other types of craft to the *Mediterranean* has also been considered:—

- a. *LCT(R)* It is considered that out of the total of thirty-six LCT (R)'s available the nine U.S., with or without three additional British LCT(R)'s, could be made available for the *Mediterranean* forthwith.

- b. *LCI(L)* Losses of LCI(L)'s up to 11th June are nine sunk and thirty-five damaged, compared with the planning figure of thirty-one sunk and fifty-one damaged. Therefore, unless the rate of losses considerably increases, twenty-four could be released by 1st July.

- c. *AKA* The ACHERNAR could be available for release by 1st July.

- d. *HQ Ship* One British HQ ship could be released by 1st July.

- e. *LSD* Three LSD's are at present being employed in *NEPTUNE* for the return of damaged craft from the beaches and their distribution to repair bases. There is already one LSD in the

Annex "A"

Mediterranean and it is understood that an additional one is required. It is considered that one LSD could be released from *NEPTUNE* by 1st July.

f. *Fighter Direction Tenders (LST)*. There are at present three Fighter Direction Tenders in *NEPTUNE*. One could be released by 1st July.

AIRBORNE FORCES

5. All airborne forces at present available are considered absolutely essential for *NEPTUNE*, and the additional U.S. airborne division due from the U.S.A. in early August or late July is equally important. There will be a continuous demand during the progress of the operation for airborne forces to help forward the advance, and large airborne operations are now being planned.

Air lift is already a limiting factor in *NEPTUNE* operations. It will not be possible to spare any lift for the *Mediterranean*.

CONCLUSIONS

6. It can be concluded that:—

a. The following force could be made available from *NEPTUNE* forces in time to take part in the operation:—

- 6 APA's
- 3 XAP's
- 6 LSI(L)'s (If replaced by equivalent personnel shipping)
- 24 LST's
- 24 LCI(L)'s
- 12 LCT(R)'s
- 1 AKA (ACHERNAR)
- 1 HQ Ship
- 1 LSD
- 1 Fighter Direction Tender (LST)

b. The above availability is subject to the proviso that there is no serious increase in losses in *NEPTUNE* ships and craft.

c. No airborne forces or air lift at present allocated to *NEPTUNE* can be made available for the *Mediterranean*.

Annex "A"

TOP SECRET

ANNEX "B"

SHAEF/17101/1/Plans 12th June, 1944

SUPREME HEADQUARTERS
ALLIED EXPEDITIONARY FORCE

MEMORANDUM

*THE EMPLOYMENT OF MEDITERRANEAN FORCES
IN AID OF "NEPTUNE"*

1. The object of this paper is to determine the best use which might be made of the available forces in the *Mediterranean* to assist *NEPTUNE*.

2. Our aim must be to deploy the maximum number of *Mediterranean* forces, both land forces and tactical air forces, against the enemy as early as possible and ensure that they have the opportunity to fight the enemy throughout the summer.

3. There are three courses open to us:—

   a. To use the available *Mediterranean* forces to reinforce the *NEPTUNE* build-up through *northwest France;* or,

   b. To carry out, with *Mediterranean* forces, an amphibious operation against the *west coast of France;* or,

   c. To carry out *ANVIL* or some similar operation in the *Mediterranean*.

REINFORCEMENT OF LODGEMENT AREA

4. Our planners estimate that the port and beach capacities in northwest *France* limit the rate of build-up to that at present planned. These estimates are probably pessimistic but, even so, it should still be possible to fill any additional port and beach capacity by bringing in additional divisions staging in the *United Kingdom* or by accelerating the build-up direct from the *United States*.

Annex "B"

5. The possibility of seizing additional beaches or ports in the *north* or *northwest* of *France* has been examined, but we believe that there are no areas in which even a two-divisional assault could be made with any prospect of success.

AMPHIBIOUS ATTACK AGAINST THE WEST COAST OF FRANCE

6. The possibility of carrying out an amphibious operation against the *west coast of France* has been examined, and we are convinced that there is no operation which is likely to offer any prospect of success. The only operation which merits serious consideration is the seizure of *Bordeaux*. *Bordeaux*, however, lies some fifty miles up the *River Gironde* which would require some ten days' minesweeping to clear. There are only two practicable beaches for a landing, each of which would take one brigade in the assault. These are on either side of the estuary, are heavily defended and the northern beach is fully exposed to the *Atlantic* swell. Air cover would have to be given by carrier-borne aircraft. Even with the assistance of airborne forces, our opinion is that the rate of build-up would be too slow to prevent our forces being overwhelmed, except under unusually favorable conditions approximating those of *RANKIN*. These we do not expect.

7. If, of course, the *southwest* of *France* were evacuated and *Bordeaux* fell into our hands, divisions from the *Mediterranean* could be moved into the *NEPTUNE* battle area through *Bordeaux*. This evacuation, however, is not likely to take place until we threaten German communications with *southwest France*, which will probably not be earlier than, say, 1st October, 1944.

ANVIL

8. There remains *ANVIL* or some similar operation against the *south coast of France*.

9. The advantages of *ANVIL* are that the available forces in the *Mediterranean*, both land forces and tactical air forces, can be deployed much earlier against the enemy than by adopting any other course. Moreover, the operation will be in closest proximity to the present location of these forces and maximum use can thus be made of the existing land and air bases. A landing in *southern France* will be closer to *OVERLORD* and likely to have more direct effect in containing enemy forces away from *OVERLORD* than other operations in the *Mediterranean*. The base established for the *ANVIL* forces

Annex "B"

TOP SECRET

in southern *France* will eventually be available for reinforcing *OVERLORD* when the Germans withdraw from southern *France*. After the capture of *Marseilles* it will not be necessary for some time, if at all, to open *Bordeaux* for the support of operations.

CONCLUSION

10. It is concluded, therefore, that *ANVIL* or some similar operation against the *south* of *France* should be mounted at the earliest possible date and certainly not later than August 10th-15th, on the assumption that sufficient forces can be made available to make the operation effective.

Annex "B"

TOP SECRET

ANNEX "C"

DRAFT TELEGRAM

Following from Combined Chiefs of Staff to General Wilson and General Eisenhower.

1. The Combined Chiefs of Staff have reviewed the relationship of Operation *OVERLORD* to operations in the Mediterranean in the light of the success of *DIADEM* and the progress of *OVERLORD*. Their views are as follows.

2. The overriding necessity is to apply to the enemy, at the earliest possible moment, all our forces in the manner best calculated to assist in the success of *OVERLORD*.

3. The destruction of the German armed forces in Italy south of the Pisa-Rimini line must be completed. There should be no withdrawal from the battle of any Allied forces that are necessary for this purpose.

4. When the Pisa-Rimini line has been reached, there will be three possible courses of action open to us:—

   a. An amphibious operation against south of France;

   b. An amphibious operation against western France;

   c. An amphibious operation at the head of the Adriatic.

5. The final choice from among the three courses in the preceding paragraph cannot be made at this moment. Which will pay us best depends on several factors, at present unknown, e.g.:—

   a. The progress of *OVERLORD* with the forces now assigned;

   b. The direction and degree of success of the forthcoming Russian offensive;

   c. The German reactions to *a* and *b* above.

The one factor common to all three courses of action is an amphibious operation, and the Combined Chiefs of Staff have decided that preparations should go forward forthwith on the greatest scale for which resources can be made available and at the earliest date.

Annex "C"

TOP SECRET

6. As to the scale of preparations, the Combined Chiefs of Staff consider that greater resources than at present contemplated should be allocated to these operations. They have in mind a three-divisional assault to be made up from landing craft already in or detailed for the Mediterranean, such craft as General Eisenhower can release without prejudice to OVERLORD and such additional assistance as could be provided from the United States. The Combined Chiefs of Staff also propose that a total lift for at least a full airborne division should be provided.

7. As to the date of the amphibious operation, the Combined Chiefs of Staff consider that the 15th August is too late and that we should aim at being ready to launch the operation by the 25th July, always provided that this does not limit the completion of the operation south of the Pisa-Rimini line.

8. As to the choice of an actual plan, the Combined Chiefs of Staff would observe that they are not inclined to favor a landing in the Marseilles area because of the strength of the coast defenses and the unprofitable line of advance up the Rhone Valley. It seems to them that the operation in France most likely to help OVERLORD would be either an initial landing at Cette designed to lead to the early capture of Bordeaux and the support of the guerrillas in the south of France, or a direct descent on the west coast of France, the object of the latter being either to open some port through which a direct build-up from the U.S.A. could be achieved or if necessary to afford direct support to the OVERLORD forces if they are not making sufficient progress.

9. It is evident that the planning and preparation of the above operations must begin forthwith, as they will require the closest coordination between AFHQ and SHAEF who are requested to submit their comments as a matter of urgency after mutual consultation.

Annex "C"

TOP SECRET

COMBINED CHIEFS OF STAFF

C.C.S. 165th Meeting

MINUTES OF MEETING HELD IN CONFERENCE ROOM "A"
WAR CABINET OFFICE, LONDON, ENGLAND
ON WEDNESDAY, 14 JUNE 1944, AT 1430.

PRESENT

United States	*British*
General G. C. Marshall, USA	Field Marshal Sir Alan F. Brooke
Admiral E. J. King, USN	Marshal of the Royal Air Force
General H. H. Arnold, USA	Sir Charles F. A. Portal
	Admiral of the Fleet
	Sir Andrew B. Cunningham

ALSO PRESENT

General Sir Hastings L. Ismay
Major Gen. R. E. Laycock

SECRETARIAT

Major Gen. L. C. Hollis
Brigadier H. Redman
Colonel A. J. McFarland, USA

TOP SECRET

1. *OPERATIONS*

The Meeting began with the reading by *ADMIRAL KING* of a dispatch which indicated a continuation of the promising start made in the Marianas operations.

A brief discussion then ensued on the progress in *OVERLORD*, which covered the following points:—

The success reported from French resistance groups;

The piecemeal deployment of four enemy panzer divisions;

The possibilities of an early enemy counterattack;

The lack of appreciation by the enemy of the importance of artificial harbors and the likelihood of a change in the enemy strategical concept as soon as the importance of these harbors was realized;

The great demolition work in progress in Cherbourg.

The advantages and disadvantages of a Quiberon Bay operation were then considered briefly and reference was made to Brest.

2. *WAR IN THE PACIFIC*

The discussion then turned to the war in the Pacific. *SIR ALAN BROOKE* referred to the brief summary that had been given by the British Chiefs of Staff at a previous meeting, and asked for the views of the United States Chiefs of Staff as to the ways in which British forces could be of maximum assistance to the United States forces in the defeat of Japan.

ADMIRAL KING gave a brief appreciation of the present extension of Japanese forces on their outer perimeter and of the importance of continuing the threats necessary to keep the enemy so extended.

A general discussion ensued which covered the following points:—

The possibilities of speeding up operations and gaining surprise by bypassing the Philippines and the Palaus and making straight for Formosa;

The importance of exploiting Allied superiority on the sea and in the air and avoiding, where possible, engagement with enemy main forces on land;

TOP SECRET

The value of Borneo, both for its oil and the denial of that oil to the enemy, and for its air bases;

The value of Amboina as a fleet base;

The concentration of Japanese forces in the area Mindanao-Celebes-Halmahera;

The possibilities of seizing Tanimbar by air action and the examination of this subject now being made;

The advantages and disadvantages of attacking Java with its good communications and its present small enemy garrison;

The positional value of Sourabaya for the British Fleet;

The possibility, through a direct advance on Formosa, of isolating many important Japanese garrisons, achieving surprise, assaulting Formosa while it is yet weak, and bringing about a major fleet action;

The capabilities, from the standpoint of the diversion and containing of enemy forces, of a British task force based on Amboina or Sourabaya;

The importance of making full use of the 10 to 1 Allied superiority expected to be achieved;

The importance, in fighting the Japanese, of doing the unexpected.

Base facilities were considered at some length, including the facilities of Indian ports. Other points considered were: the fact that India, including Ceylon, had no base that would take a battleship, whereas Brisbane and Sydney both can; the need of a British naval force for the facilities of bases such as Brisbane and Sydney, and the remoteness of Sydney; the likelihood that, after seizure of the Palaus, U.S. naval forces in the Pacific would not be dependent on Australia and might thus leave Brisbane and Sydney to a great extent available for a British task force.

SIR ANDREW CUNNINGHAM outlined the British naval force that should be available towards the end of 1944. A short discussion took place as to the possibilities of operations in the Bay of Bengal, where it appeared that a small fleet should suffice as there was no major task for a main fleet to undertake.

During consideration of the British forces likely to be available to take part in the war in the Southwest Pacific, it was pointed out that, in the initial

TOP SECRET

stages, British naval forces would expect to work under General MacArthur with Australian and New Zealand land and air forces. British forces in the Southwest Pacific would be built up from elsewhere as they became available. It would be for consideration whether any air forces could be released from Southeast Asia Command.

Full consideration was given to the question of whether or not it would be possible, in view of the acceleration of the United States operations in the Pacific, for British forces to arrive in time to be of real value to the United States operations envisaged. This included consideration of the importance of flexibility and of so placing the British effort that it would not be separated from United States effort, so that British assistance might be called in as and when found necessary.

Other items included in the afternoon's discussion were:—

The value of action by the Fourteenth Air Force to any attack on Formosa;

The fact that the United States air strength in China, including the 100 B-29's now assembled there, had reached its peak;

The importance of Formosa as a base for the operations of B-29's against the Japanese mainland;

The lack of recuperative power of Japanese air factories in comparison with those of Germany;

The possibility of by-passing Formosa and going direct to Kyushu;

The advantages of an operation direct to Kyushu from the standpoint of surprise, of the difficulty to the Japanese concentrating a large force across the mountains, and of the command of the Tsu Shima Channel that would be gained;

The possible necessity for going to Formosa in order to get supplies into China and the undesirability of either U.S. or British forces engaging Japanese land forces in China;

The possibilities of a carrier-borne strike against the mainland of Japan, the great effect on enemy shipping to be expected from such a strike, and the indifferent air defense likely to be put up.

TOP SECRET

COMBINED CHIEFS OF STAFF

C.C.S. 166th Meeting

Minutes of Meeting Held in Conference Room "A"
War Cabinet Office, London, England
on Thursday, 15 June 1944, at 1530.

PRESENT

United States

General G. C. Marshall, USA
Admiral E. J. King, USN
General H. H. Arnold, USA

British

Field Marshal Sir Alan F. Brooke
Marshal of the Royal Air Force
  Sir Charles F. A. Portal
Admiral of the Fleet
  Sir Andrew B. Cunningham

ALSO PRESENT

General Sir Hastings L. Ismay
Lt. Gen. Sir Henry Pownal
  (for part of the meeting)

SECRETARIAT

Major Gen. L. C. Hollis
Brigadier H. Redman
Colonel A. J. McFarland, USA

TOP SECRET

1. *PROGRESS OF "OVERLORD"*

The meeting began with a short discussion on the progress of Operation *OVERLORD* to date with particular reference to the fighting at Carentan, future operations in the Cherbourg Peninsula, the successful engagement in the Villers Bocage area; piecemeal engagement hitherto of enemy reinforcements as they have become available without signs of serious counterattack; the guerrilla action of the French resistance groups.

2. *FRENCH RESISTANCE GROUPS*

GENERAL MARSHALL then gave an account of a somewhat difficult interview with General Bethouart, French Chief of Staff for National Defense, from which he had just come.

A brief discussion took place on the difficulties of the Supreme Commander, Allied Expeditionary Force with regard to the control of French resistance groups owing to the restrictions that appeared to have been placed by General De Gaulle on the carrying out by General Koenig of the arrangements previously agreed upon. General Marshall read a memorandum which had been handed to him by General Bethouart.

The Combined Chiefs of Staff agreed to the dispatch of this memorandum to the Supreme Commander, Allied Expeditionary Force with a suitable covering note requesting his recommendations as to the action, if any, he might deem desirable by the Combined Chiefs of Staff. (See Annex)

3. *WAR IN THE PACIFIC*

SIR ALAN BROOKE said that the British Chiefs of Staff had given instructions this morning to their Planners to commence work on the paper that it had been agreed yesterday should be produced for the United States Chiefs of Staff on the subject. He explained that as soon as the paper was ready it would be put to the Prime Minister for his approval and then forwarded to the United States Chiefs of Staff.

4. *OPERATIONS IN SOUTHEAST ASIA COMMAND*

SIR ALAN BROOKE gave a brief appreciation of the existing situation in Southeast Asia Command.

A discussion ensued which included the following:—

The importance of clearing up the fighting in the Kohima-Imphal area as soon as possible and releasing the transport aircraft now employed there;

The establishment of a defensive position in the area Mogaung-Myitkyina and the holding of this position both during the monsoon and after;

The allocation of combat cargo groups and air commando groups to Southeast Asia Command. In this connection it was made quite clear by the United States Chiefs of Staff they had decided not to allocate any further combat groups or air commando groups until definite plans for their employment and maintenance had been established.

Discussion continued with respect to:—

The strength of the forces needed to hold Myitkyina (it appeared that a minimum of one fresh division during the monsoon and a minimum total of four divisions after the monsoon would be necessary to defend the area Mogaung-Myitkyina against the Japanese, who would have superior communications);

The possibilities of the effective cutting of Japanese rail communications in Burma once Myitkyina is established;

The importance of remembering the main issue, which was the maximum possible flow of supplies to China;

The likelihood that the Japanese would realize this issue and direct their strategy against Myitkyina; the maintenance of the Myitkyina troops; the good fighting put up by the Ramgarrh Chinese troops; the importance to the Chinese operations of the United States commando group and the steps being taken to replace them; the Japanese ability to live on the country;

The great improvement effected in the lines of communication, the lift over which promised to be trebled by November 1944, and which would then be ample for requirements;

The importance of pipeline projects already in progress;

The possibilities of airborne operations against Rangoon, the need for extra troops from outside as well as naval resources and airborne lift if such operations were to be undertaken, and the impracticability of staging such operations in time for them to have any appreciable effect on the operation now being planned in the Pacific;

The importance of concentrating as far as possible on protecting the line of communications to Assam, holding the Mogaung-Myitkyina area and maintaining the air lift to China; and of concentrating all other available British effort on the operation in the Southwest Pacific discussed at the 165th Meeting, should this line of action be agreed upon;

Estimates of the possible air lift to China;

Difficulties of the monsoon period;

The possible influence on the situation in Burma of the success of the operations envisaged in the Pacific in the autumn of 1944;

The desirability of calling upon Southeast Asia Command for an outline plan for an airborne operation for the capture of Rangoon and upon General Stilwell for the plan of operations of the Tenth and Fourteenth Air Forces.

A brief discussion took place on the different plans for amphibious operations which had been considered in the Southeast Asia Command.

In conclusion *SIR ALAN BROOKE* said that the policy in Burma at present seemed quite clear. First the Kohima-Imphal Road must be cleared, the capture of Myitkyina must be completed and a defensive position established and held in the area Mogaung-Myitkyina — the main object of all operations being the attainment of the maximum possible flow of supplies into China.

5. *CONTROL OF THE UNITED STATES TWENTIETH AIR FORCE*

SIR CHARLES PORTAL referred to the proposal put forward by the United States Chiefs of Staff in C.C.S. 501/4 for the control of the Twentieth Air Force. He said that the question had been under consideration by the British Chiefs of Staff with particular reference to the question of coordination. It had been thought that it would be desirable for the Combined Chiefs of Staff to retain control of this force with General Arnold in actual command, for two reasons: firstly, because strategic direction of the Twentieth Air Force would affect its logistic support which in turn would affect the Southeast Asia Command; secondly, because it was hoped later that British air forces would also play a part.

TOP SECRET

The British Chiefs of Staff had decided that the directive proposed by the United States Chiefs of Staff to the Twentieth Air Force could be accepted with certain provisos which Sir Charles Portal then read.

THE COMBINED CHIEFS OF STAFF:—

Approved the directive proposed by the United States Chiefs of Staff in C.C.S. 501/4 subject to the following provisos:

a. That if the Twentieth Air Force should be increased to more than four groups in China-Burma-India the British Chiefs of Staff will be consulted because of administrative problems involved.

b. That, if the Royal Air Force should take part in the operations of the Twentieth Air Force, the British Chiefs of Staff will be given a share in the strategic control, General Arnold remaining in command and functioning in a role similar to that of Sir Charles Portal in connection with the Combined Bomber Offensive.

c. That, if operations should be undertaken by the Twentieth Air Force against objectives in the Southeast Asia Command, the Supreme Allied Commander of that theater will be consulted.

TOP SECRET

ANNEX

From: Combined Chiefs of Staff

To: Supreme Commander, Allied Expeditionary Force

Memorandum from Lt. General Bethouart, French Chief of Staff of National Defense, to General Marshall, Chief of Staff, United States Army.

The Combined Chiefs of Staff will be glad of your comments on the points raised in paragraphs II and III of the attached memorandum, and your recommendations as to the action, if any, that is required of the Combined Chiefs of Staff.

In connection with paragraph III, General Bethouart stated to General Marshall orally that he was deeply concerned over the procurement of equipment.

For the Combined Chiefs of Staff:

H. REDMAN,
A. J. McFARLAND,
Combined Secretariat.

15TH JUNE 1944

TOP SECRET

London, June 14, 1944.

MEMORANDUM FOR GENERAL GEORGE C. MARSHALL,

Chief of Staff, United States Army.

I — French participation to the ANVIL operation.

A French participation to the *ANVIL* operation has been settled with General Maitland-Wilson.

Most of the French units involved in this operation are, at the present time, fighting in Italy. Their withdrawal at the appropriate moment has been foreseen.

It is asked whether the arrangements made are still valid now, and under which conditions the French divisions will be withdrawn from the Italian front.

II — Participation to the battle of the "French Forces of the Interior."

The French Forces of the Interior are, from now on, taking part to the battle, carrying out sabotage and guerrillas.

Such actions have been launched at the Allies' demand. It is requested:

1. That any action concerning the French Forces of the Interior should be taken through General Koenig, who has the necessary powers for this purpose.

   The fact that several Allied authorities are now dealing with these forces might cause errors and losses, as it already happened, if these authorities do not pass through the same French channels.

2. That General Koenig could receive all the support and the necessary means for providing arms, ammunitions, food, as well as the corresponding air force for transporting them.

   The action of the guerrillas, that has been launched at the Allies' demand, cannot be left without support, otherwise these groups would be annihilated or massacred by the enemy.

   Their abandonment or even an insufficient support from the Allies would cause a deep resentment.

Annex

TOP SECRET

III — Enlistment of young French people.

The advance in French territory is going to liberate young Frenchmen whose enlistment in the army has been foreseen by the government.

It is necessary that all Frenchmen whether they have participated or not to the armed resistance movements be cleared and screened in order that good ones join the army and constitute officered and disciplined units.

This is the best way to avoid disorder and to ensure the strongest support to the Allied military action.

A French military command and a territorial organization have been foreseen for this purpose. They will have to be set up again as soon as possible. They would be under General Koenig's command.

                                           Lieutenant General Marie-Emile BETHOUART,
                                           Chef d'état-Major de la Defense National.

Annex

OCTAGON CONFERENCE

MINUTES OF MEETINGS

OF THE

COMBINED CHIEFS OF STAFF

TOP SECRET

COMBINED CHIEFS OF STAFF

C.C.S. 172d Meeting

OCTAGON CONFERENCE

MINUTES OF MEETING HELD IN THE MAIN CONFERENCE ROOM, CHATEAU FRONTENAC HOTEL, ON 12 SEPTEMBER 1944, AT 1200.

PRESENT

United States

Admiral W. D. Leahy, USN
General G. C. Marshall, USA
Admiral E. J. King, USN
General H. H. Arnold, USA

British

Field Marshal Sir Alan F. Brooke
Marshal of the Royal Air Force
   Sir Charles F. A. Portal
Admiral of the Fleet
   Sir Andrew B. Cunningham

ALSO PRESENT

Lt. Gen. B. B. Somervell, USA
Vice Adm. R. Willson, USN
Rear Adm. C. M. Cooke, Jr., USN
Rear Adm. L. D. McCormick, USN
Major Gen. T. T. Handy, USA
Major Gen. M. S. Fairchild, USA
Major Gen. L. S. Kuter, USA

Field Marshal Sir John Dill
General Sir Hastings L. Ismay
Admiral Sir Percy Noble
Lt. Gen. G. N. Macready
Air Marshal Sir William Welsh
Major Gen. R. E. Laycock

SECRETARIAT

Major Gen. L. C. Hollis
Brig. Gen. A. J. McFarland, USA
Brigadier A. T. Cornwall-Jones
Captain E. D. Graves, Jr., USN
Commander R. D. Coleridge, RN

TOP SECRET

1. CHAIRMANSHIP OF THE COMBINED CHIEFS OF STAFF

ADMIRAL LEAHY said that the United States Chiefs of Staff would be glad if Sir Alan Brooke would take the Chair at the forthcoming series of meetings.

SIR ALAN BROOKE thanked Admiral Leahy for this proposal which he would be glad to accept.

2. PERSONNEL SHIPPING

SIR ALAN BROOKE said that he felt that the problem of the use of personnel shipping after the defeat of Germany should be examined during the Conference. There would be heavy calls for personnel shipping both for the transfer of U.S. troops other than occupational troops from Europe to the United States or the Pacific, as well as for the reorientation of British forces to the Far East. In addition the New Zealand and South African divisions and certain Canadian forces now in Europe would have to be returned to their homelands. He suggested that the experts should be instructed to examine this problem to see how best it could be met.

ADMIRAL LEAHY said that he could see no objection to this review but it would be impossible to reach any decisions during the Conference.

SIR CHARLES PORTAL, in agreeing with Admiral Leahy, said that he felt that the scope of the problem should be examined.

GENERAL SOMERVELL stated that he had only one shipping expert at present at OCTAGON but agreed with a proposal made by Sir Alan Brooke that he should discuss this matter with Lord Leathers.

THE COMBINED CHIEFS OF STAFF:—

Invited General Somervell to confer with Lord Leathers on this matter.

3. AGENDA AND HOUR OF MEETING

At the suggestion of Admiral Leahy

TOP SECRET

THE COMBINED CHIEFS OF STAFF:—

a. Agreed to meet daily from 1000 to 1300.

b. Approved the program for the Conference as set out in C.C.S. 654/6, subject to the transfer of the items for Saturday, 16 September, to Tuesday, 12 September. (Approved program subsequently circulated as C.C.S. 654/7.)

4. *SITUATION REPORT FROM SCAEF*
(SCAF 78)

SIR ALAN BROOKE said that, while agreeing in general with General Eisenhower's appreciation (SCAF 78), the British Chiefs of Staff felt that sufficient emphasis had not been laid on two points: firstly, the importance of securing sea communications and the ports of Antwerp and Rotterdam, and secondly, the importance of a strong attack being launched on the northern flank. General Eisenhower in his telegram had spoken of three possible routes of advance into Germany. In his (Sir Alan Brooke's) view the most important was the northern route of attack which should be strengthened as much as possible, the remaining two routes being retained as alternatives. The most energetic efforts should be made to secure and open the port of Antwerp as a valuable base for future operations on the northern flank. In order to open the sea approaches to Antwerp, it seemed desirable to stage an airborne operation to capture the islands at the mouth of the Schelde.

GENERAL MARSHALL said that in view of the apparent massing of German forces on the islands guarding the port of Antwerp, and the lack of cover which existed on the ground, it appeared that a more profitable operation would be the bombing of enemy positions rather than an airborne operation.

SIR ALAN BROOKE felt that bombing alone would not achieve the required results and occupying forces would have to be introduced.

SIR ALAN BROOKE presented a draft reply to SCAF 78 approving General Eisenhower's proposals and pointing out the advantages of the northern line of approach into Germany as opposed to the southern and the necessity for opening up the northwest ports, particularly Antwerp and Rotterdam.

TOP SECRET

After further discussion,

THE COMBINED CHIEFS OF STAFF:—

Approved the dispatch to the Supreme Commander, Allied Expeditionary Force of the draft telegram proposed by the British Chiefs of Staff. (Subsequently dispatched as FACS 78).

5. *SITUATION REPORT FROM THE MEDITERRANEAN*
   (MEDCOS 181 and NAF 774)

ADMIRAL LEAHY presented a statement of the views of the United States Chiefs of Staff with reference to the future role of the Fifth Army and of the Twelfth and Fifteenth Air Forces (C.C.S. 677).

GENERAL MARSHALL said that a message had just been received from the U.S. Military Attaché in Switzerland to the effect that a German withdrawal of forces in northern Italy had already begun. If this was so, it would seem that, of the two situations envisaged by General Wilson in Part II of NAF 774, situation "*a*" would be ruled out unless the Allied armies could drive ahead with great speed, and situation "*b*" would exist, that is, there would be no possibility of another major offensive till the spring.

SIR ALAN BROOKE said that as he visualized it, if the Allied armies could break through to the Plains the enemy forces remaining in northwest Italy would be badly placed. A threat to Verona would cut off these forces and might result in their retirement to the westward and later the retirement of the German forces in northeast Italy back to the Alps. It was to be hoped that a large number of these eastern forces could be broken up. The attack by the Fifth Army was planned to take place on 13 September and a successful advance north of Florence might well result in driving the enemy forces back to the Po and Piave.

The indications were that the enemy was attempting to withdraw forces from Greece and Yugoslavia, though there was some doubt whether he could succeed in getting them out through bad lines of communications threatened by the Bulgarians, Marshal Tito's army and the Greeks. The enemy might, however, get some forces out and it appeared that he was likely to endeavor to hold a line running through Yugoslavia. In such an event the enemy might be

TOP SECRET

reduced to covering the Ljubljana Gap and endeavoring to hold a line through Yugoslavia and Istria. In these circumstances any withdrawal of forces from the Fifth Army would be most regrettable.

GENERAL MARSHALL said that it was not the intention to weaken the Fifth Army at the present time.

Continuing, *SIR ALAN BROOKE* said that the forces to be maintained in Italy might later be limited by logistics and terrain. He saw, however, great advantages in a right swing at Trieste and an advance from there to Vienna. However, if German resistance was strong, he did not visualize the possibility of our forces getting through to Vienna during the winter. Even so, the seizure of the Istrian Peninsula would be valuable as a base for the spring campaign or as a base from which our forces could be introduced into Austria in the event of Germany crumbling. It had not only a military value but also political value in view of the Russian advances in the Balkans.

In view of the possibility of amphibious thrusts on the Istrian Peninsula Sir Alan Brooke asked the United States Chiefs of Staff their intention with regard to the U.S. landing craft now operating in support of *DRAGOON*.

ADMIRAL KING said that these craft were earmarked for other operations but no orders had been issued for their withdrawal. He too had in mind the possibility of amphibious operations in Istria. Naval forces on the other hand were in course of withdrawal for rehabilitation.

Unless a decision to mount an amphibious operation were taken soon the landing craft would lie idle, though required for operations in other parts of the world, for instance, against Rangoon.

In reply to a question by General Marshall, *SIR ALAN BROOKE* said that General Wilson was planning now for an amphibious operation and the picture should be much clearer in a short time, particularly if the German forces withdrew from north Italy.

There was general agreement that a decision with regard to the launching of an amphibious operation should be made by 15 October.

GENERAL MARSHALL said that if operations in the Alps were undertaken in winter there was available the *PLOUGH* Force now in south France and the necessary sleds are obtainable.

TOP SECRET

Referring to the views of the United States Chiefs of Staff on the future role of the Fifth Army, *SIR CHARLES PORTAL* said that he felt that primary emphasis should be laid on the securing of a victory in Italy. As he saw it, the possible withdrawal of units of the Fifth Army to France would be dependent on the successful outcome of the campaign in Italy.

ADMIRAL LEAHY asked if it was Sir Charles Portal's thought that these forces should be retained in Italy if General Eisenhower was in need of them in France.

SIR CHARLES PORTAL pointed out that it was a question of short-term as opposed to long-term advantages. The important point as he saw it was to prevent the German troops getting away in north Italy if it could be avoided.

ADMIRAL LEAHY said it was not the intention to withdraw troops from the Fifth Army unless the German troops withdrew.

SIR CHARLES PORTAL said that he would point out that the withdrawal of forces from an army had a greater effect on that army than the actual number of formations withdrawn, since such withdrawals had a discouraging effect on the morale of the command and of the army itself.

ADMIRAL LEAHY re-emphasized that the United States proposal was contingent on the destruction or withdrawal of a large part of the German Army.

GENERAL MARSHALL said that there was no intention in the mind of the United States Chiefs of Staff to effect the withdrawal of forces from Italy at the present time.

ADMIRAL KING confirmed that an option on the U.S. landing craft now in the Mediterranean could be retained provided a decision was reached by 15 October.

In reply to a question by Sir Alan Brooke, *GENERAL MARSHALL* confirmed that while there was no intention of moving major units of the Fifth Army at the present time, small individual units (i.e., the Japanese battalion) might be withdrawn.

TOP SECRET

After further discussion,

THE COMBINED CHIEFS OF STAFF:—

a. Agreed that no forces should be withdrawn from Italy until the outcome of General Alexander's present offensive is known.

b. Agreed that the desirability of withdrawing formations of the United States Fifth Army should be reconsidered in the light of the results of General Alexander's present offensive and of a German withdrawal in northern Italy and in the light of the views of General Eisenhower.

c. Agreed to inform General Wilson that if he wishes to retain for use in the Istrian Peninsula the amphibious lift at present in the Mediterranean, he should submit his plan therefor to the Combined Chiefs of Staff as soon as possible, and not later than 15 October; and took note that the British Chiefs of Staff would prepare a suitable message for consideration.

6. *COMBINED INTELLIGENCE REPORT ON THE SITUATION IN EUROPE*
(C.C.S. 660/1)

THE COMBINED CHIEFS OF STAFF:—

Took note of the estimate contained in C.C.S. 660/1.

7. *COMMAND OF "DRAGOON" FORCES*
(C.C.S. 674)

ADMIRAL LEAHY presented a draft telegram to General Eisenhower approving his proposals in SCAF 77 (C.C.S. 674/1).

SIR CHARLES PORTAL drew attention to a telegram (FX 28818) from General Wilson to General Devers, inquiring as to how soon General Devers' communications with General Eisenhower would be sufficient to permit General Eisenhower to assume command.

It was generally agreed that this matter must be left to the commanders concerned and that General Eisenhower's proposal to assume command of *DRAGOON* forces on 15 September would have taken account of this factor.

TOP SECRET

GENERAL MARSHALL said that while General Eisenhower had been anxious that General Devers should set up his headquarters and be able to take over the lines of communications, logistic problems and civil affairs, he also wished General Patch to continue in charge of the present battle. Undoubtedly additional U.S. troops would be transferred at a later date to General Patch from the center group of armies and further American divisions would join him through the port of Marseilles. At that time the 6th Army Group could be conveniently split, General Patch assuming command of the United States forces and the French forces forming an army of their own.

SIR ALAN BROOKE said that there was one point he would like to make. He hoped the setting up of a large headquarters by General Devers would not unduly deplete General Clark's staff organization.

GENERAL MARSHALL reassured Sir Alan Brooke on this point. General Devers' staff had been formed for some time in Corsica and General Clark's forces would not be affected.

THE COMBINED CHIEFS OF STAFF:—

Agreed to dispatch to General Eisenhower and General Wilson the message proposed by the United States Chiefs of Staff in C.C.S. 674/1. (Subsequently dispatched as FACS 76 and FAN 413, respectively.)

At this point the Combined Chiefs of Staff recessed until 1430.

8. *MACHINERY FOR COORDINATION OF UNITED STATES-SOVIET-BRITISH MILITARY EFFORT*
(C.C.S. 618/3)

SIR ALAN BROOKE explained that the proposals for improvement of liaison with the Soviets originated from a suggestion put to Mr. Harriman by Marshal Stalin some two months ago.

ADMIRAL KING said that the U.S. Planners had examined the previous British proposal (C.C.S. 618/2) and were of the opinion that while there were advantages in the establishment of a combined committee at Moscow, this would not expedite rapid coordination of operations in the field which would require separate liaison arrangements.

ADMIRAL LEAHY stressed the value of improved liaison with the Russians.

SIR ALAN BROOKE said he felt Marshal Stalin's offer should be dropped. In Moscow there were already United States and British missions and all that was required was that the Russians should appoint a suitable high-ranking officer.

SIR CHARLES PORTAL said that he felt the proposal to exchange missions between field commanders would not work. It would not be right for the Russian High Command to be represented at a field headquarters. All our own plans would flow back to Moscow and we, in turn, would gain nothing. A committee in Moscow would be a better arrangement if, indeed, the Russians could be induced to appoint a really responsible high-ranking officer. Missions in the field, he felt, would be useless and even dangerous.

ADMIRAL KING said he felt that liaison between field commanders might follow from the achievement of successful cooperation in Moscow.

After further discussion,

THE COMBINED CHIEFS OF STAFF:—

a. Approved the recommendations of the British Chiefs of Staff in C.C.S. 618/3.

b. Instructed the Secretaries to draft and circulate for approval a message to the Heads of the United States and British Military Missions in Moscow based on C.C.S. 618/3.

9. *ZONES OF OCCUPATION IN GERMANY*

SIR ALAN BROOKE suggested that the Prime Minister and the President might be invited to give consideration to the outstanding problem of the zones to be occupied by United States and British forces in Germany and to give instructions to the Combined Chiefs of Staff.

ADMIRAL LEAHY agreed. He had already mentioned this matter to the President but would do so again. He would take the line that in view of the political aspects of the problem, guidance from the heads of State was necessary.

TOP SECRET

In reply to a question by Sir John Dill, *ADMIRAL LEAHY* said that from a United States point of view there were, he felt, no military considerations. There was, however, the problem of transportation and supply of United States troops if they went into the southern zone.

SIR CHARLES PORTAL said that from the British point of view there were very considerable military implications involved and there were strong reasons why, militarily, the British Chiefs of Staff would want to occupy the northwest zone.

ADMIRAL LEAHY explained that the utilization of United States troops for occupation was politically difficult and in fact would be politically impossible with regard to France, Italy, and southern Europe. Whereas the occupation of Germany could be justified, that of France would meet with enormous difficulty.

SIR CHARLES PORTAL said there was, of course, no question of occupying France.

ADMIRAL KING said that he felt it would be easier for the United States to occupy the southwest zone if it could be arranged that the evacuation of American troops and supplies for the occupational troops could be undertaken through north German ports.

THE COMBINED CHIEFS OF STAFF:—

a. Agreed that the question of zones of occupation in Germany had such serious political implications that they were unable to make any recommendation without guidance from their respective governments.

b. Decided to report in this sense to the President and Prime Minister and, in doing so, to invite their attention to the need for an early decision on this matter.

10. *CONTROL OF STRATEGIC BOMBER FORCES IN EUROPE*
    (C.C.S. 520/3)

GENERAL ARNOLD, during consideration of the British memorandum in C.C.S. 520/3, asked why the present method of control was stated to be unsatisfactory as a long-term arrangement.

SIR CHARLES PORTAL explained that in the opening stages of *OVERLORD* the present system of control had been necessary and effective. However, with the move of General Eisenhower and Air Chief Marshal Tedder to France, they were divorced from General Spaatz' headquarters and from the Air Ministry, and strategic control by General Eisenhower became almost a formality. Air Marshal Tedder had only a small air staff and the large staffs of the Air Ministry, Bomber Command and the U.S. Strategic Air Force in Europe had, of necessity, to exercise control over the actual strategic bombing operations.

GENERAL ARNOLD asked why large staffs were necessary to control strategic bombing.

SIR CHARLES PORTAL explained that full knowledge of all available enemy intelligence and adequate and rapid methods of interpreting the results of bombing attacks were essential to the effective control of strategic bombing. In addition, it was essential to keep in close touch with the degree of enemy air opposition to be expected.

GENERAL ARNOLD asked why no mention was made of communications in the priority of targets.

SIR CHARLES PORTAL said that communications had largely become targets for medium and fighter bombers rather than strategic forces. The proposed directive on priorities was, of course, susceptible to alteration by the Combined Chiefs of Staff or at the request of General Eisenhower. In fact, the priority list set forth was, he understood, that now enforced by General Eisenhower himself.

GENERAL ARNOLD asked what would occur if General Spaatz and the Deputy Chief of the Air Staff should disagree with regard to the control of the strategic bombing forces.

SIR CHARLES PORTAL explained that in this unlikely eventuality they would refer respectively to General Arnold and himself who, if they could not give a ruling, would refer the matter to the Combined Chiefs of Staff for decision.

With regard to the declaration of an emergency by a supreme commander, *SIR CHARLES PORTAL* explained that this same procedure had been in force for approximately a year in the Mediterranean where it had worked satisfactorily. An emergency could be declared either for offense or for defense.

GENERAL ARNOLD said he was particularly interested in the full utilization of the strategic bombing force since the United States had in the United Kingdom 2970 heavy bombers and in the Mediterranean 1512 heavy bombers, making a total of 4482. Of these, 2980 were operational and each aircraft had two crews available and therefore could be used every day. Was the proposed chain of command the best setup to obtain the maximum use from this very large force?

SIR CHARLES PORTAL said he felt that it was. The Supreme Commander's role in the chain of command, which had been valuable in the first phases of *OVERLORD* was, in his opinion, no longer useful and better results would be obtained from the proposed command arrangements.

ADMIRAL LEAHY questioned the proposed directive with regard to the right of a commander in the field to get from the strategic air forces the air support which he requested. This, he felt, was essential.

SIR CHARLES PORTAL said that the system was exactly the same as had been used in the Mediterranean where the Supreme Commander had declared an emergency on only one occasion. This, as he remembered, was on the fifth day of the battle at Salerno. The declaration of an emergency by a supreme commander was in effect a direct order from the Combined Chiefs of Staff for the use of the strategic air forces as directed by the supreme commander. He said he could guarantee on the British side that the supreme commanders would always get what they needed when they needed it. The use of the emergency procedure should be regarded only as "the big stick" which could be used but probably would never have to be.

GENERAL MARSHALL suggested an alternative arrangement whereby a small assignment of strategic air might be made to supreme commanders, the remainder being controlled as suggested in the British paper.

SIR CHARLES PORTAL agreed that this was a possible solution. He felt, however, that in a real emergency the supreme commander must have all the bombers that he needed. Divided control might result in the supreme commander's allotment not being fully used on all occasions.

THE COMBINED CHIEFS OF STAFF:—

Agreed to consider this matter further at their meeting the following morning.

COMBINED CHIEFS OF STAFF

C.C.S. 173d Meeting

OCTAGON CONFERENCE

Minutes of Meeting Held in the
Main Conference Room, Chateau Frontenac Hotel,
on 13 September 1944, at 1430.

PRESENT

United States

Admiral W. D. Leahy, USN
General G. C. Marshall, USA
Admiral E. J. King, USN
General H. H. Arnold, USA

British

Field Marshal Sir Alan F. Brooke
Marshal of the Royal Air Force
  Sir Charles F. A. Portal
Admiral of the Fleet
  Sir Andrew B. Cunningham

ALSO PRESENT

Lt. Gen. B. B. Somervell, USA
Vice Adm. R. Willson, USN
Rear Adm. C. M. Cooke, Jr., USN
Rear Adm. L. D. McCormick, USN
Major Gen. T. T. Handy, USA
Major Gen. M. S. Fairchild, USA
Major Gen. L. S. Kuter, USA

Field Marshal Sir John Dill
General Sir Hastings L. Ismay
Admiral Sir Percy Noble
Lt. Gen. G. N. Macready
Air Marshal Sir William Welsh
Major Gen. R. E. Laycock

SECRETARIAT

Major Gen. L. C. Hollis
Brig. Gen. A. J. McFarland, USA
Brigadier A. T. Cornwall-Jones
Captain E. D. Graves, Jr., USN
Commander R. D. Coleridge, RN

TOP SECRET

1. *APPROVAL OF THE MINUTES OF THE 172D MEETING OF THE COMBINED CHIEFS OF STAFF*

   GENERAL MARSHALL drew attention to his statement recorded in the penultimate paragraph on page 3 of the minutes. He requested that this should be amended to read:

   "... the *PLOUGH* Force now in south France and the necessary sleds are obtainable."

   THE COMBINED CHIEFS OF STAFF:—

   Approved the conclusions of the 172d Meeting. The detailed record was amended as proposed by General Marshall and approved subject to later minor amendments.

2. *CONTROL OF THE STRATEGIC BOMBER FORCES IN EUROPE*
   (C.C.S. 520/4)

   SIR CHARLES PORTAL said that he had not had time fully to study the proposed directive. It appeared, however, to be acceptable except with regard to certain small details.

   THE COMBINED CHIEFS OF STAFF:—

   Agreed to consider C.C.S. 520/4 at their meeting to be held on the following day.

3. *MACHINERY FOR COORDINATION OF U.S.-SOVIET-BRITISH MILITARY EFFORT*
   (C.C.S. 618/4)

   THE COMBINED CHIEFS OF STAFF:—

   Agreed to the dispatch of the messages in Enclosures "A" and "B" to C.C.S. 618/4 to Generals Burrows and Deane respectively.

4. *REPORT ON THE ENEMY SITUATION IN THE PACIFIC*
   (C.C.S. 643/1)

TOP SECRET

THE COMBINED CHIEFS OF STAFF:—

Took note of the report by the Combined Intelligence Committee on the enemy situation in the Pacific-Far East (C.C.S. 643/1).

5. *GENERAL PROGRESS REPORT ON RECENT OPERATIONS IN THE PACIFIC*
(C.C.S. 676)

THE COMBINED CHIEFS OF STAFF:—

Took note of the progress report by the United States Chiefs of Staff on recent operations in the Pacific (C.C.S. 676).

6. *STRATEGY FOR THE DEFEAT OF JAPAN*
(C.C.S. 417/8)

SIR ALAN BROOKE said that the British Chiefs of Staff were in agreement with the course of action for planning purposes outlined by the United States Chiefs of Staff in C.C.S. 417/8. There was, however, one point he would like to make. In addition to the operations outlined in the paper there would, of course, be certain British operations which the British Chiefs of Staff had not yet had an opportunity to put forward. For instance, the British Fleet participating in the Pacific operations, the British Task Force in the Southwest Pacific and Operation *DRACULA*. In making provision, therefore, for the U.S. operations it should be borne in mind that there would also be certain British operations, the forces for which will require allocation of certain items of equipment for which provision should be made and a margin of requirements allowed.

SIR JOHN DILL explained that supplies would be required for British forces for the war against Japan which could not yet be requested since the operations were not yet fully approved.

ADMIRAL LEAHY said that he quite appreciated the points made by Sir Alan Brooke, but he was not clear how they could be incorporated in the existing paper.

SIR ALAN BROOKE said that all that was required was that the Combined Chiefs of Staff should take note that certain British operations against

TOP SECRET

Japan were not included in the program outlined in C.C.S. 417/8 and that requirements with regard to provision of equipment and the logistic support of these forces would be put forward at a later date.

THE COMBINED CHIEFS OF STAFF:—

a. Accepted the proposals in C.C.S. 417/8 as a basis for planning.

b. Took note that British operations against Japan, not yet approved, would require the allocation of resources and that in planning production therefor these requirements should be borne in mind.

c. Took note that the size of the British forces to be employed against Japan would be notified as soon as possible.

7. *BASIC POLICIES FOR THE "OCTAGON" CONFERENCE*
(C.C.S. 654/8)

ADMIRAL LEAHY said that it seemed to him that the U.S. and British proposals as to the wording of paragraph 6 i of C.C.S. 654 were very similar.

SIR ALAN BROOKE explained that the British wording "inescapable commitments" was aimed to cover such points as the return of Dominion forces to their homelands which was a commitment which could not be avoided.

ADMIRAL KING suggested that the two proposals should be incorporated and that the wording should read: "having regard to other agreed and/or inescapable commitments."

SIR ALAN BROOKE said that this proposal was entirely acceptable.

THE COMBINED CHIEFS OF STAFF:—

Accepted the following wording for paragraph 6 i of C.C.S. 654:

"Reorient forces from the European Theater to the Pacific and Far East, as a matter of highest priority, having regard to other agreed and/or inescapable commitments, as soon as the German situation allows."

8. *FUTURE OPERATIONS IN THE MEDITERRANEAN*
   (C.C.S. 677/1)

ADMIRAL LEAHY explained that with regard to paragraph 2 *b* of the U.S. draft of the mesage to General Wilson, it was felt that the wording "for planning the capture of the Istrian Peninsula" was more appropriate than "for the capture of the Istrian Peninsula" since the operation was not yet approved and might, in fact, never take place.

GENERAL MARSHALL explained that the words "major units" in paragraph 1 *a* had been inserted at his suggestion to cover such possible withdrawals as that of the Japanese battalion which he had mentioned the previous day.

ADMIRAL LEAHY pointed out that in the U.S. draft the date on which General Wilson was to submit his plan had been altered to 10 October. Since a decision had to be reached by the 15th it would be safer to call for the report on the 10th.

SIR ALAN BROOKE said that the U.S. draft was acceptable to the British Chiefs of Staff.

THE COMBINED CHIEFS OF STAFF:—

Agreed to dispatch to the Supreme Allied Commander, Mediterranean the draft message in Enclosure "B" to C.C.S. 677/1.
(Subsequently dispatched as FAN 415.)

9. *NEXT MEETING, COMBINED CHIEFS OF STAFF*

THE COMBINED CHIEFS OF STAFF:—

Agreed to meet at 1000 on Thursday, 14 September, and to permit photographs to be taken at that time.

COMBINED CHIEFS OF STAFF

C.C.S. 174th Meeting

OCTAGON CONFERENCE

MINUTES OF MEETING HELD IN THE
MAIN CONFERENCE ROOM, CHATEAU FRONTENAC HOTEL,
ON 14 SEPTEMBER 1944, AT 1000.

PRESENT

United States

Admiral W. D. Leahy, USN
General G. C. Marshall, USA
Admiral E. J. King, USN
General H. H. Arnold, USA

British

Field Marshal Sir Alan F. Brooke
Marshal of the Royal Air Force
  Sir Charles F. A. Portal
Admiral of the Fleet
  Sir Andrew B. Cunningham

ALSO PRESENT

Lt. Gen. B. B. Somervell, USA
Vice Adm. R. Willson, USN
Rear Adm. C. M. Cooke, Jr., USN
Rear Adm. L. D. McCormick, USN
Major Gen. T. T. Handy, USA
Major Gen. M. S. Fairchild, USA
Major Gen. L. S. Kuter, USA

Field Marshal Sir John Dill
General Sir Hastings L. Ismay
Admiral Sir Percy Noble
Lt. Gen. G. N. Macready
Air Marshal Sir William Welsh
Major Gen. R. E. Laycock

SECRETARIAT

Major Gen. L. C. Hollis
Brig. Gen. A. J. McFarland, USA
Brigadier A. T. Cornwall-Jones
Captain E. D. Graves, Jr., USN
Commander R. D. Coleridge, RN

TOP SECRET

1. *APPROVAL OF THE MINUTES OF THE 173D MEETING OF THE COMBINED CHIEFS OF STAFF*

   THE COMBINED CHIEFS OF STAFF:—

   Approved the conclusions of the 173d Meeting. The detailed record of the meeting was approved, subject to later minor amendments.

2. *CONTROL OF THE STRATEGIC BOMBER FORCES IN EUROPE*
   (C.C.S. 520/4)

   THE COMBINED CHIEFS OF STAFF:—

   Approved the directive in C.C.S. 520/4 as amended in C.C.S. 520/5. (Amended directive circulated as C.C.S. 520/6.)

3. *BRITISH PARTICIPATION IN THE PACIFIC*
   (C.C.S. 452/26 and 452/27)

   SIR ALAN BROOKE said that the British Chiefs of Staff were disturbed by the statement of the United States Chiefs of Staff in C.C.S. 452/27 with regard to British participation in the war against Japan. He realized that this paper had been written before the Plenary session on the previous day. He felt that it did not entirely coincide with the proposal put forward at that conference and accepted by the President. For political reasons it was essential that the British Fleet should take part in the main operations against Japan.

   ADMIRAL LEAHY asked if Sir Alan Brooke's point would be met by the elimination of the words, "They consider that the initial use of such a force should be on the western flank of the advance in the Southwest Pacific." It might be that the British Fleet would be used initially in the Bay of Bengal and thereafter as required by the existing situation.

   SIR ANDREW CUNNINGHAM said that the main fleet would not be required in the Bay of Bengal since there were already more British forces there than required. He agreed to the deletion proposed by Admiral Leahy.

   ADMIRAL KING also agreed to the deletion of these words which he felt were not relevant to the general case.

TOP SECRET

Continuing, *SIR ANDREW CUNNINGHAM* asked the U.S. views as to the meaning of the term "balanced forces" in the final sentence of paragraph 1 of C.C.S. 452/27. He said that the British Chiefs of Staff had in mind a force of some 4 battleships, 5 to 6 large carriers, 20 light fleet carriers and CVE's and the appropriate number of cruisers and destroyers. This he would regard as a balanced force.

ADMIRAL KING stressed that it was essential for these forces to be self-supporting.

SIR ANDREW CUNNINGHAM said that if these forces had their fleet train, they could operate unassisted for several months provided they had the necessary rear bases — probably in Australia. The provision of bases would be a matter for agreement.

ADMIRAL KING said that the practicability of employing these forces would be a matter for discussion from time to time.

ADMIRAL LEAHY said that he did not feel that the question for discussion was the practicability of employment but rather the matter of where they should be employed from time to time.

SIR ANDREW CUNNINGHAM referred to the Prime Minister's statement that he wished the British Fleet to take part in the main operations in the Pacific. Decision with regard to this was necessary since many preliminary preparations had to be made.

ADMIRAL KING suggested that the British Chiefs of Staff should put forward proposals with regard to the employment of the British Fleet.

SIR ANDREW CUNNINGHAM said that the British wish was that they should be employed in the Central Pacific.

ADMIRAL KING said that at the Plenary meeting no specific reference to the Central Pacific had been made.

SIR ALAN BROOKE said that the emphasis had been laid on the use of the British Fleet in the main effort against Japan.

TOP SECRET

ADMIRAL LEAHY said that as he saw it the main effort was at present from New Guinea to the Philippines and it would later move to the northward.

ADMIRAL KING said that he was in no position now to commit himself as to where the British Fleet could be employed.

SIR CHARLES PORTAL reminded the Combined Chiefs of Staff of the original offer made by the British Chiefs of Staff in C.C.S. 452/18, paragraph 9, which read:

> "It is our desire in accordance with His Majesty's Government's policy, that this fleet should play its full part at the earliest possible moment in the main operations against Japan wherever the greatest naval strength is required."

When the British Chiefs of Staff spoke of the main operations against Japan they did not intend to confine this meaning to Japan itself geographically but meant rather that the fleet should take part in the main operations within the theater of war wherever they might be taking place.

SIR ANDREW CUNNINGHAM stressed that the British Chiefs of Staff did not wish the British Fleet merely to take part in mopping up operations in areas falling into our hands.

ADMIRAL LEAHY said that he felt that the actual operations in which the British Fleet would take part would have to be decided in the future. It might well be that the fleet would be required for the conquest of Singapore, which he would regard as a major operation.

THE COMBINED CHIEFS OF STAFF then considered paragraph 2 of C.C.S. 452/27 referring to the use of a British Empire task force in the Southwest Pacific.

SIR CHARLES PORTAL said that the Prime Minister had offered the British Fleet for use in the main operations against Japan. By implication this paragraph accepted a naval task force for the Southwest Pacific, and was therefore contrary to the intention he had expressed.

ADMIRAL KING said that it was of course essential to have sufficient forces for the war against Japan. He was not, however, prepared to accept a British Fleet which he could not employ or support. In principle he wished

TOP SECRET

to accept the British Fleet in the Pacific but it would be entirely unacceptable for the British Main Fleet to be employed for political reasons in the Pacific and thus necessitate withdrawal of some of the United States Fleet.

SIR CHARLES PORTAL reminded Admiral King that the Prime Minister had suggested that certain of the newer British capital ships should be substituted for certain of the older U.S. ships.

SIR ANDREW CUNNINGHAM said that as he understood it the Prime Minister and President were in agreement that it was essential for British forces to take a leading part in the main operations against Japan.

ADMIRAL KING said that it was not his recollection that the President had agreed to this. He could not accept that a view expressed by the Prime Minister should be regarded as a directive to the Combined Chiefs of Staff.

SIR CHARLES PORTAL said that the Prime Minister felt it essential that it should be placed on record that he wished the British Fleet to play a major role in the operations against Japan.

SIR ALAN BROOKE said that, as he remembered it, the offer was no sooner made than accepted by the President.

ADMIRAL KING asked for specific British proposals.

SIR CHARLES PORTAL referred once more to the offer made in C.C.S. 452/18 which he had had previously quoted.

ADMIRAL LEAHY said that he could see no objection whatever to this proposal. He could not say exactly where the fleet could be employed at this moment but there would be ample opportunity for its use provided it was self-supporting.

ADMIRAL KING said that the question of the British proposal for the use the main fleet would have to be referred to the President before it could be accepted.

ADMIRAL LEAHY said that if Admiral King saw any objections to this proposal he should take the matter up himself with the President. It might not be wise to use the term "main fleet."

TOP SECRET

SIR ANDREW CUNNINGHAM said that the British Fleet had been offered by the Prime Minister and the President had accepted it. He was prepared to agree to the deletion of the word "main" from paragraph 1 of C.C.S. 452/27.

ADMIRAL KING said that the Prime Minister had also referred to the use of British air power in the Pacific.

GENERAL ARNOLD said that a definite answer with regard to British air help in the war against Japan could not be given now. The amount which could be absorbed would depend on the development of suitable facilities.

SIR CHARLES PORTAL said that it was, of course, impossible to be definite at the moment since the forces available would depend on the length of the war with Germany. What he would ask for was air facilities available in the bases in the Pacific so that the British could play their part. He would put forward a proposal for consideration.

GENERAL MARSHALL said that the best method would be a statement of numbers of aircraft and dates at which they would be available.

GENERAL ARNOLD agreed that this would be preferable.

Referring to paragraph 2 of C.C.S. 452/27, *SIR ALAN BROOKE* pointed out that this paragraph dealt with the formation of a British Empire task force which was the second alternative put forward by the British Chiefs of Staff if for any reason the support of the British Fleet in the main operations could not be accepted. Since this support had been accepted there would be no British naval forces available for the task force and British land forces could only arrive at a later date. He suggested therefore that this paragraph should be deleted.

ADMIRAL KING asked if it was intended to use the British Fleet only in the main operations and to make no contribution to a task force in the Southwest Pacific.

GENERAL MARSHALL said there were certain objections to forming a British Empire task force under General MacArthur's command at the present time. This had been proposed by General Blamey but if it were carried out between now and February of next year it would cause considerable difficulties from the point of view of land forces since the grouping of formations and the sequence of their movement had already been scheduled in accordance with future operations. The position would be different after March.

SIR ALAN BROOKE agreed that since British land forces would not be available until after Operation *DRACULA* it would be of no particular value to form a British task force now. The British Fleet could of course play a part in operations in the Southwest Pacific if they were required.

SIR ANDREW CUNNINGHAM confirmed that there would be no objection to the British Fleet working from time to time under General MacArthur's command.

GENERAL MARSHALL requested that, in order to safeguard his position with regard to the immediate formation of a task force, paragraph 2 of C.C.S. 452/27 be deleted.

SIR ALAN BROOKE agreed. General MacArthur's plans had already been made and since no British land contribution could at present be made there was no object in retaining this paragraph.

THE COMBINED CHIEFS OF STAFF:—

a. Agreed that the British Fleet should participate in the main operations against Japan in the Pacific.

b. Took note of the assurance of the British Chiefs of Staff that this fleet would be balanced and self-supporting.

c. Agreed that the method of the employment of the British Fleet in these main operations in the Pacific would be decided from time to time in accordance with the prevailing circumstances.

d. Took note that in the light of *a* above, the British Chiefs of Staff withdraw their alternative proposal to form a British Empire task force in the Southwest Pacific.

e. Invited the Chief of the Air Staff to put forward, for planning purposes, a paper containing an estimate in general terms of the contribution the Royal Air Force would be prepared to make in the main operations against Japan.

TOP SECRET

4. FUTURE OPERATIONS IN SOUTHEAST ASIA
(C.C.S. 452/28 and 452/29)
(OCTAGON-IN-9)

SIR ALAN BROOKE suggested that the situation report of the Supreme Allied Commander, Southeast Asia (OCTAGON-IN-9 of 8 September) should be noted.

ADMIRAL LEAHY agreed.

SIR ALAN BROOKE then suggested that before considering the draft directive to Admiral Mountbatten contained in C.C.S. 452/28, he should briefly outline the British views with regard to future operations in Burma. It was the British intention to endeavor to carry out operations aimed at liquidating the Burma commitment as soon as possible. This commitment was a heavy one, particularly with regard to casualties from sickness and the large numbers of men required in view of the long and tenuous lines of communication. For instance, an ordinary division amounted to some 40,000 men, whereas one particular division in Southeast Asia required approximately 90,000. The reconquest of Burma would also eliminate the commitments for the protection of the northeast frontier of India and the air route to China.

With these objects in view, operations against Rangoon had been examined. A seaborne amphibious operation was extremely difficult due to the fact that Rangoon lay some way up a river and the surrounding terrain was extremely marshy. An airborne assault had therefore been considered. By the use of airborne forces it was thought that the airfields to the north of Rangoon could be seized and that formations could then be flown in. These formations would seize the area to the north of Rangoon, then open up the river communications through Rangoon, block the Pegu route and then eliminate the Japanese in Burma by operations both from the south and from the north. If this could be achieved we should be in far better position. Forces could be released from the theater and the protection of India would be simplified.

To sum up, we should eliminate the Burma commitment, secure the air route to China, and possibly at a later date a land route, and obtain jumping-off places for further operations against Bangkok or to the Kra Peninsula and from there to Singapore.

Admiral Mountbatten had prepared a plan. This, however, had entailed removing forces from north Burma, which was felt to be unacceptable. The possibility therefore of obtaining forces from Europe had been examined. It was estimated that a decision to remove these forces would have to be taken by the first of October and that they would include the 6th Airborne Division, the 52nd Division, and the 3rd Division, from northwest Europe and three Indian divisions from Italy. There were certain difficulties with regard to this plan. The Indian troops who had been fighting for five years would have to be taken home and given three weeks' leave. This would take some time since many of them lived in extremely inaccessible parts of India, entailing in some cases a journey of a month each way to their homes. Further, India's capacity to absorb personnel was limited and had been estimated at 50,000 a month, though it was believed that this could, in certain instances, be raised to 80,000 a month. If forces were brought to India, it was estimated that two months must elapse between their arrival and the period when they would be ready to start. Every effort was being made to try and cut the time factor in this jig-saw puzzle, but there was no doubt that the moves ought to begin in October if the 15th of March was taken as the date for Operation *DRACULA*. It might be possible to postpone this date until the 1st of April, the limiting factor being the weather conditions in April rendering the airdromes north of Rangoon unserviceable.

Another possibility might be to undertake the operation with fewer forces. However, if the operation was launched and Japanese resistance was extremely strong, we should find ourselves in a difficult position since the nearest reserves would be in northwest Europe or Italy. It was felt therefore that if the operation was to be undertaken it must be undertaken with an adequate margin of strength. Operations in Europe did not permit of reaching a decision at the present time with regard to the removal of the necessary forces, i.e., three divisions from Italy and three divisions from northwest Europe. Further, there was the question of the administrative troops which would be required, particularly signal and movement personnel. These were of the utmost importance to the 21st Army Group and to General Alexander if his army advanced towards the Po. The situation was such therefore that we could not at present gamble by removing these troops. Every effort was being made to reduce the estimated time from the removal of the troops from Europe till the launching of the operation in order that a decision could be postponed and yet the operation be undertaken in the spring. Such a decision with regard to withdrawal of troops from Europe might be possible in a month's time. There were also the complications of the regulations now being instituted with regard to conditions of service for the war against Japan, the giving of leave before troops who had been fighting for many years were sent to a new theater, and the

TOP SECRET

question of the release of men who had over five years of war service. Every conceivable effort was being made to find the necessary forces to carry out DRACULA in the spring. If it were carried out, then Admiral Mountbatten's advance in the north would be limited, whereas if the operation was postponed till November, he could fight his way much further south.

SIR CHARLES PORTAL said that the air transport side of the problem was all-important. At present Admiral Mountbatten had 448 transport aircraft, and required 1200 for the Rangoon operation. Only 190 of the additional 752 required could be found from British sources, and these only from operations in Europe. The remainder would have to be provided by the United States either from Europe or from elsewhere if they were available.

At present Admiral Mountbatten had two combat cargo groups and wished to obtain the third combat cargo group by the 15th of October in order to undertake Operation CAPITAL. Further, he also required the ground echelon of the second group by that date. If Operation DRACULA were undertaken, he would require the fourth combat cargo group by mid-January and the ground echelon of the third at the same time.

GENERAL ARNOLD said that even if the fourth combat cargo group were made available to Admiral Mountbatten, he would not have enough aircraft for Operation DRACULA, and it would be necessary to divert further air forces to assist him.

SIR CHARLES PORTAL said that he noticed in C.C.S. 452/29 that the United States Chiefs of Staff were allocating the fourth combat cargo group to the Southwest Pacific. He asked that if Operation DRACULA was approved, the effect of this proposal should be examined.

GENERAL MARSHALL pointed out that this fourth combat cargo group was required for the Philippine operations, but it might be possible to send it back for the peak period of the DRACULA operation if the timings fitted. B-24 aircraft might also be used.

SIR CHARLES PORTAL said it was hoped by then to have a suitable staging point.

There was general agreement that the provision of the necessary aircraft would depend on the conclusion of hostilities in Europe.

TOP SECRET

GENERAL ARNOLD said that if hostilities in Europe had terminated, there would be 2200 U.S. transport aircraft which would become available.

SIR CHARLES PORTAL said he felt that the ground echelons for these aircraft would probably have to be taken out of Europe by December.

GENERAL ARNOLD felt that the date might be postponed since a large part of the ground echelons could be flown out in the aircraft. The ground echelon for the second combat cargo group was already on its way to Southeast Asia, and the ground echelon for the third combat cargo group could sail as soon as shipping was available.

THE COMBINED CHIEFS OF STAFF then examined the draft directive to the Supreme Allied Commander, Southeast Asia contained in C.C.S. 452/28.

ADMIRAL LEAHY put forward certain amendments proposed by the United States Chiefs of Staff. These included provision in paragraph 1 and paragraph 2 *a* for the opening of land communications with China.

GENERAL MARSHALL said that this was an important factor, and was necessary in order to introduce wheeled transport into China. It might be possible to take the short northern route though this was tortuous and difficult.

GENERAL ARNOLD said that in the last month 23,000 tons of stores had been flown into China but in view of the lack of motor transport certain of these were lying on the airfields and could not be distributed.

Referring to C.C.S. 452/29, *SIR CHARLES PORTAL* asked that the Combined Chiefs of Staff should take note that the whole feasibility of Operation *DRACULA* was dependent upon the provision of the necessary aircraft and, further, of the possibility of the transfer of the fourth combat cargo group from operations against the Philippines for a short period at the peak load of Operation *DRACULA*.

THE COMBINED CHIEFS OF STAFF:—

- *a.* Took note of the progress report on operations in the Southeast Asia Command contained in OCTAGON-IN-9.

- *b.* Approved the directive in C.C.S. 452/28 as amended during discussion. (Amended directive circulated as C.C.S. 452/30.)

TOP SECRET

 c. Took note that the British Chiefs of Staff were making every effort to overcome the problems involved in moving the necessary resources from Europe for *DRACULA* so that the operation can be carried out before the 1945 monsoon.

 d. Recognized that the ability to carry out Operation *DRACULA* would depend very largely on the provision of transport aircraft, and took note:

  (1) That the ground echelon of the second combat cargo group was already on its way to the Southeast Asia Command.

  (2) That the United States Chiefs of Staff had already assigned the third combat cargo group to Southeast Asia and that it would go out as soon as shipping was available.

  (3) That the possibility of assigning to Southeast Asia Command the fourth combat cargo group and the remaining transport aircraft required would depend on the progress of operations in Europe and in the Pacific, and that, on the whole, the prospects of making the necessary provision seemed good.

5. *PLANNING DATE FOR THE END OF THE WAR AGAINST JAPAN*
(C.C.S. 678)

 ADMIRAL LEAHY said that the memorandum by the British Chiefs of Staff dealing with the proposed date for the end of the war against Japan was acceptable to the United States Chiefs of Staff with certain amendments. It was felt that paragraph 1 *a* should be eliminated, since it was hoped that the redeployment of forces against Japan would not take two years. The United States Chiefs of Staff also felt that 18 months was a more appropriate time factor than two years. A further sentence should be added to paragraph 2, to read: "This date will be adjusted periodically to conform to the course of the war."

 GENERAL MARSHALL said that for demobilization purposes the United States Army were using a time factor of one year. This, of course, would not affect the decision with regard to the date of 18 months after the termination of hostilities with Germany for planning for production.

THE COMBINED CHIEFS OF STAFF:—

"Agreed to recommend that the date for the end of the war against Japan, for planning production and for allocation of manpower should be set at 18 months after the defeat of Germany; this date to be adjusted periodically to conform to the course of the war."

6. OPERATIONS OF THE TWENTIETH AIR FORCE

GENERAL ARNOLD made the following statement with regard to operations of the Twentieth Air Force:

"The Twentieth Air Force is designed around and includes all B-29 airplanes.

"The B-29 airplane, which is the basis of the Twentieth Air Force, is a very long range, fast, heavily armed precision day bomber. At maximum combat loading its gross weight is 140,000 pounds at which weight it operates up to 30,000-feet altitudes at a top speed of 370 miles per hour and cruises at 220 miles per hour. During a normal combat mission it burns 450 gallons per hour and at high speed consumes up to 700 gallons per hour. The airplane is operated by a crew of 11 men. A notable feature is the airplane pressurization which results in providing inside pressure equivalent to altitudes of about 8,000 feet when the airplane is actually at 30,000 feet. The most notable feature, however, is probably the central fire control features whereby three centrally located gunners handle, with precision, twelve 50-caliber machine guns and one 20 mm. cannon, all remotely controlled. In spite of its weight, this airplane can be operated from 8500-foot runways at maximum gross loadings and from 7500-foot runways when loaded to 135,000 pounds.

"The Twentieth Air Force operates directly under the United States Joint Chiefs of Staff. It is commanded by the Commanding General, Army Air Forces, who acts as the executive agent of the United States Joint Chiefs of Staff in implementing their directive for the employment of very long range bomber forces.

"Theater commanders in which elements of the Twentieth Air Force are based are responsible for logistic support and defense of Twentieth Air Force bases.

"At this time the major units of the Twentieth Air Force are the XX, XXI and XXII Bomber Commands. Each of these Bomber Commands, as a matter of fact, is a complete self-sustaining very long range air force.

TOP SECRET

"The XX Bomber Command is now based in the Southeast Asia Command in the area just west of Calcutta and operates principally from bases in the vicinity of Chengtu, China, against targets in Japan and Manchuria. It comprises four groups and had in the theater on September 11th, 155 B-29's, of which 120 are unit equipment aircraft.

"The XXI Bomber Command consists of three wings of four groups each with a total unit equipment strength of 360 B-29 aircraft. Its headquarters, ground echelons and service units, are now moving to the Marianas. All 12 groups will complete their training and move to bases in the Marianas as bases become available.

"The XXII Bomber Command, consisting of two 4-group wings, was activated on August 15th and ground echelons will be available for movement to bases in Formosa or Luzon as quickly as they can be made available. The first air echelons of the XXII Bomber Command will be ready to move in March 1945.

"The logistic requirements of the XX Bomber Command operating out of China were extremely heavy, and provision of the necessary gasoline had presented a major problem. It had, in fact, been necessary to divert some 20 B-29's to use in the role of tankers; these were now being relieved by B-24 tankers which were now en route."

GENERAL ARNOLD then outlined with the aid of a map the targets that were being brought within range of B-29's operating from the various bases either now available or which it was hoped would shortly be available.

THE COMBINED CHIEFS OF STAFF:—

Took note with interest of General Arnold's statement with respect to the Twentieth Air Force.

7. *COMMUNICATIONS TO MARSHAL STALIN AND GENERALISSIMO CHIANG KAI-SHEK*

ADMIRAL KING suggested that the Combined Chiefs of Staff should prepare for submission to the President and Prime Minister draft communications to Marshal Stalin and Generalissimo Chiang Kai-shek dealing with the broad results of the Conference. This had been done on previous occasions.

TOP SECRET

It was generally agreed that, with regard to the communication to Generalissimo Chiang Kai-shek, details of Operation *DRACULA* should not be entered into and that some broad statement should be used to the effect that amphibious operations against Lower Burma would be undertaken at the earliest possible date.

THE COMBINED CHIEFS OF STAFF:—

Directed the Secretaries to draft suitable messages to Marshal Stalin and Generalissimo Chiang Kai-shek on the results of *OCTAGON*.

8. *NEXT MEETING, COMBINED CHIEFS OF STAFF*

THE COMBINED CHIEFS OF STAFF:—

Agreed to meet at 1030 Friday, 15 September.

TOP SECRET

COMBINED CHIEFS OF STAFF

C.C.S. 175th Meeting

OCTAGON CONFERENCE

MINUTES OF MEETING HELD IN THE MAIN CONFERENCE ROOM, CHATEAU FRONTENAC HOTEL, ON 15 SEPTEMBER 1944, AT 1000.

PRESENT

United States

Admiral W. D. Leahy, USN
General G. C. Marshall, USA
Admiral E. J. King, USN
General H. H. Arnold, USA

British

Field Marshal Sir Alan F. Brooke
Marshal of the Royal Air Force
   Sir Charles F. A. Portal
Admiral of the Fleet
   Sir Andrew B. Cunningham

ALSO PRESENT

Lt. Gen. B. B. Somervell, USA
Vice Adm. R. Willson, USN
Rear Adm. C. M. Cooke, Jr., USN
Rear Adm. L. D. McCormick, USN
Major Gen. T. T. Handy, USA
Major Gen. M. S. Fairchild, USA
Major Gen. L. S. Kuter, USA

Field Marshal Sir John Dill
General Sir Hastings L. Ismay
Admiral Sir Percy Noble
Lt. Gen. G. N. Macready
Air Marshal Sir William Welsh
Major Gen. R. E. Laycock

SECRETARIAT

Major Gen. L. C. Hollis
Brig. Gen. A. J. McFarland, USA
Brigadier A. T. Cornwall-Jones
Captain E. D. Graves, Jr., USN
Commander R. D. Coleridge, RN

1. *APPROVAL OF THE MINUTES OF THE 174TH MEETING OF THE COMBINED CHIEFS OF STAFF*

ADMIRAL LEAHY said that the United States Chiefs of Staff recommend an alteration to the conclusion of Item 5 of the minutes. It was suggested that this should read:

"Agreed to recommend that for planning production and for allocation of manpower the date for the end of the war against Japan . . . ."

SIR ALAN BROOKE said that this proposal was entirely acceptable.

Continuing, *ADMIRAL LEAHY* said there was one other alteration which should be made in the final sentence to General Arnold's statement in Item 6. The number of B-29's which had been diverted to tankers should read 20 and not 40.

SIR CHARLES PORTAL said that on page 7 of the minutes his statement, as to the date on which the ground echelons for the aircraft from Europe for use in the war against Japan would have to be taken out, should read "by" December and not "in" December.

THE COMBINED CHIEFS OF STAFF:—

a. Agreed to amend the conclusion to Item 5 of C.C.S. 174th Meeting to read as follows: "Agreed to recommend that the date for the end of the war against Japan, for planning production and for allocation of manpower should be set at 18 months after the defeat of Germany; this date to be adjusted periodically to conform to the course of the war."

b. Approved the conclusions of the 174th Meeting as amended above. The detailed record of the meeting was approved subject to the amendments agreed during discussion and to later minor amendments.

2. *FINAL REPORT TO THE PRESIDENT AND PRIME MINISTER*
(C.C.S. 680)

THE COMBINED CHIEFS OF STAFF discussed and accepted certain amendments to the report.

TOP SECRET

THE COMBINED CHIEFS OF STAFF:—

Approved the final report to the President and Prime Minister, as amended in discussion.
(Subsequently circulated as C.C.S. 680/1.)

3. *COMMUNICATION OF THE RESULTS OF "OCTAGON"*
(C.C.S. 681; 681/1)

ADMIRAL LEAHY suggested the insertion in the draft letter to Marshal Stalin in C.C.S. 681 of a final paragraph (paragraph 6) to read:

"Plans for the prompt transfer of power to the Pacific Theater after the collapse of Germany were agreed upon."

SIR ALAN BROOKE accepted this amendment.

With reference to the two draft messages to Generalissimo Chiang Kai-shek in C.C.S. 681/1, *SIR ALAN BROOKE* said that on balance he preferred the shorter draft in Enclosure "B."

ADMIRAL LEAHY said that the United States Chiefs of Staff had certain deletions to suggest to the longer draft in Enclosure "A" which he would like to put forward.

ADMIRAL LEAHY read out these suggestions.

SIR ALAN BROOKE said that these amendments were acceptable.

Continuing, *ADMIRAL LEAHY* proposed that a new sentence should be added to the draft in Enclosure "A" to read as follows:

"We have agreed on future operations to intensify the offensive against the Japanese in the Pacific Theater, including the opening of a seaway into China."

SIR ALAN BROOKE said that this amendment was acceptable.

TOP SECRET

THE COMBINED CHIEFS OF STAFF:—

Subject to the amendments agreed in discussion, approved draft messages to Marshal Stalin and Generalissimo Chiang Kai-shek reporting the results of the *OCTAGON* Conference.
(Subsequently circulated as C.C.S. 681/2.)

4. *REDEPLOYMENT OF FORCES AFTER THE END OF THE WAR IN EUROPE*
(C.C.S. 679)

SIR ALAN BROOKE said that the recommendation of the United States Chiefs of Staff contained in C.C.S. 679 was acceptable. He would like the words "the combined shipping authorities" inserted after the words "Combined Military Transportation Committee" in paragraph 3.

ADMIRAL LEAHY accepted this amendment.

THE COMBINED CHIEFS OF STAFF:—

Approved C.C.S. 679 subject to insertion in the third line of paragraph 3 of the words "combined shipping authorities" after the word "Committee."

5. *COMBINED PERSONNEL MOVEMENT PROBLEM ARISING THE FIRST YEAR AFTER THE DEFEAT OF GERMANY*
(C.C.S. 675/2)

THE COMBINED CHIEFS OF STAFF had before them a memorandum by Lord Leathers and General Somervell indicating the magnitude of the combined shipping movements which might be required during the first year after the defeat of Germany.

SIR ALAN BROOKE said that Lord Leathers had explained to him that the paper was designed merely to show the magnitude of the problem rather than to give entirely accurate figures.

GENERAL SOMERVELL confirmed that this was the case.

THE COMBINED CHIEFS OF STAFF:—

Took note of C.C.S. 675/2.

6. *OPERATION "HIGHBALL"*
(C.C.S. 682)

SIR CHARLES PORTAL and *SIR ANDREW CUNNINGHAM* gave a description of Operation *HIGHBALL*. They undertook to send the United States a film on this operation.

THE COMBINED CHIEFS OF STAFF:—

Took note:

 a. That Operation *HIGHBALL* would be available in the Eastern Theater at the end of November 1944.

 b. That the British Chiefs of Staff would send an informational film and technical data to the United States Chiefs of Staff.

7. *RELEASE TO THE PRESS OF INFORMATION ON "MULBERRY"*
(SCAF 79)

SIR ALAN BROOKE said that it had been suggested that information with regard to *MULBERRY* should be released to the press. General Eisenhower was not, however, prepared to make such a release unless he was instructed to do so by the Combined Chiefs of Staff.

ADMIRAL KING said that base facilities in the Pacific were limited and it might well be that *MULBERRY* would be required in that theater, in which case it would be obviously disadvantageous if the Japanese were informed as as to their potentialities.

SIR ANDREW CUNNINGHAM agreed with Admiral King that if there was any chance of using them in the Pacific it was far wiser to release nothing to the press on *MULBERRY* for the present.

SIR ALAN BROOKE said that in view of the potentialities of *MULBERRY* for the war against Japan he agreed that security on these should be retained.

THE COMBINED CHIEFS OF STAFF:—

Agreed that security implications affecting other theaters precluded the release of information on *MULBERRY*.

8. *POSSIBLE STATEMENT TO BE MADE TO THE PRESS BY THE PRESIDENT AND PRIME MINISTER*

GENERAL MARSHALL suggested that there might be advantages in a statement being made, possibly by the President and Prime Minister, to the effect that the only difficulty encountered at the Conference was the problem of providing employment for all the Allied forces who were eager to participate in the war against Japan. The difficulty had arisen as a result of the keenness of the competition to employ the maximum possible forces for the defeat of Japan. This was a fact and issued to the press should help to undermine Japanese morale.

THE COMBINED CHIEFS OF STAFF:—

Took note that General Ismay would prepare a suitable statement for consideration.

9. *PROGRESS OF THE CAMPAIGN IN THE PACIFIC*

ADMIRAL KING outlined the extremely successful operations recently undertaken by Admiral Halsey's Task Force 38 and the Fifth Air Force against the Japanese in the Leyte area, where some 500 Japanese aircraft had been destroyed. In view of the success of these operations it had been decided, after consultation with Admiral Nimitz and General MarArthur, to advance the date of subsequently planned operations by about two months.

GENERAL MARSHALL said that he felt that the success of recent operations, particularly against the Japanese air, and the decision to advance the dates for future operations would have a decisive effect on what the Japanese could do in Burma.

GENERAL ARNOLD pointed out that the Japanese Air Force was no longer fighting with the will to win. The pilots lacked determination and even in the Philippines it seemed that the Japanese Air Force had neither the will nor the wherewithal to act offensively.

TOP SECRET

THE COMBINED CHIEFS OF STAFF:—

Took note with interest of Admiral King's remarks on the progress of the campaign in the Pacific.

10. *HOUR OF NEXT MEETING*

THE COMBINED CHIEFS OF STAFF:—

Agreed tentatively to meet at 1000 on Saturday, 16 September.

TOP SECRET

COMBINED CHIEFS OF STAFF

C.C.S. 176th Meeting

OCTAGON CONFERENCE

Minutes of Meeting Held in the
Main Conference Room, Chateau Frontenac Hotel,
on 16 September 1944, at 1100.

PRESENT

United States

Admiral W. D. Leahy, USN
General G. C. Marshall, USA
Admiral E. J. King, USN
General H. H. Arnold, USA

British

Field Marshal Sir Alan F. Brooke
Marshal of the Royal Air Force
  Sir Charles F. A. Portal
Admiral of the Fleet
  Sir Andrew B. Cunningham

ALSO PRESENT

Lt. Gen. B. B. Somervell, USA
Lt. Gen. T. T. Handy, USA
Rear Adm. C. M. Cooke, Jr., USN
Rear Adm. L. D. McCormick, USN
Maj. Gen. M. S. Fairchild, USA
Maj. Gen. L. S. Kuter, USA

Field Marshal Sir John Dill
General Sir Hastings L. Ismay
Admiral Sir Percy Noble
Lt. Gen. G. N. Macready
Air Marshal Sir William Welsh
Maj. Gen. R. E. Laycock

SECRETARIAT

Major Gen. L. C. Hollis
Brigadier Gen. A. J. McFarland, USA
Brigadier A. T. Cornwall-Jones
Captain E. D. Graves, Jr., USN
Commander R. D. Coleridge, RN

TOP SECRET

1. *APPROVAL OF THE MINUTES OF THE 175TH MEETING OF THE COMBINED CHIEFS OF STAFF*

    THE COMBINED CHIEFS OF STAFF:—

    Approved the conclusions of the 175th Meeting. The detailed record of the meeting was also approved subject to later minor amendments.

2. *"RANKIN" PLANNING IN THE MEDITERRANEAN THEATER*
    (C.C.S. 684)

    THE COMBINED CHIEFS OF STAFF:—

    Approved C.C.S. 684 (The directive to General Wilson was dispatched as FAN 418).

3. *RELEASE OF AMPHIBIOUS CRAFT FROM "OVERLORD" TO OTHER THEATERS*
    (C.C.S. 687)

    THE COMBINED CHIEFS OF STAFF:—

    Approved C.C.S. 687 (The message to SCAEF was dispatched as FACS 81).

4. *ALLOCATION OF ZONES OF OCCUPATION IN GERMANY*
    (C.C.S. 320/26)

    ADMIRAL CUNNINGHAM suggested that any naval disarmament measures for U.S. controlled ports should be under the U.S. naval member of the Central Control Commission.

    ADMIRAL KING agreed with this proposal. American control of the port of Bremen would have to include American control of a suitable area for disembarkation and staging.

    ADMIRAL CUNNINGHAM agreed. He suggested that the American area should also include Bremerhaven, some 40 or 50 miles down the river. Bremerhaven was, he understood, the port where large ships had to berth.

GENERAL SOMERVELL said that the U.S. troops would probably also have to be supplied through the ports of Antwerp and Rotterdam. It might well be desirable to set up an Inter-Allied Navigation Commission to control the Rhine.

GENERAL MARSHALL suggested that the Combined Administrative Committee might be instructed to work out the logistic details involved in the decision taken with regard to zones and the consequent maintenance of U.S. and British forces in the zones.

Certain minor amendments were then proposed to the statement of policy contained in C.C.S. 320/26. These were accepted.

THE COMBINED CHIEFS OF STAFF:—

- a. Approved the proposals in C.C.S. 320/26, subject to the minor amendments agreed in discussion. (The amended paper, as approved by the Combined Chiefs of Staff, circulated as C.C.S. 320/27.)

- b. Agreed that any naval disarmament measures for Bremen and Bremerhaven would be under the U.S. Naval Commander of the Central Control Commission.

- c. Agreed to refer C.C.S. 320/27 to the Combined Administrative Committee for examination of the logistics problems involved.

5. *SITUATION IN CHINA*

GENERAL MARSHALL informed the Combined Chiefs of Staff of the contents of a telegram recently received from General Stilwell. The Japanese were advancing on Kweilin, if indeed they had not already captured it and were therefore only 460 miles from Kunming, the China end of the air route. Further, no Chinese replacements were being provided for the Salween forces and the Generalissimo was threatening to withdraw these forces altogether if the Ledo forces did not advance to Bhamo. The Generalissimo had not yet agreed to place all Chinese forces under the direct control of General Stilwell which he had been pressed to do for some two months.

GENERAL MARSHALL then informed the Combined Chiefs of Staff of the contents of a telegram which had been sent to Chiang Kai-shek by the President urging early and vigorous action.

TOP SECRET

THE COMBINED CHIEFS OF STAFF:—

Took note of a telegram read to the meeting by General Marshall, which the President had sent to Generalissimo Chiang Kai-shek, stressing the need for action to remedy the situation in China in general and on the Salween front in particular.

6. *COMMUNIQUÉ FOR RELEASE TO THE PRESS*

SIR HASTINGS ISMAY suggested that the Combined Chiefs of Staff might wish to propose to the President and Prime Minister a paragraph dealing with the military points of the Conference for incorporation in the final press release. He presented a draft for consideration.

THE COMBINED CHIEFS OF STAFF:—

Approved the text of a short note containing suggestions as to the military substance of any communiqué that the President and the Prime Minister might wish to issue to the Press on *OCTAGON*.

7. *CONCLUDING REMARKS*

SIR ALAN BROOKE, on behalf of the British Chiefs of Staff, said he would like to express warm appreciation to the United States Chiefs of Staff for their helpful cooperation in reaching agreement on the problems which had been before them.

ADMIRAL LEAHY, in expressing thanks to Sir Alan Brooke, said that the United States Chiefs of Staff were most grateful for the helpful attitude of the British Chiefs of Staff in overcoming the minor difficulties which had initially existed.

MINUTES OF

PLENARY MEETINGS

The Minutes of the PLENARY Meetings, as transcribed herein, are from notes taken by the United States Secretary, Combined Chiefs of Staff.

TOP SECRET

OCTAGON CONFERENCE

Minutes of First Plenary Meeting Held at the Citadel, Quebec, on Wednesday, 13 September 1944, at 1145.

PRESENT

United States

The President

Admiral W. D. Leahy, USN
General G. C. Marshall, USA
Admiral E. J. King, USN
General H. H. Arnold, USA

British

The Prime Minister

Field Marshal Sir Alan F. Brooke
Marshal of the Royal Air Force
   Sir Charles F. A. Portal
Admiral of the Fleet
   Sir Andrew B. Cunningham
Field Marshal Sir John Dill
General Sir Hastings L. Ismay
Major General R. E. Laycock

SECRETARIAT

Major Gen. L. C. Hollis
Brigadier Gen. A. J. McFarland, USA

TOP SECRET

THE PRIME MINISTER, at the President's request, opened the discussion. He said that since *SEXTANT* the affairs of the United Nations had taken a revolutionary turn for the good. Everything we had touched had turned to gold, and during the last seven weeks there had been an unbroken run of military successes. The manner in which the situation had developed since the Teheran Conference gave the impression of remarkable design and precision of execution. First there had been the Anzio landing, and then, on the same day as the launching of the great Operation *OVERLORD*, we had captured Rome, which had seemed the most perfect timing. He wished to congratulate the United States Chiefs of Staff on the success of *DRAGOON*, which had produced the most gratifying results. It was already probable that eight or nine thousand prisoners had been captured, and the south and western parts of France were now being systematically cleared of the enemy. He was firmly convinced that future historians would give a great account of the period since Teheran.

THE PRESIDENT said that no little of the credit for the conception of *DRAGOON* should be attributed to Marshal Stalin. It was close to being his suggestion rather than ours.

THE PRIME MINISTER, continuing, said that he was glad to be able to record that, although the British Empire had now entered the sixth year of the war it was still keeping its end up with an over-all population, including the overseas Dominions and Colonies, of only 70,000,000 white people. The British Empire effort in Europe, counted in terms of divisions in the field, was about equal to that of the United States. This was as it should be. He was proud that the British Empire could claim equal partnership with their great ally, the United States, whom he regarded as the greatest military power in the world. The British Empire effort had now reached its peak, whereas that of their ally was ever-increasing. There was complete confidence in General Eisenhower and his relations with General Montgomery were of the best, as were those between General Montgomery and General Bradley. The part played by General W. B. Smith in directing and cementing the staffs was of the highest order. The control of operations in France was in capable hands. An efficient integrated American-British staff machine had been built up, and the battle was being brilliantly exploited.

Turning to Italy, *THE PRIME MINISTER* said that General Alexander had resumed the offensive at the end of August. Since then the Eighth Army had suffered about 8,000 and the Fifth Army about 1,000 casualties. The Fifth Army had hitherto not been so heavily engaged, but they were expected to make a thrust that very day. The British have a great stake in Italy. The army in

TOP SECRET

this theater was the largest representative British Empire Army in existence. There were in all sixteen British Empire divisions, consisting of eight British, two Canadian, one New Zealand, one South African and four British Indian divisions. He, the Prime Minister, had been anxious lest General Alexander might be shorn of certain essentials for the vigorous prosecution of his campaign. He now understood that the Combined Chiefs of Staff had agreed that there should be no withdrawals from General Alexander's Army until either Kesselring's Army had been beaten, or was on the run out of Italy.

GENERAL MARSHALL said there was no thought of withdrawing any forces until the outcome of General Alexander's present operations was known.

THE PRIME MINISTER emphasized that if the Germans were run out of Italy we should have to look for fresh fields and pastures new. It would never do for our armies to remain idle. He had always been attracted by a right-handed movement, with the purpose of giving Germany a stab in the armpit. Our objective should be Vienna. If German resistance collapsed, we should, of course, be able to reach Vienna more quickly and more easily. If not, to assist this movement, he had given considerable thought to an operation for the capture of Istria, which would include the occupation of Trieste and Fiume. He had been relieved to learn that the United States Chiefs of Staff were willing to leave in the Mediterranean certain LST's now engaged in *DRAGOON*, to provide an amphibious lift for the Adriatic operation, if this was found desirable and necessary. An added reason for this right-handed movement was the rapid encroachment of the Russians into the Balkans and the consequent dangerous spread of Russian influence in this area. He preferred to get into Vienna before the Russians did as he did not know what Russia's policy would be after she took it.

THE PRIME MINISTER then reviewed the campaign in Burma. This had been on a considerable scale. 250,000 men had been engaged, and the fighting for Imphal and Kohima had been extremely bitter. General Stilwell was to be congratulated on his brilliant operation, resulting in the capture of Myitkyina. There had been 40,000 battle casualties and 288,000 sick of which latter, happily, the great proportion recovered and returned to duty. As a result of this campaign, the air line to China had been kept open and India rendered secure from attack. It was estimated that the Japanese had lost 100,000 men in this, the largest land engagement of Japanese forces.

In spite of these successes, it was, however, most undesirable that the fighting in the jungles of Burma should go on indefinitely. For this reason, the

TOP SECRET

British Chiefs of Staff had put forward Plan *DRACULA*, which would be preceded by Plan *CAPITAL* Phase I and as much as was necessary of Phase II. Difficulties were being experienced in making available the necessary forces and transporting them to the Southeast Asia Theater in time to carry out *DRACULA* before the monsoon of 1945. The present situation in Europe, favorable as it was, did not permit a decision being taken now to withdraw forces. What was wanted was to keep an option open for as long as possible, and every effort was being directed to this end.

There were certain elements inimical to Anglo-American good relations which were putting it about that Great Britain would take no share in the war against Japan once Germany had been defeated. Far from shirking this task, the British Empire was eager to play the greatest possible part. They had every reason for doing so. Japan was as much the bitter enemy of the British Empire as of the United States. British territory had been captured in battle and grievous losses had been suffered. The offer he, the Prime Minister, now wished to make, was for the British Main Fleet to take part in the main operations against Japan under United States Supreme Command.

THE PRESIDENT said that the offer was accepted on the largest possible scale.

THE PRIME MINISTER, continuing, said there would be available a powerful and well-balanced force, including, it was hoped, at the end of next year, their newest 15-inch battleship. A fleet train of ample proportions had been built up, which would render the fleet independent for a considerable time of shore base resources. He said that the placing of a British fleet in the Central Pacific would not prevent a detachment being made to work with General MacArthur in the Southwest Pacific if this was desired. This would include air forces. There was, of course, no intention to interfere in any way with General MacArthur's command.

As a further contribution to the defeat of the enemy, the Royal Air Force would like to take a part in the heavy bombardment of Japan. A bomber force of 1500 planes could be made available for this purpose and would like a proportionate share with the four or five thousand American planes in striking at the heart of the enemy. As regards land forces, when Germany had been beaten, it would probably be possible to move six divisions from the European Theater to the East, to be followed perhaps by a further six at a later date. In Burma there were 15 divisions which might ultimately be drawn upon. He had always advocated an advance across the Bay of Bengal and operations

TOP SECRET

to recover Singapore, the loss of which had been a grievous and shameful blow to British prestige which must be avenged. It would not be good enough for Singapore to be returned to us at the peace table. We should recover it in battle. These operations would not debar the employment of small British Empire components with United States forces in the Pacific.

There was nothing cast iron in these ideas. First we should do *DRACULA*, and then survey the situation. If a better plan could be evolved, it should certainly not be ruled out in advance. Our key-word should be to engage the largest number of our own forces against the largest number of the enemy at the earliest possible moment.

THE PRESIDENT thanked the Prime Minister for his lucid and comprehensive review of the situation. It was a matter of profound satisfaction that at each succeeding conference between the American and British representatives there had been ever-increasing solidarity of outlook and identity of basic thought. Added to this there had always been an atmosphere of cordiality and friendship. Our fortunes had prospered but it was still not quite possible to forecast the date of the end of the war with Germany.

It seemed clear that the Germans were withdrawing from the Balkans and appeared likely that in Italy they would retire to the line of the Alps. The Russians were on the edge of Hungary. The Germans had shown themselves good at staging withdrawals and had been able to save large numbers of personnel although much material had been lost. If the battle went well with General Alexander, we should reach the Piave reasonably soon. All forces in Italy should be engaged to the maximum intensity.

In the west it seemed probable that the Germans would retire behind the Rhine. In his view the "West Wall" was the right bank of the Rhine which would present a formidable obstacle. He thought we should plan to force the barrier of the Rhine and then consider the situation. We should have to turn the line either from the east or from the west. For this purpose our plans must be flexible. The Germans could not yet be counted out and one more big battle would have to be fought. The operations in the East would to some extent depend on how the situation developed in Europe. He agreed that we should not remain in Burma any longer than it was necessary to clean up the Japanese in that theater. The American plan was to regain the Philippines and to dominate the mainland of Japan from the Philippines or Formosa and from bridgeheads which would be seized in China. If forces could be established on the mainland of China, China could be saved. American experience had been

TOP SECRET

that the "end run" method paid a handsome dividend. Rabaul was an example of this by-passing technique which had been employed with considerable success at small cost of life. Would it not be equally possible to by-pass Singapore by seizing an area to the north or east of it, for example, Bankok? Singapore may be very strong and he was opposed to going up against strong positions.

THE PRIME MINISTER suggested that the seizure of localities such as Penang and the Kra Isthmus or Moulmein should be studied. As far as Singapore was concerned he did not favor the by-passing method. There would undoubtedly be a large force of Japanese in the Malay Peninsula and it would help the American operations in the Pacific if we could bring these forces to action and destroy them in addition to achieving the great prize of the recapture of Singapore. If Formosa were captured, would the Japanese garrisons to the south be completely cut off?

ADMIRAL KING replied that these garrisons would be strangulated and must ultimately perish.

THE PRIME MINISTER said that all these projects were being examined and would be put in order. No decision could be taken until after Rangoon had been captured. It should not be overlooked that Marshal Stalin had volunteered a solemn undertaking at Teheran that Russia would enter the war against Japan the day that Hitler was beaten. There was no reason to doubt that Stalin would be as good as his word. The Russians undoubtedly had great ambitions in the East. If Hitler was beaten, say, by January, and Japan was confronted with the three most powerful nations in the world, they would undoubtedly have cause for reflection as to whether they could continue the fight.

THE PRESIDENT referred to the almost fanatical Japanese tenacity. In Saipan not only the soldiers but also the civilians had committed suicide rather than be taken.

SIR CHARLES PORTAL said that he hoped to have available between 600 and 800 heavy bombers for operations against the mainland of Japan. These could be supplemented by a considerable number of medium bomber squadrons.

THE PRIME MINISTER asked about the employment to be made of the British Fleet.

TOP SECRET

THE PRESIDENT said his thought was to use it in any way possible.

ADMIRAL KING said that a paper on this subject had been prepared for reference to the Combined Chiefs of Staff. The question was being actively studied.

THE PRIME MINISTER asked if it would not be better to employ the new British ships in place of battle-worn vessels of the United States.

ADMIRAL KING replied that speaking for himself, he could only say that the matter was under examination.

THE PRIME MINISTER said that the offer had been made and asked if it was accepted.

THE PRESIDENT replied in the affirmative.

THE PRIME MINISTER enquired whether an undertaking could be given for the British Air Force to participate in the main operations.

GENERAL MARSHALL said that he and General Arnold were trying to see how best to fit in the maximum number of aircraft for these operations. It was not so long ago that we were crying out for airplanes — now we had a surplus. He suggested that if the British were heavily engaged in Southeast Asia and in Malaya they would require a large proportion of their air forces for these operations. Was there a distinction between these latter opeations and the operations envisaged by Sir Charles Portal for heavy bombardment of Japan?

SIR CHARLES PORTAL replied that there was a distinction. The Lancaster bomber, if refuelled in the air, had a range nearly approaching that of the B-29. Without refuelling in the air these aircraft had a range of 800 or 900 miles.

THE PRESIDENT observed that there were certain groups in the United States, and he had no doubt that similar groups existed in Great Britain, who evinced a kindly attitude towards the Germans. Their theory was that evil could be eradicated from the German make-up and the nation could be rejuvenated by kindness.

TOP SECRET

THE PRIME MINISTER said that such sentiments would hardly be tolerated in Great Britain. The British people would demand a strong policy against the Germans. The German working man should be allowed sufficient food for his bare need, and work, but no more. The more virulent elements such as the Gestapo and the young fanatics should be deported to work in rehabilitating the devastated areas of Europe. Plans for the partition of Germany were now in the course of preparation but no final decisions had been taken.

In conclusion, *THE PRIME MINISTER* said that it was clear that a very great measure of agreement existed between the American and British Staffs.

ADMIRAL LEAHY agreed that this was so. He did not foresee any insuperable difficulties in reaching agreement on all points at issue.

TOP SECRET

OCTAGON CONFERENCE

Minutes of Second Plenary Meeting,
Held at the Citadel, Quebec, on
Saturday, 16 September 1944, at 12 noon.

PRESENT

United States

The President

Admiral W. D. Leahy, USN
General G. C. Marshall, USA
Admiral E. J. King, USN
General H. H. Arnold, USA

British

The Prime Minister

The Rt. Hon. Anthony Eden
Field Marshal Sir Alan F. Brooke
Marshal of the Royal Air Force
   Sir Charles F. A. Portal
Admiral of the Fleet
   Sir Andrew B. Cunningham
Field Marshal Sir John Dill
General Sir Hastings L. Ismay
Major Gen. R. E. Laycock

SECRETARIAT

Major Gen. L. C. Hollis
Brigadier Gen. A. J. McFarland, USA

TOP SECRET

1. *REPORT TO THE PRESIDENT AND PRIME MINISTER*

At the request of the President, *ADMIRAL LEAHY* read out the report of the Combined Chiefs of Staff to the President and Prime Minister (C.C.S. 680/1) paragraph by paragraph. A number of amendments were proposed and agreed to. These are incorporated in the final report (C.C.S. 680/2).

In addition to the agreed amendments, comments on the report were made as follows:

OPERATIONS IN ITALY

a. *Paragraph 11.*

THE PRIME MINISTER suggested that the alternative developments in the operations in Italy postulated by General Wilson were rather too rigid. There might be many shades between the rout of General Kesselring's forces and the ability of the Germans to effect an orderly withdrawal. Paragraphs 11 *a* and *b* would present a better balanced estimate if paragraph 11 *b* was amended to read "b. Kesselring's Army will succeed in effecting an orderly withdrawal, in which event it does not *at present* seem possible that we can do more than clear the Lombardy Plains this year. *Unless the enemy's resistance is markedly reduced*, difficult terrain and severe weather in the Alps during the winter would prevent another major offensive until spring 1945."

b. *Paragraph 12.*

THE PRIME MINISTER asked that the precise implication of the statement "that no major units should be withdrawn from Italy until the outcome of General Alexander's present offensive is known" might be made perfectly clear. For example, it would be quite unacceptable if paragraph 12 *a* was intended to cover an offensive only as far, say, as the Rimini Line. He assumed that the offensive contemplated would include domination of the Valley of the Po.

GENERAL MARSHALL said it was his understanding that General Alexander's present offensive included invasion of the Valley of the Po.

ADMIRAL LEAHY agreed.

TOP SECRET

c. *Paragraph 12 c.*

THE PRIME MINISTER expressed his appreciation to Admiral King for his offer to provide an amphibious lift for possible operations against the Istrian Peninsula.

ADMIRAL KING said that after taking part in operations in the Adriatic, these landing craft would be required to proceed to the Southeast Asia Theater for *DRACULA*. It was therefore of the greatest importance that General Wilson should submit his plan for the Istrian operation and a decision be taken not later than 15 October. He pointed out that there were certain other craft now in the Mediterranean which were urgently required for the Pacific.

THE PRIME MINISTER agreed that it was of the utmost importance that the matter be settled promptly.

GENERAL LAYCOCK confirmed that the additional craft referred to by Admiral King would not be wanted for the Istrian operation.

OVER-ALL OBJECTIVE FOR THE WAR AGAINST JAPAN

d. *Paragraph 21.*

THE PRIME MINISTER said he thought it quite possible that a heavy, sustained and ever-increasing air bombardment of the Japanese cities might cause Japan to capitulate. People could stand heavy bombardment only so long as they could hope that sooner or later it would come to some endurable end. There could be no such hope for Japan and all they could look forward to was the prospect of an ever-increasing weight of explosive on their centers of population.

e. *Paragraph 23.*

With reference to the term "the opening of a seaway to China," *THE PRIME MINISTER* said that he assumed this meant the seaway from the United States. He did not contemplate a sea route being opened from the south, for example, through the Sunda Strait.

ADMIRAL KING agreed with the Prime Minister's interpretation on this point.

f. Paragraph 26.

THE PRIME MINISTER said that the Canadian Government was anxious for some assurance in principle that their forces would participate in the main operations against Japan. The Canadian Government would prefer that their forces should operate in the more northerly parts of the Pacific, as their troops were unused to tropical conditions.

It was agreed that a paragraph accepting Canadian participation in principle should be inserted in the report. (See paragraph 27)

GENERAL ARNOLD pointed out that the necessity for securing suitable bases for all the forces that would be operating in the Pacific might require employment of Canadian forces in the tropics.

g. The discussion then turned to the operations in Southeast Asia, with particular reference to Operations *CAPITAL* and *DRACULA*. As regards *CAPITAL*, *THE PRIME MINISTER* said that, while he accepted the obligation of securing the air route and attaining overland communications with China, any tendency to overinsure in this operation would have the effect of ruling out *DRACULA*, which he and the British Chiefs of Staff were particularly set on carrying out before the monsoon of 1945.

h. At this point *THE PRIME MINISTER* read out a note on the provision of forces for *DRACULA* (see Annex I) in amplification of which he made certain suggestions about the timing of the movements of forces from the United States. If the United States authorities could see their way to assisting the operations in Burma with one or two divisions it would be better to move two divisions from the later schedules of the United States Army transportation to Europe than to take two divisions from General Montgomery's Army which was now actually fighting. This would bring additional troops more rapidly into action against the Japanese without withdrawing any of those already fighting in Germany. He did not ask for a decision on these proposals there and then but asked if the United States Chiefs of Staff would examine his suggestion.

GENERAL MARSHALL undertook to examine the Prime Minister's proposals. He said, however, that there was only one light division available and this had been reorganized and allocated to the European Theater at the special request of General Eisenhower. Every division in the United States was already allocated either to General Eisenhower or to the Pacific. The last divisions for the European Theater of Operations were scheduled to sail either the last week in January or the first week in February. The only way of providing United States divisions for Burma was by taking them from approved allocations. In this connection he said General Stilwell was desirous of having an American division assigned him; in fact, he wanted two if he could get them.

i. Continuing, General Marshall said that he had recently learned of an impression that the increase in the requirements for *DRACULA* had been brought about by pressure from United States authorities. After a thorough inquiry he had found that this impression was groundless. No United States authorities had advocated any such increase.

At the President's request, GENERAL MARSHALL outlined certain developments with regard to the Chinese forces. The Generalissimo contemplated withdrawing the "Y" Force across the Salween unless General Stilwell advanced on Bhamo with the Ledo Force. No replacements had been provided for the Salween Force, which had now dwindled to 14,000 men. A note had been sent by the President to the Generalissimo pointing out the consequences of the proposed action and stating that the Generalissimo must accept full responsibility therefor.

REDEPLOYMENT OF FORCES AFTER THE END OF THE WAR IN EUROPE

j. Paragraph 30.

THE PRIME MINISTER pointed out that our shipping situation would be greatly eased after the defeat of Germany by the cessation of the convoys. Lord Leathers had said that we should be able to get an additional lift of between 40 and 50 percent. The ships would be faster on passage with a much quicker turn-round at the terminal ports.

ALLOCATION OF ZONES OF OCCUPATION IN GERMANY

k. ADMIRAL LEAHY said that the Combined Chiefs of Staff had agreed on a provisional demarkation of zones of occupation in Germany. The details and implications would be required to be worked out by the experts. [An addition to the report which covered this matter (C.C.S. 320/27) was read out and agreed.]

TOP SECRET

ANNEX I: DIRECTIVE TO SUPREME ALLIED COMMANDER, SOUTHEAST ASIA

1. Admiral Mountbatten's directive was agreed, subject to certain minor amendments.

THE CONFERENCE:—

> Instructed the Secretaries to revise the report in the light of the amendments approved by the President and Prime Minister and to circulate it as an approved document.

2. *LOCATION OF THE CENTRAL TRIPARTITE CONTROL COMMISSION IN GERMANY*

THE PRESIDENT inquired whether any suggestions had been put forward for the location of the Central Tripartite Control Commission in Germany. Was this to be in Berlin or elsewhere?

MR. EDEN said that this question was under examination by the European Advisory Commission. From the administrative point of view Berlin seemed to be the best place.

3. *COMMUNICATION OF THE RESULTS OF "OCTAGON" CONFERENCE TO MARSHAL STALIN AND GENERALISSIMO CHIANG KAI-SHEK*

THE PRIME MINISTER said that he would like to add to the communication to Marshal Stalin a word on the political dangers of divergencies between Russia and the Western Allies in respect of Poland, Greece and Yugoslavia.

THE PRESIDENT said that as the communication was purely military in character and purported to give the results of the *OCTAGON* Conference, he thought it would be better if political matters were omitted.

THE PRESIDENT and *PRIME MINISTER* approved the terms of the communications to Marshal Stalin and Generalissimo Chiang Kai-shek as set out in Enclosures "A" and "B" respectively of C.C.S. 681/2.

TOP SECRET

4. RELEASE OF INFORMATION ON "MULBERRY"

THE PRIME MINISTER said that it had been suggested to him that the time had now come when information could be released to the press about *MULBERRY*. The development of the artificial harbors had been largely a British enterprise and he would naturally have liked to let the public know about them as soon as the information could safely be released. He had now been informed, however, that Admiral King thought that the release of information about *MULBERRY* might be helpful to the Japanese and might not permit full advantage being taken of these inventions in the war against Japan. The Prime Minister said he fully accepted Admiral King's view and there would consequently be no release of information to the public about *MULBERRY* at present.

5. "OCTAGON" COMMUNIQUÉ

THE CONFERENCE:—

Agreed on the terms of a communiqué to be issued to the Press that same afternoon (see Annex II).

TOP SECRET

ANNEX I

*NOTE BY THE PRIME MINISTER AND MINISTER
OF DEFENCE, DATED 16TH SEPTEMBER 1944*

1. His Majesty's Government are in full accord with the directive to Admiral Mountbatten which makes him responsible for executing the stages of Operation *CAPITAL* necessary to the security of the air route and the attainment of overland communications with China. Having regard however to the immense losses by sickness (288,000 in six months) which have attended the Burma campaign this year, they are most anxious to limit this class of operation, the burden of which falls almost wholly upon the Imperial armies, to the minimum necessary to achieve the aforesaid indispensable object. For this purpose they are resolved to strain every nerve to bring on the Operation *DRACULA* by March 15, as by cutting the Japanese communications the enemy will be forced to divide their forces. Decisive results may be obtained in a battle north of Rangoon, and the pursuit by light forces from the north may be continued without serious cost.

2. It is essential to provide five or six divisions for *DRACULA*. The 6th Airborne Division from England and a British-Indian division from Italy will start at the earliest moment irrespective of the state of the European war. It will not however be possible to withdraw any further forces from Europe before the end of organized and coherent German resistance. Admiral Mountbatten hopes by certain adjustments of his reserve divisions to withdraw two or even three divisions from the forces now facing the Japanese on the Burma front, for use in *DRACULA*. It would be of very great assistance to His Majesty's Government if the United States could place at their disposal for Operation *DRACULA* two United States light or ordinary divisions. Whether these divisions should come into action on the northern Burma front or whether they should go straight to the Operation *DRACULA* is a matter for study in time and logistics, observing that we have six months in hand before *DRACULA* D-day.

TOP SECRET

3. If such a provision were made, we should feel certain of being able to achieve *DRACULA* in time to limit the wastage to the British Imperial armies in the north and to clean up the Burma situation before the next monsoon. The destruction of the Japanese in Burma would liberate a considerable army, which could immediately attack Japanese objectives across the Bay of Bengal at whatever point or points may be considered to be most beneficial to the common cause and most likely to lead to the rapid wearing-down of Japanese troops and above all air forces.

4. If on the other hand we are not able to carry out Operation *DRACULA*, His Majesty's Government would feel they had been exposed to unnecessary sacrifices through persisting in operations ravaged by disease, and also their whole further deployment from India and Burma against the Japanese in the Malay Peninsula, et cetera, will be set back until 1946. Thus the averting of a double disaster depends upon the certainty that we can execute *DRACULA* by March 15 and, having regard to the very heavy losses we have sustained and are liable to sustain, we feel fully entitled to ask for a measure of United States assistance.

Annex I

TOP SECRET

ANNEX II

COMMUNIQUE TO THE PRESS

The President and the Prime Minister, and the Combined Chiefs of Staff held a series of meetings during which they discussed all aspects of the war against Germany and Japan. In a very short space of time they reached decisions on all points both with regard to the completion of the war in Europe, now approaching its final stages, and the destruction of the barbarians of the Pacific.

The most serious difficulty with which the Quebec Conference has been confronted has been to find room and opportunity for marshalling against Japan the massive forces which each and all of the nations concerned are ardent to engage against the enemy.

INDEX

A

ADMIRALTY ISLANDS

General progress report on recent operations in the Pacific, 113

AEGEAN (*See also* Mediterranean Theater)

Enemy situation in the Balkans, 15, 18
Naval forces to attack enemy seaborne movement in Aegean, 19

AGENDA FOR "OCTAGON"

Program for the *OCTAGON* Conference, 77, *191*

AIR FORCES (*See* Forces, Air)

AIR OPERATIONS

IN CHINA
Air forces in China to support Chinese ground forces and campaign in the Pacific, 35

IN THE EUROPEAN THEATER
Deterioration of German strategic situation, 85
General Marshall's statement regarding extensive airborne operations in connection with Operation *NEPTUNE*, *161*
Over-all mission of the strategic air forces in Europe, 50
Sir Charles Portal's statement regarding air activity in Operation *NEPTUNE*, *156, 160*
SOE/OSS operations by units of RAF Bomber Command and U.S. Strategic Air Forces in Europe, 51

IN THE MEDITERRANEAN THEATER
Strategic air force attacks in support of Russian operations, 51

IN THE PACIFIC OCEAN AREAS
CCS discussion regarding progress of the campaign in the Pacific, *228*
General Arnold's statements in reference to:
Japanese Air Force's lack of determination and will to win, *228*
Operations of the Twentieth Air Force, *219*

General progress report on recent operations in the Pacific, 109
Over-all objective in the war against Japan, 38, 136
Prime Minister's statement regarding effect of sustained air bombardment on Japanese cities, *245*

AIR ROUTES
(*See also* Lines of Communication)

Directive to Supreme Allied Commander, Southeast Asia Command for operations in Burma, 47, 137, 139

AIR SUPPLY (*See* Lines of Communication)

AIRCRAFT

General Arnold's statement regarding number of U.S. heavy bombers in the European and Mediterranean Theaters, *200*
RAF contribution in the main operations against Japan, *212*
Sir Charles Portal's statements in reference to:
British heavy bombers to be available for operations against the mainland of Japan, *240, 241*
Range of Lancaster bombers, *241*
Transport aircraft and combat cargo groups for Operations *CAPITAL* and *DRACULA*, 216, 217

AIRCRAFT ALLOCATIONS

Allocation of the two remaining combat cargo groups and air commando groups, 43
London Conference discussion regarding allocation of combat cargo and air commando groups to SEAC, *183*

ALBANIA

RANKIN planning in the Mediterranean Theater, 151

AITAPE, NEW GUINEA

General progress report on recent operations in the Pacific, 113

Note: Italic numerals refer to pages in minutes of meeting.
Plain type numerals refer to pages in C.C.S. Papers.

INDEX

ALLOCATIONS

(*See also* Aircraft Allocations)

CCS decision regarding inclusion of British requirements in production planning for operations against Japan, 204

Sir Alan Brooke's statement regarding allocation to British of requirements for Pacific operations, 203

ALPS

General Marshall's statement regarding availability of *PLOUGH* Force for operation in Alps, *193*

AMBOINA ISLAND

London Conference discussion regarding strategy in the Pacific Far-East, *179*

AMOY, CHINA

Schedule of major operations for the defeat of Japan, 1944-45, 34, 136

AMPHIBIOUS OPERATIONS

Admiral King's statement regarding amphibious operations in Istria and availability of landing craft, *193, 194*

CCS agreement that decision to mount an amphibious operation in Istria be made by 15 October, *193, 195*

Capture of the Istrian Peninsula, 121

General Marshall's statement regarding projected amphibious operation from the Mediterranean to assist *NEPTUNE*, *161*

SACMED's proposal for future strategy in Italy, 14, 18, *133*

SACSEA's strategy for operations in Burma in the near future, 24

SHAEF memo regarding employment of Mediterranean forces in support of *NEPTUNE*, 171

Sir Alan Brooke's statement regarding proposed strategy for the Mediterranean Theater, *192*

ANTWERP

CCS approve reply to SCAEF's report on intentions in the near future, *192*

Progress report on Operation *OVERLORD*, *4, 9*

SCAEF's intentions for the near future, *5, 9, 133*

Sir Alan Brooke's statement regarding situation report from SCAEF and operation to capture islands at mouth of the Schelde, *191*

"ANVIL" (See "*DRAGOON*")

APAMAMA ISLAND

General progress report on recent operations in the Pacific, 111

ARAKAN COAST

Progress report of operations in SEAC, 22

ARNOLD, GENERAL H. H.

Statements in reference to:
Availability of transport aircraft, *162*
British participation in the Pacific, *212*
Control of strategic bomber forces in Europe, *198*
Future operations in Southeast Asia, *216*
Japanese Air Force's lack of determination and will to win, *228*
Number of U.S. heavy bombers in the European and Mediterranean Theater, *200*
Operations of the Twentieth Air Force, *219*

ARTIFICIAL HARBORS

CCS decision regarding release to the Press of information on *MULBERRY*, 227

Importance of artificial harbors, 178

Prime Minister's statement regarding release to the Press of information on *MULBERRY*, *249*

Release of *MULBERRY* stories to the Press, 28, 29, 227, *249*

AUSTRALIA

Base facilities for U.S. and British naval forces in the Pacific, 179

Sir Alan Brooke's statements regarding British assistance in the defeat of Japan, *163, 178, 182*

Note: Italic numerals refer to pages in minutes of meeting.
Plain type numerals refer to pages in C.C.S. Papers.

INDEX

AUSTRIA

Employment of U.S., French, Indian and Italian forces for *RANKIN* Operation in Mediterranean Theater, 152

RANKIN planning in the Mediterranean Theater, 151

Prime Minister's statement regarding thrust to Vienna, *237*

Sir Alan Brooke's statement regarding proposed strategy for the Mediterranean Theater, *192*

B

B-24 AIRCRAFT

Employment of B-24 aircraft in the role of tankers, *220*

Employment of in Operation *DRACULA*, *216*

B-29 AIRCRAFT

General Marshall's statement regarding Japanese advance in central China and B-29 stores at Chengtu, *157*

Operation of Twentieth Air Force, *219*

VLR bomber operations against Japan Proper, 35

BALKAN AIR FORCE

Enemy situation in the Balkans, 15, 18

BALKANS

Admiral King's statement regarding amphibious operations in Istria and availability of landing craft, *193, 194*

Deterioration of German strategic situation, 85

Enemy situation in the Balkans, 15, 18

Execution of the over-all strategic concept, 134

Forces available for employment in the Balkans, 18, 134

London Conference discussion regarding operations in the Balkans, *156*

Prime Minister's statement regarding encroachment of the Russians into the Balkans, *237*

SACMED's proposal for future strategy in Italy, 14, 18, 133

Sir Alan Brooke's statements in reference to:
  Hitler's strategy in the Balkans, *157*
  Proposed strategy for the Mediterranean Theater, *192*

BALTIC SEA

Sir Andrew Cunningham's statement regarding enemy naval forces in the Baltic and Mediterranean, *160*

BANGKOK

CCS discussion regarding future operations in Southeast Asia, *214*

BAY OF BENGAL

CCS discussion regarding British participation in the Pacific, *208*

BAY OF BISCAY

London Conference decision that plans be prepared for alternate objectives in the Mediterranean Theater, *162, 166, 174*

BIAK ISLAND

General Marshall's remarks regarding air base at Biak, *157*

General progress report on recent operations in the Pacific, 114

BONIN ISLANDS

Japanese intentions in Bonins, 63, 75

Schedule of major operations for the defeat of Japan, 1944-45, 35, 136

BORNEO ISLAND

London Conference discussion regarding strategy in the Pacific-Far East, *179*

BOULOGNE, FRANCE

Progress report on Operation *OVERLORD*, 4, 9

Note: Italic numerals refer to pages in minutes of meeting.
Plain type numerals refer to pages in C.C.S. Papers.

INDEX

BRADLEY, GENERAL OMAR N.

Prime Minister's statement regarding role of the British Empire in the war and efficiency of American-British staff machine, 236

BREMEN, GERMANY

Naval disarmament measures for U.S. controlled ports, 232, 233

BREMERHAVEN, GERMANY

Naval disarmament measures for U.S. controlled ports, 232, 233

BREST, FRANCE

Development of lines of communication for OVERLORD, 7, 9
SCAEF's intentions for the near future, 6, 9, 133

BRITTANY, FRANCE

Progress report on Operation OVERLORD, 4, 9

BROOKE, FIELD MARSHAL SIR ALAN

Statements in reference to:
  Allocations for British requirements in Pacific operations, 203
  Amphibious operations from Mediterranean Theater, 160
  British assistance in the defeat of Japan, 163, 178, 182
  British participation in the Pacific, 208
  Casualties from sickness in Burma, 214
  Command of DRAGOON forces, 196
  Concluding remarks regarding OCTAGON Conference, 234
  Depletion of General Clark's staff organization on change of command, DRAGOON forces, 196
  Enemy situation in Italy, 156
  Future operations in Southeast Asia, 214
  Hitler's strategy in the Balkans, 157
  Machinery for coordination of U.S.-Soviet-British military effort, 196
  Operations in Burma, 157, 182
  Personnel shipping problem following defeat of Germany, 190
  Progress of Operation NEPTUNE, 156
  Proposed strategy for the Mediterranean Theater, 192
  Release of information on MULBERRY, 227
  Situation report from SCAEF; and operation to capture islands at mouth of the Schelde, 191
  Strategic policy in Burma, 184
  Wording for paragraph 6 (i), "Basic Policies for the OCTAGON Conference," 204
  Zones of occupation in Germany, 197

BUILD-UP

Sir Alan Brooke's statement regarding progress of Operation NEPTUNE, 156

BULGARIA

Deterioration of German strategic situation, 88
RANKIN planning in the Mediterranean Theater, 150

BURMA (See also Southeast Asia)

CCS discussion regarding future operations in Southeast Asia, 214
Directive to Supreme Allied Commander, Southeast Asia Command for operations in Burma, 47, 137, 139, 217
Japanese intentions in Burma, 63, 74
Japanese situation in Burma, 22, 24
London Conference discussion re:
  Strategy in Burma, 183
  Strategy in the Pacific-Far East, 163
Note by the Prime Minister and Minister of Defence regarding future operations in Burma and provision of forces, 250
President's review of strategic situation of the United Nations, 239
Prime Minister's statement regarding campaign in Burma, 237
Progress report of operations in SEAC, 22
Reorientation of forces from Europe for operations in Southeast Asia, 215, 218
SACSEA's strategy for operations in Burma in the near future, 24

Note: Italic numerals refer to pages in minutes of meeting.
Plain type numerals refer to pages in C.C.S. Papers.

INDEX

BURMA *(Cont'd)*

Sir Alan Brooke's remarks in reference to:
  Casualties from sickness in Burma, *214*
  Operations in Burma, *157, 183*
  Strategic policy in Burma, *184*
Statement with regard to Operation HIGHBALL, 148

C

CCS DECISIONS (See Decisions)

CALAIS, FRANCE

Progress report on Operation OVERLORD, 4, 9

CANADA

British Empire participation in the Pacific, 137, *246*

"CAPITAL"

CCS discussion regarding future operations in Southeast Asia, *214*
Directive to Supreme Allied Commander, Southeast Asia Command for operations in Burma, 47, 137, 139, *217*
Note by the Prime Minister and Minister of Defence in regard to future operations in Burma and provision of forces, 250
Prime Minister's statements in reference to:
  Campaign in Burma, *237*
  Obligations in China and desire to carry out operations before the monsoon of 1945, *246*
Transport aircraft and combat cargo groups for Operations CAPITAL and DRACULA, 216, *218*

CASUALTIES

In Burma, *214*
Prime Minister's statements in reference to:
  British stake in Italy, *236*
  Campaign in Burma, *237*

CELEBES ISLAND

London Conference discussion regarding strategy in the Pacific-Far-East, *179*

CENTRAL CONTROL COMMISSION

Naval disarmament measures for U.S. controlled ports, *232, 233*
Plenary Meeting statements regarding location of the Central Tripartite Control Commission in Germany, *248*

CENTRAL PACIFIC (See Pacific, Central)

CETTE, FRANCE

London Conference decision that plans be prepared for alternate objectives in the Mediterranean Theater, *162, 166, 174*

CEYLON

Base facilities for U.S. and British naval forces in the Pacific, *179*

CHANNEL ISLANDS

Operation against the Channel Islands, 7, 9

CHIANG KAI-SHEK, GENERALISSIMO

Communication of the results of OCTAGON Conference, 145, *220, 225, 248*

CHINA (See also Southeast Asia)

Air forces in China to support Chinese ground forces and campaign in the Pacific, 35
Approved operations in Southeast Asia, 137
Basic undertakings in support of overall strategic concept, 132
Communication of results of OCTAGON Conference to Generalissimo Chiang Kai-shek, 145, *220, 225, 248*
Directive to Supreme Allied Commander, Southeast Asia Command for operations in Burma, 47, 137, 139

Note: Italic numerals refer to pages in minutes of meeting.
Plain type numerals refer to pages in C.C.S. Papers.

INDEX

CHINA (Cont'd)

General Marshall's statements in reference to:
Japanese advance in central China and B-29 stores at Chengtu, 157
Situation in China, 233, 247
Japanese intentions in China, 63, 73
London Conference discussion regarding strategy in the Pacific-Far East, 163
Prime Minister's statement regarding obligation in China and desire to carry out operation before monsoon of 1945, 246
Schedule of major operations for defeat of Japan, 1944-45, 34, 136
Sir Alan Brooke's statements regarding British assistance in the defeat of Japan, 163, 178, 182
VLR bomber operations against Japan Proper to be continued, 35

CIVIL AFFAIRS

Arrangements for occupation in Greece in event of German withdrawal, 16, 134

COLLABORATION WITH THE U.S.S.R.

CCS instructions to Generals Deane and Burrows for negotiation of a Tripartite Military Committee in Moscow, 56, 135, 202
Machinery for coordination of U.S.-Soviet-British military effort, 54, 196

COMBINED BOMBER OFFENSIVE

Control of strategic bomber forces in Europe, 49, 132
Execution of the over-all strategic concept, 132
Over-all mission of the strategic air forces in Europe, 50
SCAEF report on air operations from the United Kingdom, 5, 8

COMBINED BRITISH-U.S.-SOVIET COMMITTEE

CCS instructions to Generals Deane and Burrows for negotiation of a Tripartite Military Committee in Moscow, 56, 135, 202
Machinery for coordination of U.S.-Soviet-British military effort, 54

COMMAND

"DRAGOON" FORCES
Assumption of command of DRAGOON forces by Supreme Commander, Allied Expeditionary Force, 92, 95, 135, 195
Transfer of operational control of DRAGOON forces, 6, 13

STRATEGIC AIR FORCES IN EUROPE
CCS approve directive for control of strategic bomber forces in Europe, 208
Control of strategic bomber forces in Europe, 49, 132, 198

TWENTIETH AIR FORCE
London Conference decision regarding control of the U.S. Twentieth Air Force, 185
Sir Charles Portal's remark regarding control of the U.S. Twentieth Air Force, 184

"CROSSBOW"

Prospects of Germany introducing new secret weapon, 89
Report on effort against CROSSBOW, 5
Sir Charles Portal's remarks regarding CROSSBOW attacks, 166

CUNNINGHAM, ADM. SIR ANDREW B.

Statements in reference to:
British naval forces available in the Pacific toward end of 1944, 179
British participation in the Pacific, 208
Enemy naval forces in the Baltic and Mediterranean, 160
Naval disarmament measures for U.S. controlled ports, 232
Naval situation in Operation NEPTUNE, 156
Release to the Press of information on MULBERRY, 227

D

DATES (See Target Dates)

DECEPTION

Disposition of enemy strength in Italy, 14

Note: Italic numerals refer to pages in minutes of meeting.
Plain type numerals refer to pages in C.C.S. Papers.

INDEX

DECISIONS

CANADA
Plenary decision to accept, in principle, Canada's participation in war against Japan, *246*

COMMAND
Command of *DRAGOON* forces, *196*

COORDINATION WITH U.S.S.R.
Machinery for coordination with U.S.S.R. in the military effort, *197, 202*

EUROPEAN THEATER
CCS approve reply to SCAEF's report on intentions in near future, *192*

CCS note CIC report on the situation in Europe, *195*

FORCES
CCS note that British will announce size of British forces to be employed against Japan, *204*

Withdrawal of forces from Mediterranean, *195, 205*

GERMANY
CAdC directed to make examination of the logistics problems involved in approved allocation of zones of occupation in Germany, *233*

Disarmament measures for Bremen and Bremerhaven, *233*

Plenary Meeting agreement that details for the allocation of zones of occupation in Germany be worked out by the experts, *247*

Zones of occupation in Germany, *198, 233*

"HIGHBALL"
CCS take note of British statement regarding Operation *HIGHBALL*, *227*

JAPAN (*See also* Pacific Ocean Areas)
CCS agreed planning date for end of war against Japan, *219*

LANDING SHIPS AND CRAFT
CCS approve dispatch of message to SCAEF regarding release of amphibious craft from *OVERLORD* to other theaters, *232*

MEDITERRANEAN THEATER
CCS agree that decision for mounting an amphibious operation in Istria be made by 15 October, *193, 195*

London Conference decision to mount a 3-divisional lift amphibious assault from the Mediterranean, target date 25 July, *162*

London Conference decision that plans be prepared for alternate objectives in the Mediterranean Theater, *162, 166, 174*

"OCTAGON"
CCS approve final report to President and Prime Minister (C.C.S. 680/1), *225*

Messages for dispatch to Stalin and Chiang Kai-shek, *221, 226*

President and Prime Minister approve final report, *244*

Press statement for *OCTAGON* Conference, *228, 234, 249, 252*

Program for *OCTAGON* Conference, *191*

Wording for paragraph 6 (i), "Basic Policies for the *OCTAGON* Conference," *204*

PACIFIC OCEAN AREAS
CCS acceptance, for planning purposes, of schedule of operations for defeat of Japan, *204*

Enemy situation in Pacific, *202*

General progress report on recent operations in the Pacific, *203*

Participation of the British Fleet in the main operations against Japan in the Pacific, *213*

PRODUCTION
CCS decision regarding production planning to include British requirements for operations against Japan, *204*

"RANKIN"
Directive to General Wilson for *RANKIN* planning in Mediterranean Theater, *232*

REDEPLOYMENT
CCS approve proposal for study on redeployment of forces after the end of the war in Europe, *226*

CCS take note of General Somervell and Lord Leathers report on the combined personnel movement problem arising the first year after the defeat of Germany, *227*

SOUTHEAST ASIA
CCS take note of SACSEA's report on operations (OCTAGON-IN-9), *217*

Note: Italic numerals refer to pages in minutes of meeting.
Plain type numerals refer to pages in C.C.S. Papers.

INDEX

DECISIONS *(Cont'd)*

    CCS approve directive for operations in SEAC, *217*

    Plenary Meeting agreement to amend and approve the directive to SACSEA, *248*

  STRATEGIC AIR FORCE

    CCS approve directive for control of strategic bomber forces in Europe, *208*

  TWENTIETH AIR FORCE

    CCS take note of General Arnold's statements regarding Twentieth Air Force, *220*

    London Conference decision regarding control of the Twentieth Air Force, *185*

DEMOBILIZATION

  Combined personnel movement problems arising during the first year after the defeat of Germany, 103

"DIADEM" (*See* Italy)

DILL, FIELD MARSHAL SIR JOHN

  Sir John Dill's statement regarding allocation of British requirements for Pacific operations, *203*

DIRECTIVES

  To Supreme Allied Commander, Southeast Asia Command, 46, 137, 139, *217*

  For control of strategic bomber forces in Europe, 49, *208*

DISARMAMENT

  Naval disarmament measures for U.S. controlled ports, *232, 233*

  Plans for Operation *TALISMAN*, 7

DODECANESE ISLANDS

  Employment of U.S., French, Indian and Italian forces for *RANKIN* Operation in Mediterranean Theater, 152

  London Conference discussion regarding operations in Balkans, *156*

  RANKIN planning in the Mediterranean Theater, 150

"DRACULA"

  Approved operations in Southeast Asia, 137

  CCS discussion regarding future operations in Southeast Asia, *214*

  Combined memorandum on troop movements, covering the period October 1944 to March 1945, 99

  Directive to Supreme Allied Commander, Southeast Asia Command for operations in Burma, 46, 137, 139, *217*

  Prime Minister's statements in reference to:

    Campaign in Burma, *237*

    Obligation in China and desire to carry out operation before the monsoon of 1945, *246*

    Provision of forces for *DRACULA*, *246, 250*

  Reorientation of forces from Europe for operations in Southeast Asia, *215, 218*

  Strategy for operations in Burma in the near future, 24

  Transport aircraft and combat cargo groups for Operations *CAPITAL* and *DRACULA*, 216, 217

"DRAGOON"

  Assumption of command of *DRAGOON* forces by Supreme Commander, Allied Expeditionary Force, 92, 95, 135, *195*

  General Marshall's statements in reference to:

    General Devers' staff organization, *196*

    Mounting the projected amphibious operation from the Mediterranean to assist *NEPTUNE*, *161*

  General tactical plan of Commander, Seventh Army, 12

  London Conference decision to mount a 3-divisional lift amphibious assault from the Mediterranean, target date 25 July, *162*

  President's statement attributing credit for conception of *DRAGOON* Operation to Marshal Stalin, *236*

Note: Italic numerals refer to pages in minutes of meeting.
Plain type numerals refer to pages in C.C.S. Papers.

INDEX

"DRAGOON" (Cont'd)

Prime Minister's opening statement, reviewing the successes of the Allied Nations, 236

Progress report on Operation DRAGOON and operations in Mediterranean Theater, 12, 17

Report on advance of the Seventh Army, 4

Sir Alan Brooke's statements in reference to:
  Amphibious operations from Mediterranean Theater, 160
  Depletion of General Clark's staff organization on change of command, DRAGOON forces, 196

SHAEF memoranda in reference to:
  Employment of Mediterranean forces in support of NEPTUNE, 171
  Release of airborne forces from Operation NEPTUNE, 170
  Release of shipping and craft from Operation NEPTUNE, 168

Transfer of operational control of DRAGOON forces, 6, 13

E

EAST INDIES

Japanese intentions in East Indies, 63, 74

EDEN, ANTHONY

Statement regarding location of the Central Tripartite Control Commission in Germany, 248

EIGHTH ARMY

Plans for major offensive in Italy, 14, 17, 133

EISENHOWER, GENERAL D. D.

Prime Minister's statement regarding role of the British Empire in the war and efficiency of American-British staff machine, 236

ENEMY SITUATION

GERMANY

CCS note CIC report on the situation in Europe, 195

Enemy situation in the Balkans, 15, 18

General Marshall's remarks regarding enemy formations on the Pisa-Rimini line, 156

Prospects of a German collapse or surrender (as of 8 Sept 1944), 82

SCAEF report on enemy resistance in European Theater, 4

Sir Alan Brooke's remarks in reference to:
  Enemy situation in Italy, 156
  Progress of Operation NEPTUNE, 156

JAPAN

CCS take note of CIC report on enemy situation in Pacific, 202

Estimate of the enemy situation, Pacific-Far East (as of 8 Sept 1944), 60

ENIWETOK

See Marshall Islands

EUROPEAN THEATER

CCS:
  Approve reply to SCAEF's report on intentions in near future, 192
  Note CIC report on the situation in Europe, 195

Control of strategic bomber forces in Europe, 50, 132, 198, 208

Execution of over-all strategic concept, 132

General Arnold's statement regarding number of U.S. heavy bombers in European and Mediterranean Theaters, 200

General Marshall's statements regarding operation to capture islands at mouth of the Schelde, 191

President's review of the strategic situation of the United Nations, 239

Progress report on Operation OVERLORD, 4, 9

SCAEF reports on:
  Air operations from the U.K., 5, 8
  Enemy resistance in European Theater, 4

Note: Italic numerals refer to pages in minutes of meeting.
Plain type numerals refer to pages in C.C.S. Papers.

INDEX

EUROPEAN THEATER (Cont'd)

Naval operations in Operation *OVERLORD*, 5

Sir Alan Brooke's statements in reference to:
  Progress of Operation *NEPTUNE*, *156*
  Situation report from SCAEF, and operation to capture islands at mouth of the Schelde, *191*

Sir Andrew Cunningham's review of naval situation in Operation *NEPTUNE*, *156*

Sir Andrew Cunningham's statement regarding enemy naval forces in the Baltic and Mediterranean, *160*

Strategic air force attacks in support of Russian operation, 51

F

FAR EAST

Estimate of enemy situation, Pacific-Far East (as of 8 Sept 1944), 60

London Conference discussion regarding strategy in Pacific-Far East, *163, 178, 179*

Sir Alan Brooke's statements regarding British assistance in the defeat of Japan, *163, 178, 182*

Statement with regard to Operation *HIGHBALL*, 148

FIFTEENTH AIR FORCE

Employment of the Fifth Army, Twelfth and Fifteenth Air Forces, 118, 121, 134

FIFTH ARMY

CCS discussion regarding withdrawal of forces from Italy, *193, 194*

Employment of the Fifth Army, Twelfth and Fifteenth Air Forces, 118, 120, 134

General Marshall's statement regarding withdrawal of Fifth Army from Italy, *193, 194*

Plans for major offensive in Italy, 14, 17, 133

Sir Alan Brooke's statement regarding proposed strategy for Mediterranean Theater, *192*

FINLAND

Deterioration of German strategic situation, 88

FINSCHHAFEN, NEW GUINEA

General progress report on recent operations in the Pacific, 114

FIRST SPECIAL SERVICE FORCE

General Marshall's statement regarding availability of *PLOUGH* Force for operation in the Alps, *193*

FORCES

COMMAND OF

Assumption of command of *DRAGOON* forces by Supreme Commander, Allied Expeditionary Force, 92, 95, 135, *195*

Transfer of operational control of *DRAGOON* forces, 6, 13

IN THE EUROPEAN THEATER

Admiral Leahy's statement regarding use of U.S. troops for occupation of France, *198*

IN THE MEDITERRANEAN THEATER

Availability of forces, *RANKIN* Operation in Mediterranean Theater, 151

CCS decision regarding withdrawal of U.S. units from Mediterranean and planning for capture of Istrian Peninsula, 205

Employment of U.S., French, Indian and Italian forces for *RANKIN* Operation in Mediterranean Theater, 152

Forces available for employment in the Balkans, 18, 134

General Marshall's statements regarding withdrawal of U.S. units from Mediterranean, *193, 194, 205, 237*

London Conference decision to mount a 3-divisional lift amphibious assault from Mediterranean; target date 25 July, *162*

Prime Minister's statement regarding British stake in Italy, *236*

SHAEF memo regarding employment of Mediterranean forces in support of *NEPTUNE*, 171

Note: Italic numerals refer to pages in minutes of meeting.
Plain type numerals refer to pages in C.C.S. Papers.

INDEX

FORCES *(Cont'd)*

IN THE PACIFIC OCEAN AREAS
- CCS decision regarding participation of British Fleet in main operations against Japan in the Pacific, 213
- CCS discussion regarding British participation in Pacific, 208
- Contribution of the RAF in main operations against Japan, 213
- Plenary decision to accept, in principle, Canada's participation in the war against Japan, 246
- President's acceptance of Prime Minister's offer for British participation in the war against Japan, 238
- Prime Minister's statement regarding British participation in the war against Japan, 238
- Sir Alan Brooke's statements regarding British assistance in defeat of Japan, 163, 178, 182

IN SOUTHEAST ASIA
- General Marshall's statements in reference to:
  - Provision of U.S. forces for operations in Burma, 246
  - Situation in China, 233, 247
- London Conference discussion re strategy in Burma, 183
- Note by Prime Minister and Minister of Defence in regard to future operations in Burma and provision of forces, 250
- Prime Minister's statements in reference to:
  - Campaign in Burma, 237
  - Provision of forces for DRACULA, 246, 250
- Reorientation of forces from Europe for operations in Southeast Asia, 215, 218
- Transport aircraft and combat cargo groups for Operations CAPITAL and DRACULA, 216, 217

REDEPLOYMENT OF
- CCS approve proposal for study on redeployment of forces after the end of the war in Europe, 226

FORCES, AIR

IN THE MEDITERRANEAN
- Tactical air force operations from the Mediterranean Theater, 13

IN THE PACIFIC OCEAN AREAS
- British Empire participation in the Pacific, 137
- General Marshall's statement regarding employment of British Air Force in the Pacific, 241
- Prime Minister's statement regarding British forces to be available for employment in the Pacific, 238, 241

IN SOUTHEAST ASIA
- Air forces in China to support Chinese ground forces and campaign in the Pacific, 35
- Allocation of the two remaining combat cargo groups and two remaining air comando groups, 44
- London Conference discussion regarding allocation of combat cargo groups and air commando groups to SEAC, 183

JAPANESE
- Military factors governing Japanese strategy, 70

FORCES, AIRBORNE

- SCAEF's intentions for the near future, 6, 9, 133
- SHAEF's memo regarding release of airborne forces from Operation NEPTUNE, 170

FORCES, GROUND

- Military factors governing Japanese strategy, 72

FORCES, NAVAL

IN THE MEDITERRANEAN
- Naval forces to attack enemy seaborne movement in the Aegean, 19

IN THE PACIFIC OCEAN AREAS
- British Empire participation in the Pacific, 137
- British participation in the war against Japan, 40, 41
- Factors governing Japanese strategy, 71
- Prime Minister's statement regarding British forces to be available for employment in the Pacific, 238
- Sir Andrew Cunningham's statement re British naval forces available in the Pacific toward end of 1944, 179

Note: Italic numerals refer to pages in minutes of meeting.
Plain type numerals refer to pages in C.C.S. Papers.

INDEX

FORMOSA

Admiral King's statement regarding strangulation of Japanese forces to the south, if Formosa were captured, *240*

Forces to be employed against Japan, 203

Japanese intentions in Formosa, 63, 75

London Conference discussion regarding strategy in the Pacific-Far East, *163, 178, 179*

Schedule of major operations for the defeat of Japan, 1944-45, 34, 136

FOURTEENTH AIR FORCE

London Conference discussion regarding strategy in the Pacific-Far East, *180*

FRANCE

Admiral Leahy's statement regarding use of U.S. troops for occupation of France, *198*

Basic undertakings in support of over-all strategic concept, 131

CCS discusion regarding withdrawal of the Fifth Army from Italy, *193*

Deterioration of German strategic situation, 85

Employment of the Fifth Army, Twelfth and Fifteenth Air Forces, 118, 121, 134

Employment of the French Forces of the Interior, *182, 187*

Employment of the French Forces of the Interior in Operation *DRAGOON*, 12

Employment of U.S., French, Indian and Italian forces for *RANKIN* Operation, in Mediterranean Theater, 152

Execution of the over-all strategic concept, 132

Progress report on Operation *DRAGOON* and operations in the Mediterranean Theater, 12, 17

Progress report on Operation *OVERLORD*, 4, 9

Report on advance of the Seventh Army, 4

FRANKFURT, GERMANY

SCAEF's intentions for the near future, *9, 133*

G

GERMANY

Allocation of U.S. and U.K. zones of occupation in Germany, 32, 138, *197, 198, 232, 233*

Basic undertakings in support of over-all strategic concept, 131

CCS discussion in regard to naval disarmament measures for U.S. controlled ports, *232*

Deterioration of German strategic situation, 85

Estimate of German strategy, 85

Fighting effectiveness of German Air Force, 51

General Somervell's statement regarding Inter-Allied Navigation Commission to control the Rhine, *233*

Over-all mission of the strategic air forces in Europe, 50

Over-all objective in the war against the Axis, 131

Over-all strategic concept for the prosecution of the war, 131, 132

Plans for Operation *TALISMAN*, 7

Plenary Meeting agreement that details for the allocation of zones of occupation in Germany be worked out by the experts, *247*

Plenary Meeting statements regarding location of the Central Tripartite Control Commission in Germany, *248*

Political and psychological factors in the German situation, 87, 89

Prospects of a German collapse or surrender (as of 8 Sept 1944), 83

Prospects of Germany introducing new secret weapon, 89

SCAEF's intentions for the near future, 5, 9, *133*

SCAEF report on enemy resistance in European Theater, 4

Sir Alan Brooke's remarks regarding Hitler's strategy in the Balkans, *156*

Statements of Prime Minister and President re treatment of Germany, *241*

Symptoms of German collapse or surrender, 90

GILBERT ISLANDS

General progress report on recent operations in the Pacific, 111

Note: Italic numerals refer to pages in minutes of meeting.
Plain type numerals refer to pages in C.C.S. Papers.

INDEX

GREECE

Employment of U.S., French, Indian and Italian forces for *RANKIN* Operation in Mediterranean Theater, 152

Enemy situation in the Balkans, 15, 18

Forces available for employment in the Balkans, 16, 134

Occupation of Greece in event of German withdrawal, 16, 134

RANKIN planning in the Mediterranan Theater, 150

GREEN ISLAND

General progress report on recent operations in the Pacific, 112

H

HALMAHERA ISLAND

Japanese intentions in Halmahera, 62, 75

"HIGHBALL"

Statement with regard to Operation *HIGHBALL*, 148, 227

HOLLAND (*See* Netherlands)

HOLLANDIA, NEW GUINEA

General progress report on recent operations in the Pacific, 113

HUMP TONNAGE

General Marshall's remarks regarding Japanese advance in central China and B-29 stores at Chengtu, 157

London Conference discussion regarding strategy in Burma, 183

Sir Alan Brooke's remarks in reference to:
  Operations in Burma, 157, 182
  Strategic policy in Burma, 184

HUNGARY

RANKIN planning in the Mediterranean Theater, 151

I

IMPHAL

Sir Alan Brooke's remarks in reference to:
  Operations in Burma, 157, 182
  Strategic policy in Burma, 184

INDIA

Base facilities for U.S. and British naval forces in the Pacific, 179

Combined memorandum on troop movements covering the period October 1944 to March 1945, 100

Employment of U.S., French, Indian and Italian forces for *RANKIN* Operation in Mediterranean Theater, 152

INTELLIGENCE

Estimate of the enemy situation, Pacific-Far East (as of 8 Sept 1944), 60, 202

Morale of Japanese populace, 61, 64

Prospects of a German collapse or surrender (as of 8 Sept 1944), 82, 195

INTER-ALLIED NAVIGATION COMMISSION

General Somervell's statement regarding Inter-Allied Navigation Commission to control the Rhine, 233

ISMAY, SIR HASTINGS

Statement for the Press regarding *OCTAGON* Conference, 228, 234

ISTRIAN PENINSULA

Admiral King's statement regarding amphibious operations in Istria and availability of landing craft, 193, 194

Capture of the Istrian Peninsula, 121

CCS agree that decision to mounting an amphibious operation in Istria be made by 15 October, 193, 195

CCS discussion regarding future operations in the Mediterranean and capture of the Istrian Peninsula, 205

London Conference decision that plans be prepared for alternate objectives in the Mediterranean Theater, 162, 166, 174

Note: Italic numerals refer to pages in minutes of meeting.
Plain type numerals refer to pages in C.C.S. Papers.

INDEX

ISTRIAN PENINSULA (Cont'd)

    Plenary Meeting discussion regarding amphibious craft for Istrian Peninsula operation, 245

    Prime Minister's statement regarding strategy in the Mediterranean Theater, *237*

    Sir Alan Brooke's statement regarding proposed strategy for the Mediterranean Theater, *192*

    Sir Charles Portal's remarks regarding an advance northeast via Istria, *161*

ITALY

    Admiral King's remarks regarding operations in Italy, *161*

    Basic undertakings in support of over-all strategic concept, 131

    Deterioration of German strategic situation, 85

    Disposition of enemy strength in Italy, 14

    Employment of the Fifth Army, Twelfth and Fifteenth Air Forces, 118, 121, 134

    Employment of U.S., French, Indian and Italian forces for *RANKIN* Operation in Mediterranean Theater, 152

    Execution of the over-all strategic concept, 131

    General Marshall's remarks in reference to:

        Enemy formations on the Pisa-Rimini line, *156*

        Present strategic situation in Italy, *192*

    Plans for major offensive in Italy, 14, 17, 133

    Plenary Meeting conclusion regarding invasion of the valley of the Po, *244*

    President's review of the strategic situation of the United Nations, *239*

    Prime Minister's statements in reference to:

        British stake in Italy, *236*

        Strategy in the Mediterranean Theater, *237*

    Sir Alan Brooke's remarks in reference to:

        Amphibious operations from Mediterranean Theater, *160*

        Enemy situation in Italy, *156*

        Proposed strategy for the Mediterranean Theater, *192*

    Withdrawal of forces from the Mediterranean, *193, 194, 237*

J

JAPAN

    Admiral King's remarks regarding operations in the Pacific, *157, 167, 178*

    Allocation of resources for British operations against Japan, 136

    Basic undertakings in support of over-all strategic concept, 131

    British Empire participation in the Pacific, 40, 41, 137

    CCS discussion regarding strategy for the defeat of Japan, 203

    Estimate of the enemy situation, Pacific-Far East (as of 8 Sept 1944), 60

    Japanese intentions, 63, 73

    Japanese production and shipping, 61, 66, 67, 68

    Japanese situation in Burma, 22, 24

    Japanese strategy, 62

    Military factors governing Japanese strategy, 70, 71, 72

    Morale of Japanese populace, 61, 64

    Naval and air superiority to be exploited, wherever possible, to avoid commitment to costly land campaign, 35, 136

    Over-all objective in the war against the Axis, 131

    Over-all objective in the war against Japan, 38, 136

    Over-all strategic concept for the prosecution of the war, 131

    Planning date for the end of the war against Japan, 125, 138

    Plenary decision to accept, in principle, Canada's participation in the war against Japan, *246*

    Political and psychological factors in Japanese propaganda, 64

    Presidents' acceptance of Prime Minister's offer for British participation in the war against Japan, *238*

    President's statement regarding Japanese tenacity, *240*

Note: Italic numerals refer to pages in minutes of meeting.
Plain type numerals refer to pages in C.C.S. Papers.

INDEX

JAPAN (Cont'd)

    Prime Minister's statements in reference to:

        British participation in the war against Japan, 237

        Effect of sustained air bombardment on Japanese cities, 245

    Schedule of major operations for the defeat of Japan, 1944-45, 34, 136, *203*

    Sir Alan Brooke's remarks regarding British assistance in the defeat of Japan, *163, 178, 182*

    Unremitting submarine warfare against Japanese shipping to be continued, 35, 136

JAVA

    London Conference discussion regarding strategy in the Pacific-Far East, *179*

K

KALEMYO, BURMA

    Strategy for operations in Burma in the near future, 24

KALEWA, BURMA

    Strategy for operations in Burma in the near future, 24

KING, ADMIRAL E. J.

    Statements in reference to:

        Amphibious operations in Istria and availability of landing craft, *193, 194*

        British participation in the Pacific, *208*

        Logistic difficulties in the Pacific, *163*

        Machinery for coordination of U.S.-Soviet-British military effort, *196*

        Naval disarmament measures for U.S. controlled ports, *232*

        Operations in Italy; and the importance of capturing Le Havre, *161*

        Operations in the Pacific, *157, 167, 178*

        Progress of the campaign in the Pacific, *228*

        Release to the Press of information on MULBERRY, *227*

        Strangulation of Japanese forces to the south, if Formosa were captured, *240*

        Wording for paragraph 6 (i), "Basic Policies for the OCTAGON Conference," *204*

        Zones of occupation in Germany, *198*

KRA ISTHMUS

    CCS discussion regarding future operations in Southeast Asia, *214*

    Prime Minister's statement regarding strategy in the Pacific and an operation against Singapore, *238*

KURILES

    Admiral King's remarks regarding operations in the Pacific, *157, 167, 178*

    General progress report on recent operations in the Pacific, 111

    Japanese intentions in the Kuriles, 63, 73

KWAJALEIN ATOLLS

    General progress report on recent operations in the Pacific, 111

KYUSHU ISLAND, JAPAN

    London Conference discussion regarding strategy in the Pacific-Far East, *180*

    Schedule of major operations for the defeat of Japan, 1944-45, 35, 136

L

LANDING SHIPS AND CRAFT

    For capture of the Istrian Peninsula, 121, *193, 194, 195, 245*

    Message to SCAEF with regard to release of amphibious craft from OVERLORD to other theaters, 154, *232*

    Prime Minister's statement regarding strategy in the Mediterranean Theater, *237*

    SHAEF memo regarding release of shipping and craft from Operation NEPTUNE, 168

Note: Italic numerals refer to pages in minutes of meeting.
Plain type numerals refer to pages in C.C.S. Papers.

INDEX

LEAHY, ADMIRAL WILLIAM D.

Statements with reference to:
- British participation in the Pacific, 208
- Control of strategic bomber forces in Europe, 200
- Future operations in the Mediterranean and capture of the Istrian Peninsula, 205
- Future operations in Southeast Asia, 214
- Machinery for coordination of U.S.-Soviet-British military effort, 197
- Planning date for end of war against Japan, 218
- Strategy for the defeat of Japan, 203
- Withdrawal of the Fifth Army from Italy, 194
- Wording for paragraph 6 (i) "Basic Policies for the OCTAGON Conference," 204

LE HAVRE, FRANCE

- Admiral King's remarks regarding the importance of capturing Le Havre, 161
- Development of lines of communication for OVERLORD, 7, 9
- Progress report on Operation OVERLORD, 4, 9
- SCAEF's intentions for the near future, 5, 9, 133

LEIPZIG, GERMANY

- SCAEF's intentions for the near future, 7, 9, 133

LEYTE, PHILIPPINE ISLANDS

- Schedule of major operations for defeat of Japan, 1944-45, 34, 136

LIAISON

- CCS discussion regarding machinery for coordination of U.S.-Soviet-British military effort, 196

LINES OF COMMUNICATION

- Approved operations in Southeast Asia, 137
- Basic undertakings in support of overall strategic concept, 131
- Development of lines of communication for OVERLORD, 7, 9
- London Conference discussion regarding strategy in Burma, 184
- Plenary Meeting discussion regarding opening of a seaway to China, 245
- Report on Operation DRAGOON and operations in the Mediterranean Theater, 12
- Sir Alan Brooke's remarks regarding British assistance in the defeat of Japan, 163 178, 182

LJUBLJANA GAP

- SACMED's proposal for future strategy in Italy, 15, 18, 134

LOGISTICS

- Admiral King's remarks regarding logistic difficulties in the Pacific, 163
- CCS agree that CAdC be directed to make examination of the logistics problems involved in approved allocation of zones of occupation in Germany, 233
- CCS decision regarding production planning to include British requirements for operations against Japan, 204
- Development of lines of communication for OVERLORD, 7, 9
- General Arnold's statements regarding operations of the Twentieth Air Force, 219

LONDON CONFERENCE

ARTIFICIAL HARBORS, 178

CHINA
- General Marshall's remarks regarding Japanese advance in central China and B-29 stores at Chengtu, 157

FORCES
- General Marshall's remarks regarding employment of the French Forces of the Interior, 182, 187
- Sir Andrew Cunningham's statements in reference to:
    - British naval forces available in the Pacific toward end of 1944, 179
    - Enemy naval forces in the Baltic and Mediterranean, 160

Note: Italic numerals refer to pages in minutes of meeting.
Plain type numerals refer to pages in C.C.S. Papers.

INDEX

LONDON CONFERENCE (Cont'd)

MANPOWER
London Conference discussion regarding U.S. manpower difficulties, *157*

OPERATIONS IN EUROPEAN THEATER
Admiral King's remarks regarding the importance of capturing Le Havre, *161*
General Marshall's remarks regarding extensive airborne operations in connection with Operation *NEPTUNE*, *161*
Progress in Operation *OVERLORD*, *160, 178, 182*
Sir Alan Brooke's remarks regarding progress of Operation *NEPTUNE*, *156*
Sir Andrew Cunningham's review of naval situation in Operation *NEPTUNE*, *156*
Sir Charles Portal's remarks in reference to:
  Air activity in Operation *NEPTUNE*, *156, 160*
  CROSSBOW attacks, *166*

OPERATIONS IN MEDITERRANEAN THEATER
Admiral King's remarks regarding operations in Italy, *161*
Decision to mount a 3-divisional lift amphibious assault from the Mediterranean; target date 25 July, *162*
Decision that plans be prepared for alternate objectives in the Mediterranean Theater, *162, 166, 174*
Discussion regarding operations in the Balkans, *156*
General Marshall's remarks in reference to:
  Enemy formations on the Pisa-Rimini line, *156*
  Mounting the projected amphibious operation from the Mediterranean to assist *NEPTUNE*, *161*
Sir Alan Brooke's remaks in reference to:
  Amphibious operations from Mediterranean Theater, *160*
  Enemy situation in Italy, *156*
  Hitler's strategy in Balkans, *157*
Sir Charles Portal's remarks regarding an advance northeast via Istria, *161*

OPERATIONS IN THE PACIFIC OCEAN AREAS
Admiral King's remarks in reference to:
  Operations in the Pacific, *157, 167, 178*
  Logistic difficulties in the Pacific, *163*
Base facilities for U.S. and British naval forces in the Pacific, *179*
Discussion regarding strategy in the Pacific-Far East, *163, 178, 179*
General Marshall's remarks in reference to:
  Air base at Biak, *157*
  Stepping up the tempo of operations in the Pacific, *163*
Sir Alan Brooke's remarks regarding British assistance in the defeat of Japan, *163, 178, 182*

OPERATIONS IN SOUTHEAST ASIA
Sir Alan Brooke's remarks regarding operations in Burma, *157, 183*

TRANSPORT AIRCRAFT
Discussion regarding allocation of combat cargo and air commando groups to SEAC, *183*
General Arnold's remarks regarding availability of transport aircraft, *162*

TWENTIETH AIR FORCE
Control of the U.S. Twentieth Air Force, *184*

LOS NEGROS ISLAND

General progress report on recent operations in the Pacific, 113

LOSS RATE

Admiral King's remarks regarding operations in the Pacific, *157, 167, 178*
Japanese production and shipping, 61, 66, 67, 68
SCAEF report on naval operations in Operation *OVERLORD*, 5

LUZON, PHILIPPINE ISLANDS

Japanese intentions in Luzon, 63, 75
Schedule of major operations for the defeat of Japan, 1944-45, 34, 136

Note: Italic numerals refer to pages in minutes of meeting.
Plain type numerals refer to pages in C.C.S. Papers.

INDEX

LYONS, FRANCE

General tactical plan of Commander, Seventh Army, 12

M

MAGDEBURG, GERMANY

SCAEF's intentions for the near future, 7, 9, 133

MAJURO ATOLLS

General progress report on recent operations in the Pacific, 111

MAKIN ISLAND

General progress report on recent operations in the Pacific, 111

MALAY PENINSULA

Japanese intentions in Malaya, 63, 74
Prime Minister's statement regarding strategy in the Pacific and an operation against Singapore, 238

MANCHURIA

Japanese intentions in Manchuria, 63, 73

MANPOWER

Deterioration of German strategic situation, 85
London Conference discussion regarding U.S. manpower difficulties, 157
Planning date for the end of the war against Japan, 125, 138, *218*

MAPS

Allocation of zones of occupation in Germany, opposite page 32
Progress report on operations in the Pacific, opposite page 116

MARIANAS

Admiral King's remarks regarding operations in the Pacific, 157, 167 178
General progress report on recent operations in the Pacific, 111
VLR bomber operations against Japan Proper to be continued, 35

MARSEILLES, FRANCE

Progress report on Operation *DRAGOON* and operations in the Mediterranean Theater, 12, 17

MARSHALL, GENERAL G. C.

Statements in reference to:
Air base at Biak, *157*
Allocation of zones of occupation in Germany, *233*
Availability of *PLOUGH* Force for operation in the Alps, *193*
British participation in the Pacific, *212*
Command of *DRAGOON* forces, *196*
Control of strategic bomber forces in Europe, *200*
Employment of British Air Forces in the Pacific, *241*
Employment of the French Forces of the Interior, *182*, *187*
Enemy formations on the Pisa-Rimini line, *156*
Extensive airborne operations in connection with Operation *NEPTUNE*, *161*
Future operations in Southeast Asia, *216*
General Devers' staff organization, *196*
Japanese advance in central China and B-29 stores at Chengtu, *157*
Mounting the projected amphibious operation from the Mediterranean to assist *NEPTUNE*, *161*
Operation to capture islands at mouth of the Schelde, *191*
Planning date for the end of the war against Japan, *218*
Present strategic situation in Italy, *192*
Progress of the campaign in the Pacific, *228*
Provision of U.S. forces for operations in Burma, *246*
Situation in China, *233*, *247*
Stepping up the tempo of operations in the Pacific, *163*
Withdrawal of U.S. units from the Mediterranean, *193*, *194*, *205*, *237*

MARSHALL ISLANDS

General progress report on recent operations in the Pacific, 111

Note: Italic numerals refer to pages in minutes of meeting.
Plain type numerals refer to pages in C.C.S. Papers.

INDEX

MEDITERRANEAN THEATER

Admiral King's statement regarding amphibious operations in Istria and availability of landing craft, *193, 194*

Availability of forces, *RANKIN* Operation in the Mediterranean Theater, 151

Capture of the Istrian Peninsula, 121, *193, 194, 205*

Disposition of enemy strength in Italy, 14

Employment of U.S., French, Indian and Italian forces for *RANKIN* Operation in Mediterranean Theater, 152

Execution of the over-all strategic concept, 133

Forces available for employment in the Balkans, 15, 134

Future operations in the Mediterranean, 118, 119

General Arnold's statement regarding number of U.S. heavy bombers in the European and Mediterranean Theaters, *200*

General Marshall's statements in reference to:
    Availability of *PLOUGH* Force for operation in the Alps, *193*
    Enemy formations on the Pisa-Rimini line, *156*
    Mounting the projected amphibious operation from the Mediterranean to assist *NEPTUNE, 161*
    Present strategic situation in Italy, *192*

London Conference decision to mount a 3-divisional lift amphibious assault from the Mediterranean; target date 25 July, *162*

London Conference decision that plans be prepared for alternate objectives in the Mediterranean Theater, *162, 166, 174*

Naval forces to attack enemy seaborne movement in the Aegean, 19

Plans for major offensive in Italy, 14, 17, 133

Prime Minister's statements in reference to:
    British stake in Italy, *236*
    Strategy in the Mediterranean Theater, *237*
    Successes of the Allied Nations, *236*

Progress report on Operation *DRAGOON* and operations in the Mediterranean Theater, 12, 17

RANKIN planning in the Mediterranean Theater, 150, *232*

SACMED's proposal for future strategy in Italy, 14, 17, 133

SHAEF memo regarding the employment of Mediterranean forces in support of *NEPTUNE, 171*

Sir Alan Brooke's remarks in reference to:
    Amphibious operations from Mediterranean Theater, *160*
    Enemy situation in Italy, *156*
    Proposed strategy for the Mediterranean Theater, *192*

Tactical air force operations from the Mediterranean Theater, 13

Withdrawal of U.S. forces from the Mediterranean, *193, 194, 205, 237*

MESSAGES TO MARSHAL STALIN AND THE GENERALISSIMO, *142, 220, 225, 248*

MIDDLE EAST

Employment of U.S., French, Indian and Italian forces for *RANKIN* Operation in Mediterranean Theater, 152

Forces available for employment in the Balkans, 18, 134

MILITARY GOVERNMENT

CCS discussion regarding:
    Naval disarmament measures for U.S. controlled ports in Germany, *232, 233*
    Zones of occupation in Germany, *197*

General Somervell's statement regarding Inter-Allied Navigation Commission to control the Rhine, *233*

MINDANAO, PHILIPPINE ISLANDS

Japanese intentions in Mindanao, 63, 75

London Conference discussion regarding strategy in the Pacific-Far East, *179*

MOGAUNG, BURMA

Operations in Burma in the near future, 24

MONTGOMERY, GEN. SIR BERNARD L.

Prime Minister's statement regarding role of the British Empire in the war and efficiency of American-British staff machine, *236*

Note: Italic numerals refer to pages in minutes of meeting.
Plain type numerals refer to pages in C.C.S. Papers.

INDEX

MORALE

CCS discussion regarding withdrawal of the Fifth Army from Italy, *194*

Political and psychological factors in the German situation, 87, 89

MOULMEIN, BURMA

Prime Minister's statement regarding strategy in the Pacific and an operation against Singapore, *240*

"MULBERRY" (See Artificial Harbors)

MYITKYINA, BURMA

Directive to Supreme Allied Commander, Southeast Asia Command for operations in Burma, 47, 137, 139

London Conference discussion regarding strategy in Burma, *183*

Operations in Burma in the near future, 24

Sir Alan Brooke's remarks in reference to:

    Operations in Burma, *157, 183*

    Strategic policy in Burma, *184*

N

NAVAL FORCES (See Forces, Naval)

"NEPTUNE" (See "OVERLORD")

NETHERLANDS

Progress report on Operation *OVERLORD* 4, 9

NEUTRAL COUNTRIES

Deterioration of German strategic situation, 85

NEW BRITAIN

General progress report on recent operations in the Pacific, 112

NOEMFOOR ISLAND

General progress report on recent operations in the Pacific, 114

NORTHERN COMBAT AREA COMMAND

Progress report of operations in SEAC, 23

NORWAY

Operation into Norway, 8

O

O.S.S.

SOE/OSS operations undertaken by units of RAF Bomber Command and U.S. Strategic Air Forces in Europe, 51

"OCTAGON" CONFERENCE

Basic policies for the *OCTAGON* Conference, 80

Communication of the results of *OCTAGON* Conference to Marshal Stalin, and Generalissimo Chiang Kai-shek, 142, *248*

Concluding remarks regarding *OCTAGON* Conference, *234*

Program for the *OCTAGON* Conference, 77

Report to the President and Prime Minister, 130, *224*

Statement for the Press regarding *OCTAGON* Conference, *228, 234, 249, 252*

OVER-ALL OBJECTIVE

Over-all objective in the war against the Axis, 131

Over-all objective in the war against Japan, 38, 136

"OVERLORD"

Command of *DRAGOON* forces, 92, 95, 135, *195*

General Marshall's remarks in reference to:

    Employment of the French Forces of the Interior, *182, 187*

    Extensive airborne operations in connection with Operation *NEPTUNE*, *161*

    Operation to capture islands at mouth of the Schelde, *191*

Note: Italic numerals refer to pages in minutes of meeting.
Plain type numerals refer to pages in C.C.S. Papers.

INDEX

"OVERLORD" (Cont'd)

Operation against the Channel Islands, 7

Prime Minister's opening statement reviewing the successes of the Allied Nations, *236*

Prime Minister's statement regarding role of the British Empire in the war and efficiency of American-British staff machine, *236*

Progress in Operation OVERLORD, *160, 178, 182*

Progress report on Operation OVERLORD (9 Sept 1944), 4, 9

Release of amphibious craft from OVERLORD to other theaters, 154, *232*

SCAEF's intentions for the near future, 5, 9, *132, 191*

SCAEF's report on naval operations in Operation OVERLORD, 5

SHAEF memoranda in reference to:

Employment of Mediterranean forces in support of NEPTUNE, 171

Release of airborne forces from Operation NEPTUNE, 170

Release of shipping and craft from Operation NEPTUNE, 168

Sir Alan Brooke's remarks in reference to:

Progress of Operation NEPTUNE, *156*

Situation report from SCAEF, and operation to capture islands at mouth of the Schelde, *191*

Sir Andrew Cunningham's review of naval situation in Operation NEPTUNE, *156*

Sir Charles Portal's remarks regarding air activity in Operation NEPTUNE, *156, 160*

P

PACIFIC OCEAN AREAS

Admiral King's remarks in reference to:
Logistic difficulties in the Pacific, *163*
Operations in the Pacific, *157, 167, 178*
Strangulation of Japanese forces to the south, if Formosa were captured, *240*

Air forces in China to support Chinese ground forces and campaign in the Pacific, 35

Base facilities for U.S. and British naval forces available in the Pacific toward end of 1944, 179

British Empire participation in the Pacific, 137

British participation in the Pacific, 208, 212, 238

CCS accept, for planning purposes, schedule of operations for defeat of Japan, 204

CCS discussion regarding progress of the campaign in the Pacific, *228*

CCS discussion regarding strategy for the defeat of Japan, *203*

Contribution of the RAF in the main operations against Japan, *213*

Employment of British Air Force in the Pacific, *241*

Estimate of the enemy situation, Pacific-Far East (as of 8 Sept 1944), 60, *202*

General Arnold's statement regarding Japanese Air Force's lack of determination and will to win, *228*

General Marshall's remarks in reference to:

Air base at Biak, *157*

Stepping up the tempo of operations in the Pacific, *163*

General progress report on recent operations in the Pacific, 110, *203*

London Conference decision regarding control of the Twentieth Air Force, *185*

London Conference discussion regarding strategy in the Pacific-Far East, *163, 178, 179*

Naval and air superiority to be exploited, wherever possible, to avoid commitment to costly land campaign, 35, *136*

Over-all objective in the war against Japan, 38, *136*

President's review of the strategic situation of the United Nations, *239*

Prime Minister's statements in reference to:

British forces to be available for employment in the Pacific, *238, 241*

Russian entry into the war against Japan, *240*

Sir Alan Brooke's statements in reference to:

Allocation of British requirements for Pacific operations, *203*

British assistance in the defeat of Japan, *163, 178, 182*

Note: Italic numerals refer to pages in minutes of meeting.
Plain type numerals refer to pages in C.C.S. Papers.

TOP SECRET

INDEX

PACIFIC OCEAN AREAS *(Cont'd)*

Sir Andrew Cunningham's statement regarding British naval forces available in the Pacific toward end of 1944, *179*

Sir Charles Portal's statement regarding British heavy bombers to be available for operations against the mainland of Japan, *240, 241*

Submarine warfare against Japanese shipping, 35, 136

PACIFIC, CENTRAL

Japanese intentions in Central Pacific, 63, 75

Progress report on recent operations in, 111

PACIFIC, NORTH

Japanese intentions in North Pacific, 63, 73

Progress report on recent operations in the Pacific, 111

PACIFIC, SOUTH

Progress report on recent operations in the Pacific, 112

PACIFIC, SOUTHWEST

Allocation of the two remaining combat cargo groups and the two remaining commando groups, 44

British participation in the war against Japan, 40, 41, *208*

Progress report on recent operations in the Pacific, 112

PALAU ISLANDS

Admiral King's remarks regarding operations in the Pacific, *157, 167, 178*

General progress report on recent operations in the Pacific, 111

Japanese intentions in the Palaus, 63, 75

PARAMUSHIRU

General progress report on recent operations in the Pacific, 111

PETROLEUM

Japanese production and shipping, 62, 66, 67, 68

PHILIPPINES

General progress report on recent operations in the Pacific, 112

Japanese Air Force's lack of determination and will to win, *228*

London Conference discussion regarding strategy in the Pacific-Far East, *178*

Schedule of major operations for the defeat of Japan, 1944-45, 34, 136

Transport aircraft and combat cargo groups, *217, 218*

PIPELINES

London Conference discussion regarding strategy in Burma, *183*

PLANNING

Allocation of resources for British operations against Japan, 137

Alternate objectives in the Mediterranean Theater, *162, 166, 174*

Capture of the Istrian Peninsula, 121

Logistics problems involved in approved allocation of zones of occupation in Germany, *233*

Planning date for the end of the war against Japan, 124, 138, *218*

RANKIN planning in the Mediterranean Theater, 150

Redeployment of forces after the end of the war in Europe, 124, 137

PO VALLEY

Plenary Meeting conclusion regarding invasion of the valley of the Po, *244*

"POINTBLANK"

SCAEF report on air operations from the U.K., 5, 8

POLAND

Deterioration of German strategic situation, 85

Note: Italic numerals refer to pages in minutes of meeting.
Plain type numerals refer to pages in C.C.S. Papers.

INDEX

PORT DE BOUC, FRANCE

Progress report on Operation *DRAGOON* and operations in the Mediterranean Theater, *12, 17*

PORT FACILITIES

Base facilities for U.S. and British naval forces in the Pacific, *179*
Development of lines of communication for *OVERLORD*, *7, 9*

PORTAL, SIR CHARLES

Statements in reference to:
   Advance northeast via Istria, *161*
   Air activity in Operation *NEPTUNE*, *156, 160*
   British heavy bombers to be available for operations against the mainland of Japan, *240, 241*
   British participation in the Pacific, *210*
   Command of *DRAGOON* forces, *195*
   Control of strategic bomber forces in Europe, *199*
   Control of the U.S. Twentieth Air Force, *184*
   CROSSBOW attacks, *166*
   Future operations in Southeast Asia, *216*
   Machinery for coordination of U.S.-Soviet-British military effort, *197*
   Range of Lancaster bombers, *241*
   Withdrawal of the Fifth Army from Italy, *194*
   Zones of occupation in Germany, *198*

POST HOSTILITIES

Planning date for the end of the war against Japan, *125, 138*

PRESIDENT OF THE UNITED STATES

Report to the President and Prime Minister, 131, *224, 244*
Statements in reference to:
   British participation in the war against Japan, *238*
   Credit for conception of *DRAGOON* Operation, *236*
   Japanese tenacity, *240*
   Location of the Central Tripartite Control Commission in Germany, *248*
   Strategic situation of the United Nations, *239*
   Treatment of Germany, *241*

PRESS RELEASE

Information on *MULBERRY*, 227, *249*
Statement for the Press regarding *OCTAGON* Conference, 228, 234, *249, 252*

PRIME MINISTER OF THE UNITED KINGDOM

Report to the President and Prime Minister, 131, *224, 244*
Statements in reference to:
   British participation in the war against Japan, *237, 238, 241*
   British stake in Italy, *236*
   Campaign in Burma, *237*
   Deployment of forces after the end of the war in Europe, *247*
   Effect of sustained air bombardment on Japanese cities, *245*
   Encroachment of the Russians into the Balkans, *237*
   Note by the Prime Minister and Minister of Defence in regard to future operations in Burma and provision of forces, 250
   Obligation in China and desire to carry out Operation *DRACULA* before the monsoon of 1945, *246*
   Provision of forces for *DRACULA*, *246* 250
   Release of information on *MULBERRY* to the Press, *249*
   Role of the British Empire in the war and efficiency of American-British staff machine, *236*
   Russian entry into the war against Japan, *240*
   Strategy in the Mediterranean Theater, *237*
   Strategy in the Pacific and an operation against Singapore, *238*
   Successes of the Allied Nations, *236*
   Treatment of Germany, *241*

Note: Italic numerals refer to pages in minutes of meeting.
Plain type numerals refer to pages in C.C.S. Papers.

INDEX

PRIORITY

Basic policies for the OCTAGON Conference, 80

Combined personnel movement problems arising during the first year after the defeat of Germany, 103

Memorandum on troop movements, covering the period October 1944 to March 1945, 99

Over-all mission of the strategic air forces in Europe, 50

Priorities for personnel shipping subsequent to termination of hostilities in Europe, 98

PRISONERS OF WAR

Progress report on Operation DRAGOON and operations in the Mediterranean Theater, 12

PRODUCTION

Basic undertakings in support of over-all strategic concept, 132

British operations against Japan will require planning for the allocation of resources, 137, *203*

Deterioration of German strategic situation, 88

Japanese production and shipping, 61, 66, 67, 68

Planning date for the end of the war against Japan, 125, 138, *218*

PROGRESS REPORTS

CCS discussion regarding progress of the campaign in the Pacific, *228*

General progress report on recent operations in the Pacific, 110, *203*

Progress report on Operation DRAGOON and operations in the Mediterranean Theater, 12, 17

Progress report on Operation OVERLORD, 4, 9, *191*

Progress report of operations in SEAC, 22

PSYCHOLOGICAL WARFARE

Operation against the Channel Islands, 7

Political and psychological factors in German situation, 87, 89

Political and psychological factors in Japanese propaganda, 64

Statement for the Press re OCTAGON Conference, *228, 234*

R

RANGOON, BURMA

CCS discussion regarding future operations in Southeast Asia, *214*

London Conference discussion regarding strategy in Burma, *183*

"RANKIN"

Availability of forces, RANKIN Operation in the Mediterranean Theater, 151

Employment of U.S., French, Indian and Italian forces for RANKIN Operation in Mediterranean Theater, 152

RANKIN planning in the Mediterranean Theater, 150

"RATWEEK"

Enemy situation in the Balkans, 15, 18

REDEPLOYMENT

Availability of personnel shipping, 107

Basic policies for the OCTAGON Conference, 80

Basic undertakings in support of over-all strategic concept, 132

Combined personnel movement problems arising during the first year after the defeat of Germany, 103, *226*

General Marshall's statement regarding provision of U.S. forces for operations in Burma, *246*

Memorandum on troop movements, covering the period October 1944 to March 1945, 99

Planning date for the end of the war against Japan, 125, 137

Prime Minister's statements in reference to:

    Campaign in Burma, *237*

    Deployment of forces after the end of the war in Europe, *247*

    Provision of forces for DRACULA, *246, 250*

Priorities for personnel shipping subsequent to termination of hostilities in Europe, 98

Note: Italic numerals refer to pages in minutes of meeting.
Plain type numerals refer to pages in C.C.S. Papers.

INDEX

REDEPLOYMENT *(Cont'd)*

Reorientation of forces from Europe for operations in Southeast Asia, 215, 218

Sir Alan Brooke's remarks regarding personnel shipping problem following defeat of Germany, *190*

Study on redeployment of forces after the end of the war in Europe, 128, 137, *226*

RELIEF AND REHABILITATION

Arrangements for occupation in Greece in event of German withdrawal, 16, 134

Forces available for employment in the Balkans, 16, 134

REPATRIATION

Combined personnel movement problems arising during the first year after the defeat of Germany, 103

Plans for Operation *TALISMAN*, 7

Sir Alan Brooke's remarks regarding shipping problem following defeat of Germany, *190*

Study on redeployment of forces after the end of the war in Europe, 128, 137

RESISTANCE GROUPS

General Marshall's remarks re employment of the French Forces of the Interior, *182, 187*

ROTTERDAM, HOLLAND

SCAEF's intentions for the near future, 6, 9, 133, *191*

Sir Alan Brooke's statement regarding situation report from SCAEF; and operation to capture islands at mouth of the Schelde, *191*

RUHR

SCAEF's intentions for the near future, 5, 9, 133

RUMANIA

Deterioration of German strategic situation, 88

RANKIN planning in the Mediterranean Theater, 151

RUSSIA (*See* U.S.S.R.)

RYUKYU ISLANDS

Schedule of major operations for the defeat of Japan, 1944-45, 35, 136

S

SAAR

SCAEF's intentions for the near future, 5, 9, 133

SAKHALIN ISLAND

Japanese intentions in Sakhalin, 63, 73

SARANGANI BAY, PHILIPPINE ISLANDS

Schedule of major operations for the defeat of Japan, 1944-45, 34, 136

SATELLITE COUNTRIES

Deterioration of German strategic situation, 88

SECRET WEAPONS

Prospects of Germany introducing new secret weapon, 89

SEVENTH ARMY

Command of *DRAGOON* forces, 93, 95, 135

Progress report on Operation *DRAGOON* and operations in the Mediterranean Theater, *12, 17*

Report on advance of the Seventh Army, *4*

SHIMUSHU

General progress report on recent operations in the Pacific, 111

Note: Italic numerals refer to pages in minutes of meeting.
Plain type numerals refer to pages in C.C.S. Papers.

INDEX

SHIPPING

Japanese production and shipping, 61, 66, 67, 68
Submarine warfare against Japanese shipping, 35, 136

SHIPPING, PERSONNEL

Availability of personnel shipping, 107
Combined personnel movement problems arising during the first year after the defeat of Germany, 103, *226*
Memorandum on troop movements, covering the period October 1944 to March 1945, 99
Priorities for personnel shipping subsequent to termination of hostilities in Europe, 98
Sir Alan Brooke's remarks regarding personnel shipping problem following defeat of Germany, *190*
Study on redeployment of forces after the end of the war in Europe, 128, 137

SIEGFRIED LINE

SCAEF's intentions for the near future, 5, 9, 133

SINGAPORE

British participation in the Pacific, *208*
Future operations from Southeast Asia, *214*
Prime Minister's statement regarding strategy in the Pacific and an operation against Singapore, *238*

SIXTH ARMY

General progress report on recent operations in the Pacific, 113

SMITH, GENERAL W. B.

Prime Minister's statement regarding role of the British Empire in the war and efficiency of American-British staff machine, *236*

SOMERVELL, GENERAL B. B.

General Somervell's statement regarding Inter-Allied Navigation Commission to control the Rhine, *233*

SOURABAYA, JAVA

London Conference discussion regarding strategy in the Pacific-Far East, *179*

SOUTHEAST ASIA

Allocation of the two remaining combat cargo groups and air commando groups, 44
CCS discussion regarding future operations in Southeast Asia, *214*
CCS take note of British statement regarding Operation HIGHBALL, *227*
Directive to Supreme Allied Commander, Southeast Asia Command for operations in Burma, 46, 137, 139, *217*, *248*
London Conference discussion in reference to:
  Allocation of combat cargo and air commando groups to SEAC, *183*
  Strategy in Burma, *183*
  Strategy in the Pacific-Far East, *163*, *178*, *179*
Prime Minister's statements in reference to:
  Campaign in Burma, *237*
  Obligation in China and desire to carry out Operation DRACULA before the monsoon of 1945, *246*
Progress report of operations in SEAC, 22
Reorientation of forces from Europe for operations in Southeast Asia, 215, 218
Sir Alan Brooke's remarks in reference to:
  Operations in Burma, *157*, *183*
  Strategic policy in Burma, *184*
Strategy for operations in Burma in the near future, 24
Transport aircraft and combat cargo groups for Operations CAPITAL and DRACULA, 216, 217

SPECIAL OPERATIONS EXECUTIVE

SOE/OSS operations undertaken by units of RAF Bomber Command and U.S. Strategic Air Forces in Europe, 51

Note: Italic numerals refer to pages in minutes of meeting.
Plain type numerals refer to pages in C.C.S. Papers.

INDEX

STALIN, MARSHAL

Communication of the results of *OCTAGON* Conference to Marshal Stalin and Generalissimo Chiang Kai-shek, 142, *220, 225, 248*

President's statement attributing credit for conception of *DRAGOON* Operation to Marshal Stalin, *236*

STRATEGIC AIR FORCES IN EUROPE

Control of strategic bomber forces in Europe, 50, 132, *198, 208*

Over-all mission of the strategic air forces in Europe, 50

STRATEGY

BASIC POLICIES

Basic policies for the *OCTAGON* Conference, 80

Basic undertakings in support of over-all strategic concept, 131

Execution of the over-all strategic concept, 132

Over-all objective in the war against the Axis, 131

Over-all strategic concept for the prosecution of the war, 131, 132

IN THE EUROPEAN THEATER

Estimate of German strategy, 85

Operation against the Channel Islands, 7

Operation into Norway, 8

Over-all mission of the strategic air forces in Europe, 50

SCAEF's intentions for the near future, 5, 9, 133

IN THE MEDITERRANEAN THEATER

CCS decision to dispatch message to SACMED regarding withdrawal of U.S. units in Mediterranean, 205

CCS discussion regarding future operations in the Mediterranean, 205

Capture of the Istrian Peninsula, 121, 205

Future operations in the Mediterranean, 118, 119

General Marshall's statement regarding availability of *PLOUGH* Force for operation in the Alps, *193*

General tactical plan of Commander, Seventh Army, 12

Naval forces to attack enemy seaborne movement in the Aegean, 19

Plans for major offensive in Italy, 14, 17, 133

Plenary Meeting conclusion regarding invasion of the valley of the Po, *244*

Prime Minister's statement regarding strategy in the Mediterranean Theater, *236*

SACMED's proposal for future strategy in Italy, 14, 17, 133

Sir Alan Brooke's remarks in reference to:

Hitler's strategy in the Balkans, *157*

Proposed strategy for the Mediterranean Theater, *192*

IN THE PACIFIC OCEAN AREAS

Admiral King's statement regarding strangulation of Japanese forces to the south, if Formosa were captured, *240*

CCS acceptance, for planning purposes, of schedule of operations for defeat of Japan, 204

CCS discussion regarding strategy for the defeat of Japan, 203

Japanese intentions, 63, 73

Japanese strategy, 62

London Conference discussion regarding strategy in the Pacific-Far East, *163, 178, 179*

Naval and air superiority to be exploited wherever possible, to avoid commitment to costly land campaign, 35, 136

Over-all objective in the war against Japan, 38, 136

Prime Minister's statement regarding strategy in the Pacific and an operation against Singapore, *238*

Strategy of major operations for the defeat of Japan, 1944-45, 34, 136

IN SOUTHEAST ASIA

CCS discussion regarding future operations in Southeast Asia, *214*

Directive to Supreme Allied Commander, Southeast Asia Command for operations in Burma, 46, 137, 139

London Conference discussion regarding strategy in Burma, *183*

Note: Italic numerals refer to pages in minutes of meeting.
Plain type numerals refer to pages in C.C.S. Papers.

INDEX

STRATEGY (Cont'd)

IN SOUTHEAST ASIA (Cont'd)

Prime Minister's statement regarding obligation in China and desire to carry out Operation DRACULA before the monsoon of 1945, 246

Sir Alan Brooke's remarks regarding strategic policy in Burma, *184*

Strategy for operations in Burma in the near future, 24

SUMATRA

Japanese intentions in Sumatra, 63, 74

SUPREME HEADQUARTERS, ALLIED EXPEDITIONARY FORCE

Memoranda in reference to:
Employment of Mediterranean forces in support of NEPTUNE, 171
Release of airborne forces from Operation NEPTUNE, 170
Release of shipping and craft from Operation NEPTUNE, 168
Progress report on Operation OVERLORD, 4, 9
Transfer of operational control of DRAGOON forces, 6, 13

SURRENDER

Plans for Operation TALISMAN, 7
Prospects of a German collapse or surrender (as of 8 Sept 1944), 90

T

"TALISMAN"

Plans for Operation TALISMAN, 7

TANIMBAR

London Conference discussion regarding strategy in the Pacific-Far East, *179*

TARAWA ISLAND

General progress report on recent operations in the Pacific, 111

TARGET DATES

CCS discussion regarding progress of the campaign in the Pacific, *228*
General Marshall's remark regarding stepping up the tempo of operations in the Pacific, *163*
London Conference decision to mount a 3-divisional lift amphibious assault from the Mediterranean; target date 25 July, *162*
Planning date for the end of the war against Japan, 125, 138
Schedule of major operations for the defeat of Japan, 1944-45, 34, 136, *203*

TARGETS

Over-all mission of the strategic air forces in Europe, 50

TOKYO

Schedule of major operations for the defeat of Japan, 1944-45, 34, 136

TOULON

Progress report on Operation DRAGOON and operations in the Mediterranean Theater, 12, 17

TRANSPORT AIRCRAFT

Allocation of the two remaining combat cargo groups and the two remaining air commando groups, 44
General Arnold's remarks regarding availability of transport aircraft, *162*
London Conference discussion regarding allocation of combat cargo and air commando groups to SEAC, *182*

TRIESTE, ITALY

SACMED's proposal for future strategy in Italy, 15, 17, 134
Sir Alan Brooke's statement regarding proposed strategy for the Mediterranean Theater, *193*

Note: Italic numerals refer to pages in minutes of meeting.
Plain type numerals refer to pages in C.C.S. Papers.

INDEX

TROOP MOVEMENTS

Combined personnel movement problems arising during the first year after the defeat of Germany, 103

Memorandum on troop movements, covering the period October 1944 to March 1945, 99

Priorities for personnel shipping subsequent to termination of hostilities in Europe, 98

TRUK

General progress report on recent operations in the Pacific, 112

TWELFTH AIR FORCE

Command of *DRAGOON* forces, 93, 95, 135

Employment of the Fifth Army, Twelfth and Fifteenth Air Forces, 118, 121, 134

TWENTIETH AIR FORCE

Control of the U.S. Twentieth Air Force, *184*

General Arnold's statements regarding operations of the U.S. Twentieth Air Force, *219*

U

U-BOAT WARFARE

Deterioration of German strategic situation, 86

General progress report on recent operations in the Pacific, 112

Sir Andrew Cunningham's remarks regarding enemy naval forces in the Baltic and Mediterranean, *160*

Sir Andrew Cunningham's review of naval situation in Operation *NEPTUNE*, *156*

Submarine warfare against Japanese shipping, 35, 136

U.S.S.R.

Basic undertakings in support of over-all strategic concept, 132

Communication of the results of *OCTAGON* Conference to Marshal Stalin and Generalissimo Chiang Kai-shek, 142, *220, 225, 248*

Entry of Russia into the war against Japan, 35

Machinery for coordination of U.S.-Soviet-British military effort, 54, 56, 135, *196, 197, 202*

Over-all objective in the war against the Axis, 131

Over-all strategic concept for the prosecution of the war, 131

Prime Minister's statements in reference to:
  Encroachment of the Russians into the Balkans *237*
  Russian entry into the war against Japan, *240*

Strategic air force attacks in support of Russian operation, 51

UNITED KINGDOM

Allocation of resources for British operations against Japan, 137

Allocation of U.S. and U.K. zones of occupation in Germany, 32, 138

Basic undertakings in support of over-all strategic concept, 131

British participation in the war against Japan, 40, 41, 137, *208, 212*

CCS decision regarding participation of the British Fleet in the main operations against Japan in the Pacific, 213

Contribution of the RAF in the main operations against Japan, 213, *238*

Machinery for coordination of U.S.-Soviet-British military effort, 56, *196, 197*

V

VENEZIA GIUILIA, ITALY

RANKIN planning in the Mediterranean Theater, 151

Note: Italic numerals refer to pages in minutes of meeting.
Plain type numerals refer to pages in C.C.S. Papers.

INDEX

VERY LONG RANGE AIRCRAFT

VLR bomber operations against Japan Proper to be continued, 35

VIENNA, AUSTRIA

Prime Minister's statement regarding strategy in the Mediterranean Theater, *237*

Sir Alan Brooke's statement regarding proposed strategy for the Mediterranean Theater, *193*

W

WAKDE ISLAND

General progress report on recent operations in the Pacific, 113

Y

YUGOSLAVIA

London Conference discussion regarding operations in the Balkans, *156*

RANKIN planning in the Mediterranean Theater, 151

YUNNAN FORCE

Progress report of operations in SEAC, 23

Z

ZONES OF OCCUPATION

Allocation of U.S. and U.K. zones of occupation in Germany, 32, 138, *197, 198, 232, 233*

CCS agree that CAdC be directed to make examination of the logistics problems involved in approved allocations of zones of occupation in Germany, *233*

Plenary Meeting agreement that details for the allocation of zones of occupation in Germany be worked out by the experts, *247*

Note: Italic numerals refer to pages in minutes of meeting.
Plain type numerals refer to pages in C.C.S. Papers.

www.ingramcontent.com/pod-product-compliance
Lightning Source LLC
Chambersburg PA
CBHW060336010526

44117CB00017B/2856